505

unbelievably

STUPID

web p@ges

2nd Edition

DAN CROWLEY

SOURCEBOOKS HYSTERIA™
AN IMPRINT OF SOURCEBOOKS, INC.®
NAPERVILLE, ILLINOIS

Published by Sourcebooks Hysteria, an imprint of Sourcebooks, Inc.

P.O. Box 4410, Naperville, Illinois 60567-4410

(630) 961-3900

FAX: (630) 961-2168

www.sourcebooks.com

ISBN 13: 978-1-4022-1090-7

ISBN 10: 1-4022-1090-6

Previous edition cataloged as follows:

Crowley, Dan.

505 unbelievably stupid Web pages / by Dan Crowley.

p. cm.

ISBN 1-4022-0142-7 (alk. paper)

1. Web sites—Directories. 2. Internet addresses—Directories. 3. Trivia—Computer network resources—Directories. I. Title: Five hundred and five unbelievably stupid Web pages. II. Title.

ZA4225.C76 2003

025.04—dc21

2003005077

Printed and bound in the United States of America

VP 10 9 8 7 6 5 4 3 2 1

To my family, living and gone

Table of Contents

Introduction

What if I told you that there was a web page, somewhere out there on the vast world known as the Internet, dedicated to the worship of an all-powerful deity known as the Flying Spaghetti Monster?

There is such a page.

What if I told you that another web page warns people of the danger of the "Nega-Scooby Doo Gang," a group that is comprised of the evil alternates of the lovable *Scooby Doo* characters?

It exists. I'm not kidding.

The Internet has become a great source of information. You can find a concert schedule for your favorite band or you can book a flight to the Caribbean. You can even go head to head with someone on the other side of the world in a game of cards or chess.

However, there are many web pages on the Internet that seem to have no use at all. One wonders why people would dedicate themselves to such worthless causes.

There is a game I play on Google, called Googlewhacking. Here's how it works: you go to www.google.com and type in a two-word phrase for something you know isn't going to get many responses, if any. An example would be "Swedish rappers." When I was working on the first edition of this book back in 2003, a search for Swedish rappers turned up 1,820 matches. If you think that's amazing, try searching today. You'll get a mind-boggling 182,000 matches—one hundred times more than four years ago! There's even an article on Wikipedia (a popular online encyclopedia with tons of information on almost anything) about Swedish hip-hop, with a list of several dozen artists!

Surprised? You should be. I, for one, have never heard of, much less listened to, a Swedish rapper. And yet, it seems to be an entire sub-genre of music, and you can learn all about it on the Internet. And, like the list of stupid things Paris Hilton has done, it keeps growing and growing.

If you look harder, you'll find web pages that display how stupid some people can be. "101 Uses for AOL Disks" is another one of my favorites. It shows you some actual uses for the countless America Online CDs that appear in your mailbox and every electronics store, attempting to add members to the AOL ranks. (Hey, AOL, maybe you should focus more on marketing to people who actually want to use your product.)

The more I looked, the more I became fascinated with how many unusual, bizarre, and downright idiotic web pages there are. In addition, there are many "serious" sites that are unintentionally funny. So I decided to dedicate my time to finding these web pages and giving them some much-needed attention. Deserved, maybe not, but needed, yes. Most were meant to give someone a laugh, after all. Why shouldn't they get attention?

Now that I've shown you some humorous examples, it's time for you to go off and do some fun web-surfing of your own. Throughout the book, I include descriptions of the sites as well as my own comments. I have given each site an abnormality rating, a stupidity rating, and an entertainment rating. Each is rated on a scale of 1 to 10, (1 being the least abnormal/stupid/entertaining, 10 being the most). So, ladies and gentlemen, join me as we count down 505 Unbelievably Stupid Web Pages, in no particular order. Enjoy!

Dead Sites—
Where Did They Go?

These websites may or may not exist once you go to look for them. The fluid nature of the Web dictates that I cannot guarantee that the sites will be in service at the time of publication. I have done my best to make sure that most are current as of this writing. Those sites that have gone to Internet Heaven (or Internet Hell, as the case may be) are still included as a record of their incredibly pathetic existence and a timeless tribute to their extreme stupidity and uselessness.

If the address listed in the book does not work, try searching for the site using a search engine such as Google, as the site may have changed its address since the printing of the book. Sites such as Google and the Way Back Machine (www.archive.org) also have cached images of websites, so that you can view what a website looked like even if it no longer exists. Please also visit www.stupid webpages.com to receive updates of which sites are dead and which sites have changed addresses.

505

The Virtual Stapler
www.virtualstapler.com

Love staplers? Well, then, this is the page for you.

This page features a gallery of stapler models from different years, including comments on how they work, as if they need any. The "1968 Swingline," the "Drexel Odyssey," and the "Max Hong Kong Booklet Stapler" are just a few of the models. They also have an FAQ on the mechanics of staplers and questions on how you can find those annoying things when they get lost. Letters from outsiders having stapler problems or other queries are encouraged, as they post these in a letters section (one letter was trying to make these people realize how moronic the idea of a stapler web page is, but they'd have none of it). They have an entire section devoted to the surprisingly many times they've been noticed by the media, along with comments they've received. They're currently working on a section that features staplers that appeared in movies, and finally, the ultimate in stupidity for this page: Stapler Poetry.

COMMENTS: I've never realized how much attention people can put into such a mundane, inanimate object. Well, I guess now I know that there's much more to staplers than I realized. These people have gone to the point where they love staplers to death. And I thought it was just an office tool.

ABNORMALITY: 3 STUPIDITY: 7 ENTERTAINMENT: 6

504

Dishwasher Pete
www.outwestnewspaper.com/pete.html

This is an article about a man named Dishwasher Pete. His goal is groundbreaking, yet simple: wash dishes in every state in the USA. He not only washes dishes, he writes about it in a self-published newsletter. Boy, I'd really love to get a subscription today! This article tells a great deal about Pete and what he's done so far, like washing dishes at a Montana ski resort. Talk about luxury—washing dishes at a ski resort!

COMMENTS: It's a noble goal just to travel to every state in the U.S. But no, he just had to add dishwashing to that goal! I tell you, if that isn't a stupid tack-on to a goal like that, I don't know what is.

ABNORMALITY: 7 STUPIDITY: 8 ENTERTAINMENT: 6

503

The Dark Side of the Scooby Doo Gang
www.ccs00.com/cdc/scooby/darkside

There's the real Scooby Doo gang, and then there's the Nega-Scooby Doo Gang.
That's right. The Nega-Scooby Doo Gang is comprised of the real group's evil counterparts. The web page has profiles on "Evil-Minded Velma," "Hot Stuff Freddy," "Dark Daphne," "Devil Doo," and "Disgruntled Shaggy." The funniest profile, in my opinion, is the sixth one: Scrappy Doo! They claim that Scrappy is a double agent whose objectives are to "annoy the real Scooby Doo Gang," "REALLY annoy the real Scooby Doo Gang," and "REALLY REALLY annoy the real Scooby Doo Gang" (sounds about right to me). They even have a picture of "the Misery Machine," the vehicle of the Nega-Scooby Doo Gang. A section for fan art and stories is also included.

COMMENTS: I like this page. The concept is funny, and the part about Scrappy Doo really agreed with me. People who dislike Scooby Doo will especially get a kick out of this site.

ABNORMALITY: 8 STUPIDITY: 7 ENTERTAINMENT: 8

502

How to Drive Like a Moron!
www.doggiesnot.com

Do you hate people who are moronic drivers? If you do, blame this page.
How to Drive Like a Moron has all the rules of how to be an annoying moron while on the road. General rules, highway rules, maintenance tips, shopping-center parking lots, pedestrians…you name it, this page has a "tutorial" for it. Among the general rules are, "When there's traffic behind you, always drive eight to twenty miles per hour below the posted limit," "You always have the right of way," and "Women are encouraged to put on their makeup while driving." Among the other features are "Report a Moron," and a section where you can read these reports.

COMMENTS: This site is most amusing for those who enjoy annoying others on the road. Even if you're a good driver, you'll get a laugh out of the "rules" on this site. Or you could be offended. Either one. Once again, a must-see for all people who drive like idiots and those who hate them.

ABNORMALITY: 5 STUPIDITY: 8 ENTERTAINMENT: 8

501   Stupid People
www.geocities.com/SouthBeach/Sands/7085

This page is a tribute to how stupid some people can be. I would have put it at No. 1 if these pages were put in some kind of order. The page is a collection of tales of, well, stupid people. From the dumb girl who thought there were fifty-one states to the woman who backed up on a highway to drive down her missed exit to the person who sued Budweiser for his "lack of success with women," these tales tell it all. They're divided into categories including classmates, criminals, coworkers, drivers, headlines, and even laws. (San Francisco prohibits walking an elephant down Market Street unless it's on a leash. Really! This is a real law!)

COMMENTS: This page is good fun all around. I personally always get a laugh out of the stupidity of others. Visit it and you're sure to get more than your share of laughs. I highly recommend this page, whether you're not stupid or you think you're not stupid (you may think so, but…).

ABNORMALITY: 7 STUPIDITY: 9 ENTERTAINMENT: 9

---

500   Benway's Stupid Pages
www.legal-mp3.co.uk/Stupid/stupid.html

This page is very hard to describe. Once again, stupid is the best word (that is the name of this book, ain't it?). You click on a link, then you are presented with a series of stupid text messages. Heck, there's even a warning saying that the page contains no useful information whatsoever and that you should only use it if you're bored beyond recognition. They willingly admit that!

COMMENTS: The maker of this site is messed up. He must not have had much to do at all when he made this. In fact, this is probably a site where you will only be entertained due to its abnormality and stupidity. Only visit this site if you are "very, very bored."

ABNORMALITY: 8 STUPIDITY: 10 ENTERTAINMENT: 4

499

All Too Flat
www.alltooflat.com

Yet another collection of jokes and stupidity. This page is also divided into sections: funny, serious, geeky, and pranks. There are subsections also, including "The Bible According to Cheese," "Ask the Fish," "Help Me Name My…," "Scientist Trading Cards," and much more. This site can take up a lot of your time if you intend to see it all, since there are archives of various features and lots of media. Wondering why they chose the name All Too Flat? They have a section on that, too. (I'd certainly pick "all too flat" over "intellisloth.com.")

COMMENTS: This site has a lot of decent laughs. It's quite extensive, as I said earlier, so take some time to look at it. It's definitely a site to visit when looking for a lot of funny information. What's more, you can kinda tell that nerds built this site, which makes it all the more stupid.

ABNORMALITY: 5 STUPIDITY: 9 ENTERTAINMENT: 8

498

Furby Autopsy
www.phobe.com/furby

I suspect that many children have disassembled their Furbies after they got bored with the senseless rambling of those annoying things. But the people at this site have actually performed an autopsy on one of the furry robotic toys.

At the Furby Autopsy page, you can see the autopsy of the Furby Toh-Loo-Ka. They list virtually everything about the Furby, from what parts made him say the annoying things he said to a whole FAQ on theories of how it might be possible to hack a Furby and make him talk like Beavis and Butthead or command him to move and slaughter stuffed animals using a laptop computer. Maybe you can even program one to destroy Microsoft!

COMMENTS: Now that I think about it, would it really be classified as an autopsy, even though a Furby was never alive in the first place? My hope is that Microsoft is destroyed, and that a mysterious Furby is found at the crime scene…. Anyway, I'd recommend visiting this site if you ever wondered how Furbies acted so annoying.

ABNORMALITY: 9 STUPIDITY: 8 ENTERTAINMENT: 6

497

Marshmallow Bunny Survival Tests
www.keypad.org/bunnies

They're fun to eat, but apparently somebody got bored with this plain concept and decided to try something else.

It's the Marshmallow Bunny Survival Tests. These sick individuals have gotten a few of those cute little marshmallow bunnies we get at Easter and they've subjected them to tests such as the "Laser Exposure Endurance," the "Slow Application of Heat Test," the "Hot Tub Test," and much more. Each test name links to a separate page containing an analysis and a few photographs from the test.

COMMENTS: It makes me sad to see those lovable little bunnies suffer so much. What did they ever do to us?! Huh?! It makes me all teary and sad.... Seriously, though, this website is somewhat amusing for those who enjoy those trivial objects. I guess they're not just only good for Easter.

ABNORMALITY: 9 STUPIDITY: 9 ENTERTAINMENT: 5

496

How to Keep an Idiot Busy
www.pagetutor.com/idiot/idiot.html

This website is extremely simple, yet very fun. A button is placed on the screen, and the closer you get to it, the farther it goes away from your cursor. It is possible to catch it; however, people who are not very computer competent will have their work cut out for them.

COMMENTS: This site is pretty fun, despite how simple it is. I like to continually click the button when I "catch" it, as if I were an axe murderer chopping up a victim. But wait a minute…because I like it, am I considered an idiot? No! Why did I fall for something so stupid?! I must go wallow in shame now; I have disgraced myself.

ABNORMALITY: 9 STUPIDITY: 9 ENTERTAINMENT: 6

495

101 Uses for AOL Disks
www.earthplaza.com/aoldisks

AOL disks.

They appear in your mailbox and in almost every electronics store. Their numbers are in the thousands, perhaps millions, and nobody has any use for them.

Until now.

This website shows you all the things you can do with those annoying little things. From constructing a life-size Stonehenge replica to using them for drink coasters, this page offers you 101 uses, some of them halfway serious, for AOL disks.

COMMENTS: After viewing this page, you might want to pick up a package or two of these things. I mean, it's not like anyone's going to miss them, right? How many bazillion AOL disks are there? I bet if you could line all of them up, they'd circle the Earth. Hey, there's a use! But seriously, if you're looking for a good laugh or some way to use the annoying disks, go to this page.

ABNORMALITY: 6   STUPIDITY: 8   ENTERTAINMENT: 7

494

Dyslexic Gerbil Society
www.geocities.com/Petsburgh/Fair/8006

This site claims there's a new demographic debilitated by dyslexia. Gerbils?!?! The International Society for the Prevention of Cruelty to Dyslexic Newborn Gerbils is, inexplicably, in its fifth year of existence. The society is "devoted to the plight of the helpless infant gerbils that come into this harsh world unable to learn, write, or even communicate with their families." See case studies with subjects like "Benny," who "tragically died due to overwhelming torture due to his mutation and handicap." This torture involved "fetching sessions" in the "back room" involving "a 1" diameter PVC pipe, Vaseline, gerbil food, and 'Benny.' The site says that they cannot reveal the details due to the "confidentiality" of the experiments, but they encourage you to "use your imagination." I'd rather not, thank you.

COMMENTS: How exactly do gerbils suffer by not being able to read or write? I'd think they'd be more content to run on their wheels or play with their toys. What do non-dyslexic gerbils read anyway? Heavy stuff, like Shakespeare, Tolstoy, or Orwell? Or do they like more flaky stuff, like *The Secret* (the pseudo-New Age self-help philosophy that's only popular because Oprah endorsed it)? Given those choices, maybe the dyslexic gerbils are lucky.

ABNORMALITY: 9   STUPIDITY: 9   ENTERTAINMENT: 5

493

SPAM.com
www.spam.com

Yes, the official site of everyone's favorite lunchmeat! They feature the origins of SPAM, the SPAM family tree, SPAM in history, SPAM gear, and a form to order SPAM! There's even a section on the three (yes, three!) "Spammobiles," including a large recreational vehicle painted to look like a giant blue can of Spam. Each vehicle features electric sandwich grills to prepare SPAMBURGER hamburgers. Each Spammobile is, of course, manned by a "crew of trained Spambassadors."

COMMENTS: This is an official product page, believe it or not, so a lot of careful consideration has gone into this site. That, in itself, is proof of its stupidity; no great amount of time should be spent on SPAM. It's an icky luncheon meat! It tastes bad; it's in a can. What more proof do you want? Even though I've never tasted it…still! I've met people who have. SPAM is people! SPAM is people!!! Okay, maybe not.…

ABNORMALITY: 7   STUPIDITY: 9   ENTERTAINMENT: 3

492

The Slightly Less Than Official Spork Page
www.members.tripod.com/~sporkk

Spork! Ah, those lovable utensils. This page praises everything that is great about these useful eating tools. You'll find a definition of a Spork, uses for Sporks, and much more information on Sporks. They also have a section of locations to buy Sporks, and a definition of a technique called "fooning" that you can use with Sporks. There are even links to other Spork pages! Who would think there are others?

COMMENTS: Who would dedicate their time to building a temple to Sporks? Is it because Taco Bell uses them? Was that lovable Chihuahua that cute? I mean, I loved the "Yo Quiero Taco Bell" thing, but did he have that power? Is it possible that dog lured people into subconsciously displaying their love for Taco Bell in a Spork website? Could it have been a failed plot for Taco Bell to take over the world, which they are now attempting to conceal? Okay, I'm getting to be a bit too much of a conspiracy theorist there.…

ABNORMALITY: 9   STUPIDITY: 9   ENTERTAINMENT: 4

491   Gingerbread Menace

members.iconn.net/~phantom/gbmgobad.htm

Killer gingerbread men!

This page chronicles attacks by those deceptively cute little gingerbread men. There are a number of stories, some viewer-submitted, about when gingerbread men snap (no pun intended). There are a surprising number of stories, including attacks "On Christmas Eve," "Vampire Gingerbread Men," "Trailer Park Gingers," "Senseless Attack on a Milkman," and much more. Pictures are also included. What's even more surprising is that some of the stories are very well written.

COMMENTS: Who knew that gingerbread men could be so dangerous? They lure you with their great smell and cute smiles around the "most wonderful time of the year." Then, when you least expect it, BOOM! I shudder just thinking about it. This site is fairly funny, but it's not something that's up there on my list. Still, you might want to take a look.

ABNORMALITY: 7 STUPIDITY: 8 ENTERTAINMENT: 5

---

490   The Oracle of Bacon

www.oracleofbacon.org

Ever notice how Kevin Bacon appears in a whole lot of movies? No? Well, you will after you take a visit to the "Oracle of Bacon." It's quite simple: you type in a name of a celebrity, and the Oracle will show you how that person is linked to Kevin Bacon in movies. For example, if you type in Sarah Michelle Gellar, it will say, "Sarah Michelle Gellar was in *Scream 2* with Luke Wilson." Then it will say, "Luke Wilson was in *My Dog Skip* with Kevin Bacon." You'll be surprised at how many people are linked to Kevin Bacon this way. The fact that this is a fairly common game doesn't diminish the amazingly huge scope of actors, past and present, connected through the Oracle of Bacon.

COMMENTS: This page is only a little abnormal and a little stupid, but it is extremely fun. For the serious movie fan or even the casual flick viewer, you will be surprised that even old-time movie stars like Humphrey Bogart or silent-film star Douglas Fairbanks can be linked to Kevin Bacon.

ABNORMALITY: 1 STUPIDITY: 2 ENTERTAINMENT: 9

489

Official Sizzling Saucer Lady Report
www.geocities.com/sizzling_saucer_lady_ssl

"Beware! The Alien Threat is closer than you think." At least, according to the Sizzling Saucer Lady Report, an "alien watchdog site about alien visitors known as SSL Aliens from that which is Beyond Planet Earth." This site has all the information you'll need on the alien threat. Learn about alien culture, alien sightings, and, of course, alien abductions. But there's more: alien advertisements, and even alien personal ads! An adult human woman might want to respond to the ad by an "Evil Alien Overlord" who seeks an enterprising female "for genetic transformation and mind control as well as be my slave-Queen."

COMMENTS: The OSSLR is good for a laugh or two, if only because it pokes fun at all the crazy theories that people actually think are true.

ABNORMALITY: 8 STUPIDITY: 8 ENTERTAINMENT: 8

488

Amish Laptop
www.mystique.net/amish.html

The Amish people have built their first computer! But wait, the Amish "don't use electricity, and they don't have phones," so how can this be true? This site brings you top-secret info straight from the "Amish Technology Resource Center located in a remote underground bunker in Intercourse, Pennsylvania."

Well, not really. But the picture of the "computer" is an interesting thing to take a look at. It is basically a wooden abacus in a box with beads, chalk, slate, and other ancient learning tools. A chicken powers the "laptop," and it uses a "can and string" modem to connect to the outside world. The Amish may frown upon technology, but according to the site, "the laptop is by no means technology." And, in case you were wondering, it is *not* Windows compatible.

COMMENTS: Amish technology, what a concept! What's next, honest and ethical politicians? Even scarier is the fact that the Amish are not stopping with this laptop. "Future beadware includes a butter churn simulator, a virtual barn builder, and a quilt designer." Luddites beware!

ABNORMALITY: 7 STUPIDITY: 8 ENTERTAINMENT: 7

487

The Official National Enquirer Website
www.nationalenquirer.com

This is the one periodical where, unlike all others, what's in it is probably not true. Here, you can catch up on all the latest gossip. You're sure to find up-to-date trash regarding scandal-sheet favorites like Paris Hilton, Lindsay Lohan, Barry Bonds, Oprah, and Liz. Get the scoop on the battles with booze, who's getting fat or thin, and the latest fashion disaster. And of course, don't forget the cheating and custody battles, like the one over recently deceased Anna Nicole Smith's baby. Sadly enough, Anna would have probably been a better parent than any of the potential fathers in this case, including Howard K. "Not-That-Sleazy-Radio-Host" Stern.

COMMENTS: Chances are, if something outrageous or even semi-controversial happens to a star, this wild and wacky weekly tabloid will be there to "report" it. If you actually derive some enjoyment out of this rag, do two things: one, visit this site regularly, and two, tell me why you do.

ABNORMALITY: 8 STUPIDITY: 7 ENTERTAINMENT: 8

486

The Payphone Project
www.payphone-project.com

This website has an entire list of articles regarding payphones, from the article about prepaid phone cards to the first ever "submarine phone booth." Where do you put the quarters in a wet suit? There are several fascinating photo galleries. Pictures range from "Payphones of Copenhagen" to a payphone outside a Hollywood adult book store to a line of payphones at the "Vince Lombardi Rest Stop" on the New Jersey Turnpike. "These phone booths smelled absolutely nasty. Evidence suggests that these phone booths double as bathrooms." Only in New Jersey could you come up with the idea of smelly phone booths as a tribute to a legendary football genius!

COMMENTS: I'm going to attempt to explain this website in a rational and sane way, with a firmly logical premise. It's a secret place where Superman can look to find a phone booth to change into his costume. No, that's not it. It's a valuable public service for travelers without cell phones. Nah. Wait, it's another stupid, inane, and meaningless website. Yes! That's it!

ABNORMALITY: 8 STUPIDITY: 7 ENTERTAINMENT: 8

485
Fixing Your Website
www.webpagesthatsuck.com/mysterymeat navigation.html

This web page is unusual. It is apparently trying to offer website advice while explaining how web pages are just trying to make money and have no other purpose…at least I think that's the message. Either that or they just threw something together when they weren't thinking straight. See if you understand the message. Anyway, this web page has a lot of rambling text and pictures that are sure to generate a laugh or two. It is divided into different "Mystery Meat" sections. I think the people who made this site were paranoid, stupid, or both.

COMMENTS: I've never seen a website whose purpose is so unclear. Maybe it's me, but I just don't get it.

ABNORMALITY: 9 STUPIDITY: 7 ENTERTAINMENT: 6

484
Top 10 Stupidest Lists
www.davesite.com/humor/top10

Ever seen those top-ten lists on TV? Well, now there are lists like that for stupidity. At Top 10 Stupidest Lists, you can view dozens of top-ten lists of stupidity. "Top 10 Stupid Things to Do with a Newspaper" is one such list. In it are examples like "Put it by the toilet in case you run out of toilet paper," or "Sit down in your armchair and pretend to read it in case your in-laws show up." Another funny one is "Top 10 Stupidest Ways to Answer the Telephone," one of which is "Pizza Hut Japan, how may we help you?" There are tons of lists just like these to fit any taste in humor.

COMMENTS: Some of the lists are pretty funny, but you can tell that a good portion of them, maybe about half, are poorly done. At least they admit their stupidity, unlike many other sites listed in this book. Nevertheless, it is a pretty funny site.

ABNORMALITY: 4 STUPIDITY: 8 ENTERTAINMENT: 8

483

B's Cucumber Pages
www.lpl.arizona.edu/~bcohen/cucumbers/info

This is the site to go to when you want to know something about cucumbers. Anything and everything on cucumbers is here, including the fact that a cucumber is a fruit. Oh my! I never knew! For education, there is a "Brief History of Cucumbers." There is even a recipe file containing the ingredients for cucumber lemonade and cucumber mousse. Wow, yummy!

COMMENTS: Actually, I don't think this website was meant to be funny, but it is. The .edu extension proves that it was probably made by some college geeks who were really into gardening. But hey, different strokes for different folks, right?

ABNORMALITY: 6 STUPIDITY: 8 ENTERTAINMENT: 5

482

Mr. T versus Everything
www.mrtvseverything.com

Ever wanted to see the invincible Mr. T fight someone? Wonder how it would turn out? Well, then this site is for you.

Like Grudge Match (see number 456), this site features links to pages that pit Mr. T against virtually anyone or anything imaginable, and I do mean anything, from Mr. T vs. Hitler, John Wayne, Austin Powers, AC/DC, or the Australian Parliament to Mr. T vs. Eminem. There's even a section for Mr. T vs. Santa! Each site is a series of pictures of Mr. T fighting something all while saying his famous catchphrases. Most of them are actually very funny. My favorite is Mr. T vs. Al Gore, where Al Gore is building a doomsday machine and Mr. T is the only one who can stop him. If you visit the site, I highly recommend checking that one out.

COMMENTS: I pity da fool who mess with me! I'm gonna bust you down, sucka! If you want to see Mr. T pitted against almost any famous figure (and some not so famous ones), check out Mr. T versus Everything. And remember, kids; don't mess with Mr. T. As you'll find in Mr. T vs. Elmo, "that's not going to tickle"!

ABNORMALITY: 7 STUPIDITY: 9 ENTERTAINMENT: 10

481

The Infamous
Expperpale

www.perp.com/whale

This website tells you the entire story of when a beached, rotting whale was intentionally exploded. The whole story is here, complete with actual news video. You see, the Oregon authorities couldn't figure out what to do with the smelly, decomposing whale. They couldn't tow it or burn it, so they decided to blow it up and hope that seagulls would eat the pieces. Except the explosion didn't quite go right. You'll have to see it to believe it.

I'm not quite sure what the purpose of the site is, or where they got the whole exploding-whale idea for that matter. It might not even be true, as the site mentions that many people thought this was an urban legend. I'm not sure, although the news footage does look real. I guess it just shows that some people love blowing anything up.

COMMENTS: Man oh man, is this site screwed up. It's a disgrace! It's ridiculous! Oh well. Watch out for flying blubber!

ABNORMALITY: 8 STUPIDITY: 9 ENTERTAINMENT: 3

480

The Ghostwatcher
www.ghostwatcher.com

Ever wanted to go ghost hunting?

If you answered yes, head on over to this site. Apparently, this paranoid guy decided to put cameras up all over his house. He claimed that he "heard things he couldn't explain." (We all do, bud; that doesn't mean we have to set up cameras.) So, random visitors called "Watchers" watch the cameras and report any unusual activity. You can browse the archives for unusual incidents or you can watch the house yourself. What's more, this site is pretty serious.

COMMENTS: This is definitely one weird site. If you look at the photos, you wonder what happened to them. I mean, it's not like he really has ghosts, right? Ghosts are not real, except for the ghosts of stars who are way past their prime, like Mr. T. (I pity da fool who don't like my old shows! Give me work!)

ABNORMALITY: 9 STUPIDITY: 3 ENTERTAINMENT: 8

479

Evil Plan Generator
http://members.tripod.com/mrpuzuzu/plan.html

Ever had your heart set on World Domination? Destroying the Earth? Sounds like a good idea, but how would you do it? That's where the Evil Plan Generator comes in. This devious device allows you to customize your crafty scheme to the fullest. Determine your objective and motive, then move on to your type of henchmen (choices include the Undead, Animal Minions, and Mean English Teachers). Then choose your base of operations (Air Fortress, Amusement Park, and Underground Secret Headquarters of Doom are just a few options). From there, you can construct the three stages of your plan, your targets, and finally your ideal Superweapon that will destroy all that is right in the world. The end result is a short but workable evil plan propagated precisely for you.

COMMENTS: If you've ever pondered an evil plan of some sort (and haven't we all?), this site will be perfect for you. Every evil super villain cliché can be included in your plan, along with some fun extra options. My only complaint is that the end result is a little too generic. Still, the Evil Plan Generator is fun, at least for the first few times.

ABNORMALITY: 5 STUPIDITY: 8 ENTERTAINMENT: 8

478

Ultimate Taxi
www.ultimatetaxi.com

This website is home to the world's greatest Internet broadcasting taxi cab.

On this wacky page, you'll find all you need to know about the ultimate taxi cab and its famous riders. This wild and crazy vehicle cruises the streets of Aspen, Colorado, a famous celebrity hangout. The special features in this taxi include fiber-optic lights, four red lasers, one green laser projector, a Sony Notebook computer, an "Aironet 2 Megabit high-speed wireless LAN," and various other novelties and pieces of high-tech equipment. Most interesting is the photo gallery show of the many celebrities who have been taken for a ride, from George Lucas to Clint Eastwood to Jerry Seinfeld and more.

COMMENTS: Now wait just a minute; how can all that technology fit into a taxi cab? I wonder. Think about it: they say it has a "Dry Ice Fog Machine" and "12 Mini-Stage Lights." I don't think all of that can fit into one car. Heck, I'd have trouble fitting all that in one small apartment!

ABNORMALITY: 7 STUPIDITY: 9 ENTERTAINMENT: 6

477

Pick the Worst
www.picktheworst.com

The concept behind this site is simple: you are given two options, and you must choose which is the worst of the two. For example, you can choose between "learning you were stolen at birth by rich people" or "learning you were sold at birth by poor people." Another example is "political commercials" or "herpes commercials." Now that's a tough choice! One leaves you with an unpleasant, irritated, and shameful feeling…and the other is about a venereal disease. One that I really didn't understand was "eating cereal without milk" or "having pancakes without syrup." I can see how the dry pancakes would be bad, but I like eating my cereal without milk.

COMMENTS: These questions really make you think. Some are casual, some are kind of gross, and others are heavy stuff. Psychology buffs would have a field day with the answers people give for these questions. Forced choices reveal a lot about a person's subconscious mind—and they're fun. The most disturbing one for me was "having to choose which one of your children should live" or "being forced to watch the movie Gigli." In my mind, the only choice would be "sorry, kids!"

ABNORMALITY: 9 STUPIDITY: 9 ENTERTAINMENT: 6

476

Geek Quiz
www.geekquiz.com

Quizzes galore are on this site!
Here, you can find all the quizzes you could want and some you don't (no, you don't have to do all of them). Quizzes include the Star Wars Quiz to test your knowledge of the Force; the Math Quiz, which stays true to the site's domain name; and the Dead Celebrity Quiz, which tests your knowledge of famous (and infamous) dead celebrities.

COMMENTS: This website is definitely good for a laugh. But mostly, it's great for testing your knowledge of topics you've always known you're an expert in. Or at least, topics you think you know well. Don't be too confident in your skills, young Padawan.

ABNORMALITY: 5 STUPIDITY: 7 ENTERTAINMENT: 8

475

Will It Blend?
www.willitblend.com

This is an "extreme blending" site. They take ingredients or objects that most people would never put in a blender, then attempt to blend the objects while a video recorder runs. The site has two sections, "try this at home" and "don't try this at home." The majority of the experiments are in the "don't try this at home" section, and include objects such as glow sticks, magnets, and tape measures. There's also a video that claims to blend diamonds, but they confess in the description that, in reality, cubic zirconia were blended; they were "playing along" because they saw "how happy [we] were." Playing along. Right. In reality, this site is just a giant commercial for a brand of blenders called "Blendtec," as the name is plastered all over the site along with wishy-washy promotional language.

COMMENTS: What a scam this site is! It masquerades as a cool video series, but they're really just peddling their product. It's like a high-class infomercial. "High class" as in an elaborate scam for a product that stinks. Will it blend? Unless you're looking for a commercial for a crappy blender, don't bother finding out.

ABNORMALITY: 6 STUPIDITY: 8 ENTERTAINMENT: 4

474

Foam Bath Fish Time
www.savetz.com/fishtime/fishtime.cgi?-5

They're foam, they're fish, and they can tell time!

You heard me right! When you go to this website, you can click on your time zone, and four foam fishies will appear on top showing your time in military time (I didn't know fish were enlisted in the U.S. Navy). Talk about technology! You may already have a clock, but this is a fish clock. It's better than an ordinary clock. And it's foam, too.

COMMENTS: In all seriousness, this is a site that's only worth spending a few minutes on. You laugh at first, but then it'll get boring. Sadly, that's the case for many things these days. It's kind of amusing, though. Check it out once, but I'll make a safe bet that you won't return.

ABNORMALITY: 7 STUPIDITY: 9 ENTERTAINMENT: 5

473

Santa Claus:
The Great Impostor
www.av1611.org/othpubls/santa.html

This site states that Santa Claus is not only an impostor as a Christmas symbol, but also a tool of Satan! The site references dozens of obscure Bible verses that supposedly warn against a "deceiver" and talk about Satan ruling the Earth from the sky. Satan preys on the weak, specifically children; hence, Santa is Satan in disguise. There are also rants about other terrible tools of Satan: Harry Potter, the Internet, public schools, and rock and roll music—specifically, George Harrison from the Beatles. Now I can understand Marilyn Manson as being Satanic, but...the Beatles? "Hey Jude" and "Yellow Submarine" as sinful anthems?

COMMENTS: To think that Santa Claus is a Satanic figure is, to be frank, nuts. Santa is an innocent holiday icon, specifically intended to make kids happy. On the other hand, Santa is an anagram of Satan!!! But, I'm gonna cut Santa some slack, and you should too. We don't want to be on his naughty list come Christmastime.

ABNORMALITY: 8 STUPIDITY: 5 ENTERTAINMENT: 8

472

The "Should I Stalk
William Shatner?" Test
www.apeculture.com/games/shatner.htm

One word: why? I don't know, but apparently these people have devised some sort of test to help you figure out if you're "dedicated" enough to stalk William Shatner. Such a nice test, isn't it? With multiple choice questions like "Those priceline.com ads are…" and answers like "b. Proof that Shatner understands the comic potential of his iconic status" and "d. a blinding, white light, beckoning me," that's just scary.

COMMENTS: I think I'd be the last person who'd want to stalk William Shatner. Not only does his speaking style scare me, but I'm afraid he'll start saying, "DennyCrane, DennyCrane" (his catchphrase from *Boston Legal*) over and over again until I go insane. If you want a good laugh, take this test, but if you decide to actually stalk the Shatman, you need help. Serious help.

ABNORMALITY: 7 STUPIDITY: 8 ENTERTAINMENT: 8

471

PhoneSpell
www.phonespell.org

On this site, you type in a phone number and it will tell you what it spells. Take the number 1-800-555-5525 (do *not* call this number, I have no idea what it is, if it exists). It spells "Jake" or "Lake" for the last four numbers. Interesting, no? This site is quite simple, but at the same time, it's surprisingly fun.

COMMENTS: For such a simple concept, this is an awesomely addicting site. Try all sorts of numbers! Try your friend's numbers, your number, a local store number, Microsoft's customer support number, or any number. When you're done with that, try names, words, and phrases. The fun doesn't stop!

ABNORMALITY: 5 STUPIDITY: 8 ENTERTAINMENT: 8

470

The World's Most High-Tech Urinal
www.johnchow.com/the-worlds-most-high-tech-urinal

If you thought automatically-flushing urinals were fancy, wait until you see this. The purpose of this product is to, um, relieve the problem of drunken men urinating on the street at night. Usually they're the ones who partied a little too hard and don't have the logical capacity to "go" in a more acceptable place. This potty is programmed to plunge below the street during the day, and then hydraulically lift up to street level during the night. The urinal has no doors, meaning it doesn't get all nasty like porta potties, nor does it become a hangout for hookers and hopheads. These high-tech lavatories are already standard in places like the Netherlands and London. Those Europeans have thought of everything, haven't they?

COMMENTS: I recommend checking this one out. This thing is actually a great idea. I say that after using many portable toilets at my sister's cross-country meets when I was younger. Those have to be the most disgusting two-by-two-foot spaces on the face of the Earth. The smell is worse than a hippie who hasn't showered in fifteen years. By the way, if you ever meet somebody like that, spray him—with a bottle of Febreze. It works wonders—I know from experience (don't ask).

ABNORMALITY: 8 STUPIDITY: 5 ENTERTAINMENT: 8

469

This page is exactly what it says it is: dumb jokes.

On this page are a few dozen jokes on a lot of different subjects. Topics include "Cellular Phone Jokes" (I myself have never heard a cellular phone joke) to "A Bill Gates Joke" (ah, the best kind!). There's also stuff everybody can use, like the aptly named "Useless Information!" You can find all this and more at Dumb Jokes.

COMMENTS: This site is another one that's good for a laugh. Or two. Or three. Or twenty-three. You decide how many you want to view. The jokes are well thought out, so you might want to drop by this site when you're looking for a genuine laugh or two. There are no archives, but there are a lot of jokes.

ABNORMALITY: 4 STUPIDITY: 8 ENTERTAINMENT: 8

468

Virtual Stupidity!
www.picknowl.com.au/homepages/cyton/default.htm

This is yet another collection of stupid jokes (there seems to be no end… and there probably won't be). The jokes are pretty funny, and there are lots of them to keep your funny bone satisfied. Jokes include "things to do with a 300 bps modem" (which would transmit less than a five-word Microsoft Word document), "why you should never buy a Macintosh" (good ol' Bill wants to see that that never happens), and much more.

COMMENTS: You'll be busy with this site for a while. I can't express enough how much this site is similar to the one I reviewed before this one. Still, there are different jokes, so visit them both.

ABNORMALITY: 5 STUPIDITY: 9 ENTERTAINMENT: 8

467

Dancing Bush
www.miniclip.com/dancingbush.htm

For those whose computers can handle it, this site is a must-see. It shows George W. Bush dancing the groovy disco. During his routine, you can add disco lights, spotlights, a dance floor, and other features to the video clip. You can make George do a variety of dance moves, like the moonwalk, the splits, and the funky chicken. Now this is the Internet at its finest!

COMMENTS: Who knew that the president was such a good dancer? Well, it must be a nice escape. He doesn't have to worry about stress-inducing things like spelling, grammar, or justifying the war in Iraq while he's on the dance floor, now does he? The music also adds a nice touch, so make sure your speakers are active. Love him or hate him, you've got to admit: He's got the moves.

ABNORMALITY: 7 STUPIDITY: 8 ENTERTAINMENT: 9

466

FreakyDreams.com
www.freakydreams.com/freaky.htm

This website interprets your dreams…kind of.

It's quite simple, really. Just type in a dream you've had (or haven't had) and this website will "interpret" your dream. Most of the time, the interpretation isn't remotely relevant to the dream though, so don't take the answers too seriously. (In fact, a phone psychic can give you better interpretations than this site.) Even so, this is another site with endless possibilities.

COMMENTS: This website is pretty amusing. Whether you're looking for divine answers or a good laugh, this is the place to go. Who knows? Maybe you'll get lucky and will actually find that answer you're looking for…or not.

ABNORMALITY: 6 STUPIDITY: 7 ENTERTAINMENT: 8

465

Sox: Sock Monkey with a Harley

www.homestead.com/soxmonkey/scrapbook.html

He's a sock, he's a monkey, and he's got a Harley!

This page tells the story of "Sox, the Sock Monkey with a Harley." It shows several photos of a rather crudely put-together sock monkey on a toy motorcycle (when I could be entertained by sock puppets and toy motorcycles…those were the days). The monkey has a leather jacket on, and it says his favorite food is birthday cake. (What does he do when it's not his birthday?)

COMMENTS: Another pitiful site. This site is so stupid it's not even funny. I can only wonder what weirdo thought this up. He or she must have been so bored this was the only thing to do to keep from going crazy.

ABNORMALITY: 7 STUPIDITY: 10 ENTERTAINMENT: 2

464

Redneck Adventures of Mutt and Jeff

Members.tripod.com/~merilu88/index.html

The adventures of the rednecks are here!

Well, not really. This is a site featuring some photos and stories from a redneck family. There are photos of the trailer park they live in, photos of their home, a redneck family tree, and other random photos, stories, and tidbits of information. All that's missing is a picture of a road-kill buffet.

COMMENTS: This site is extremely stupid, yet funny at the same time. It's funny to see how these hicks lead their lives. Maybe it's just me, but I liked it. Maybe it's from watching all of that Jeff Foxworthy stuff.

ABNORMALITY: 6 STUPIDITY: 10 ENTERTAINMENT: 7

463

The Most Neglected Site on the Web

www.mostneglectedsite.com

This is one site that I guarantee will still be there when you read this.

This site prides itself on one thing: it never changes. Period. They created this site one day then left it the way it was. Forever. They have a lot of features that ordinary stupid web pages have, but they're extremely limited and are, naturally, never updated. You may feel cheated, but hey, that's the point.

COMMENTS: Kudos to this site: I first found it four years ago, and it still hasn't changed. No doubt its creators have forgotten all about it and moved on to better (or worse) things in life. Laziness? Maybe. But maybe letting go of your creation and moving on is a good thing. Whatever the case, this is one result of negligence we can take pleasure in.

ABNORMALITY: 8 STUPIDITY: 9 ENTERTAINMENT: 6

462

Patent of the Week

www.patentoftheweek.com

On this website, you can see a lot of weird, bizarre, and crazy inventions.

At the "Patent of the Week" website, you can see unusual patents for inventions that have come up over the years. From the "Device for Accelerated Growth" to the "Feminine Undergarment with Calendar," this website has almost all of the wacky patents you can think of. If you have Adobe Acrobat Reader, you can even see the blueprints for these devices.

COMMENTS: This website is hilarious! When you see all these strange patents, you'll laugh at how incredibly useless they are. There are things in here that nobody, and I mean nobody, can use. It's stupid, and naturally, it's a great site to visit!

ABNORMALITY: 8 STUPIDITY: 8 ENTERTAINMENT: 8

461

Poke Alex in the Eye: The Game
www.pokealexintheeye.com

At this bizarre website, you can poke a freckled-face geek named Alex in the eye. They have three difficulty levels: one where he's poked automatically (there's not a lot of purpose in that, though), one where you poke him and he doesn't resist (also not that hard), and another where he dodges your pokes (*now* we're getting somewhere). It's pretty amusing to see somebody get poked in the eye repeatedly, somehow…

COMMENTS: This web page is somewhat funny. And I'm using "somewhat" generously. For a few seconds you can be entertained by poking somebody in the eye, but then this site loses its appeal.

ABNORMALITY: 7 STUPIDITY: 9 ENTERTAINMENT: 6

460

Virtual Bubble Wrap
www.virtual-bubblewrap.com

Do you like playing with bubble wrap? (You know, that fun stuff that comes in packages.) Do you love hearing the joyous sound of popping bubble wrap, but packages just don't come often enough for you to enjoy it on a daily basis? If so, head on over to this site! It features a whole sheet for your popping pleasure. When you're done, click the Reload button and you'll have a whole new sheet ready to go!

COMMENTS: I love popping bubble wrap. Who doesn't like it? There is not a person I know who does not enjoy this blissfully bubbly material. It drives some people crazy, though…wait a minute, did I just contradict myself?

ABNORMALITY: 6 STUPIDITY: 8 ENTERTAINMENT: 8

459

Cybercones.com
www.cybercones.com

Ice cream! We all love it, and now it's on the Web!

On this site, you select a number of options to make your very own virtual ice cream cone. You can select from M&Ms, sprinkles, and caramel and hot-fudge toppings, as well as strawberry, chocolate, and vanilla flavors (mmm…makes my stomach growl just thinking about it). At the end, you click on a button, and voila! Your ice cream cone is visible, ready for eating…er…viewing.

COMMENTS: This website is fun despite its simple concept. It makes you hungry, naturally. Good for when you want a laugh or two, but not a page to mark under your favorites.

ABNORMALITY: 5 STUPIDITY: 7 ENTERTAINMENT: 6

458

Net Disaster: Destroy the Web!
www.netdisaster.com

Have you ever found a website that really pushed your buttons? Did you ever want to destroy that website, but your hacker skills weren't up to snuff, or you just didn't want to get in trouble (or both)? Not to worry—Net Disaster has you covered. This website allows you to type in any website—I used Yahoo.com as a guinea pig (no offense, Yahoo)—then decimate it with your choice of destructive disasters. Choose from nukes, meteors, dinosaurs, or alien invasion. You can choose to have Net Disaster destroy the site automatically, or you can use your mouse to destroy the site yourself. (Is that even a choice?) A variety of categories, including nature, technology, creatures, and "dirty," also allow you to defile the website with a number of disgusting bodily fluids. Not all of the methods are destructive, though. The "flower power" option simply lets you cover the website in a colorful floral bouquet. Groovy, man.

COMMENTS: This is a great place to visit if you find a website you really don't like. Use it on your nauseating employer's site, a company whose product let you down, even your own website! Better yet, use it on one of the other sites in this book. I highly recommend Carrot Top's website (see number 1). You know that wretched redhead deserves it.

ABNORMALITY: 7 STUPIDITY: 6 ENTERTAINMENT: 8

457

Cyberparodies.com
www.cyberparodies.com

This website is full of hilarious parodies of modern-day songs. Some of them are actually quite funny and well written in terms of humor. They have songs available such as "My Name Is Al Bundy" (parody of Eminem's "My Name Is") or "MP3 Killed the Media Star" (nice idea for a parody, but it doesn't rhyme that well).

COMMENTS: Their selection is somewhat limited, but it's still a funny page that you should visit. Some of the songs are quite creative. After all, you can't go wrong with a parody called "I Hate Jar Jar Binks" (parody of Joan Jett's "I Love Rock and Roll").

ABNORMALITY: 5 STUPIDITY: 8 ENTERTAINMENT: 7

456

Grudge Match
www.grudge-match.com

What would it be like if the A-Team and MacGyver fought it out in a steel-covered battlefield? Who would win? Would it be close? What would contribute to the outcome? Grudge Match answers this and many other questions on their site. They have comprehensive predictions for Flipper vs. Jaws, the Death Star vs. the *Enterprise* (Death Star all the way!), the Headless Horseman vs. the Terminator (no contest, the Terminator would whip the Horseman's butt), and much more.

COMMENTS: This is funny! It's like they're giving a preview for a professional wrestling match. With all the commentary and analyzing, it sounds as serious as wrestling announcers. The only difference is this isn't real…wait a minute, that's not a difference!

ABNORMALITY: 5 STUPIDITY: 8 ENTERTAINMENT: 8

455

Elibs.com
www.elibs.com/e/myelibs

Patty had a little monkey, her fleece was pink as snow. It followed her to Abu Dabi one day. It made the children Funkalize and play, to see a monkey at Abu Dabi.

That's my nursery rhyme that I made on Elibs.com. If you've ever done Mad Libs, where you fill in a name, verb, noun, and so on, to complete a story, then you know what this is. For those of you who don't, take my word for it; it's a blast!

COMMENTS: This site is only limited by your creativity. It can be as stupid or as intelligent as you want it to be. From Nancy Pelosi flying to Alaska to Britney Spears jumping to the moon, anything can happen in an elib. There's also already completed elibs for your viewing pleasure. The ratings for abnormality and stupidity vary, because how weird or dumb your elib is will be up to you.

ABNORMALITY: 1–10 STUPIDITY: 1–10 ENTERTAINMENT: 9

454

The Illustrated Guide to Breaking Your Computer
Members.aol.com/spoons1000/break/index.html

Is there such a thing as the "right" way to break your computer? If so, this page shows it. This comprehensive, step-by-step guide shows how to properly make sure your computer will never be able to function again (no offense, buddy, but I don't need a manual to do that; trust me). All the tools you need are listed and there are some helpful photographs, too (as if you need it).

COMMENTS: What defines the right way to break a computer? Style? Rage? Or is it just a matter of procedure? Apparently, the latter. Still, I had absolutely no idea that there were certain procedures to follow when breaking a computer. Well, I guess now I know.

ABNORMALITY: 7 STUPIDITY: 9 ENTERTAINMENT: 6

453

This is for all those who get a kick out of making fun of cops. It's a funny collection of cartoons, real-life tales (like the time when a hunter found a severed head, but it turned out to be a mannequin), top-ten lists, and much more mocking and laughing at the folks who keep the peace. Law-breakers are made fun of here too; they have a rather…creative assortment of terrorist photos (don't ask).

COMMENTS: This site just shows that you can never take anything too seriously; a fine piece of advice, in my humble opinion. This really isn't just police humor, as a side note; it mocks both sides of the law with equal enthusiasm. Please do check out the terrorist photos. You'll either be appalled or you'll love them.

ABNORMALITY: 6 STUPIDITY: 8 ENTERTAINMENT: 8

452

Great Mobile Homes of Mississippi
www.drbukk.com/gmhom/park.html

Yet another glimpse into the fascinating world of the rednecks. This site shows several dwellings of this fascinating group of people. View everything, from the luxurious doublewide trailers (now *that's* good livin') to the modest singlewides, and don't forget the freewheeling "real" mobile homes themselves (which are, of course, the core of this site). Anyone looking to learn more about this vanishing culture should check out this site.

COMMENTS: A funny set of photos, including a funny, albeit staged, redneck family photo. There are plenty of redneck photos here showing almost everything about their southern culture, from their sub-par dental hygiene to the homes themselves. This is a good one to visit for a laugh or two or just to pity these interesting people.

ABNORMALITY: 7 STUPIDITY: 9 ENTERTAINMENT: 6

451   Citizen's Self-Arrest Form
www.ou.edu/oupd/selfarr2.htm

This is a self-arrest form. On it, you'll find everything you need to arrest yourself. Just tell them the crime you committed, a few details, your name, and some other information, and you'll be behind bars before you know it. Normally I would describe the whole site, but instead I'll mention that it's only this particular section that's humorous. The rest of the site is actually quite serious…I think. Funny, serious, you decide.

COMMENTS: My opinion on this site is that the presentation makes it stupid enough to be in this book, whatever its intentions. I am very confused about this one. That makes it stupid in my opinion. The bottom line is that anyone who is stupid enough to fill out this form deserves to be behind bars. Book 'em, Danno!

ABNORMALITY: 8 STUPIDITY: 8 ENTERTAINMENT: 7

---

450   Mark's Apology Note Generator
www.karmafarm.com/formletter.html

Do you hate to apologize? Are you not very good with words? Do you just not like admitting that you were wrong? If so, never fear! This site does it for you. Choose from an assortment of statements, and this site will generate a fully functional apology note, ready for you to take to your girlfriend, mother, or any significant other. Check out the women's version, too; it's pretty funny.

COMMENTS: This is actually quite funny when you do it. I'd only advise sending it to yourself, though. You never know how suspicious the receiver will interpret it to be. Just a friendly warning.

ABNORMALITY: 7 STUPIDITY: 8 ENTERTAINMENT: 7

449

Totally Useless Office Skills
www.jlc.net/~useless

This is the kind of thing I deal with: totally useless and stupid information—only this stuff you can do at the office! Bored when you have nothing to do? Never fear; totally Useless Office Skills are here! There's a new one each day. For example, the Endless Fax. Make two copies of an obnoxious message, tape the ends together, start the fax, and after the first sheet comes out, tape the other ends to make a loop. It's endless!

COMMENTS: This is the type of stuff I love. However, this site is poorly maintained and in need of a lot of additional features, such as archives. But it's still somewhat funny. As a side note, there is a book with these tricks. If you like the book you're reading right now and you need some entertainment for your cubicle, knock yourself out.

ABNORMALITY: 8 STUPIDITY: 9 ENTERTAINMENT: 6

448

The Squirrel Clan
www.hevanet.com/benh/sqclan/index.html

They're cute, they're lovable, and they're on the Web! This website is about squirrels, and why we should do nothing less than worship the ground they walk, er, crawl on. This site includes a Q&A, pictures, reasons why squirrels are more intelligent than us, and a comprehensive plan to help squirrels take over the world. Will the squirrels rule the world? We'll just have to wait and see.

COMMENTS: There are different types of stupidity, but this one has a little bit of everything. Squirrels achieving world domination…what a noble cause. About as noble as an episode of the *Howard Stern* show. The bottom line is that squirrels, while fascinating creatures, probably aren't animals we should bow down to.

ABNORMALITY: 8 STUPIDITY: 9 ENTERTAINMENT: 6

447

The Official
Jerry Springer Website
www.jerryspringertv.com

Jerry! Jerry! Jerry! Yes, this is *the* official site of America's—no, the world's—sleaziest talk show...if you can call this trash a talk show. The *Jerry Springer* official website contains gear for sale, as well as recent episode synopses, such as "My Momma Stole My Man!" or "You'll Never Marry My Son!" Those are some of the mild ones; I excluded the really raunchy ones out of common decency and to keep this book PG rated (at most).

COMMENTS: This rating isn't so much based on the site, but really for the show itself. I mean, Jerry Springer is *the* American icon of stupidity! He attracts trailer-park trash and rednecks to a taping like flies to a bug zapper. Anyway, Jerry Springer *is* stupidity, that much is clear from watching thirty seconds of the show. And there's no final thought needed for that one.

ABNORMALITY: 9 STUPIDITY: 10 ENTERTAINMENT: 7

446

The Official Nerdity
Test Homepage
Home.rochester.rr.com/jbennett/nerd

Do you think you're a nerd? Do you ever wonder how close you are to being a nerd? Did you ever want to take a big test to find out? For those of you who want these things, head to the Official Nerdity Test. It contains a very long and detailed nerdity test (is "nerdity" a word?) that can determine to what extent you are or aren't a nerd.

COMMENTS: Is being a nerd a bad or a good thing? Is it both? What would the majority of the population want to be? In any case, this site is fun, and a lot of the questions on the test are quite creative. I took it and got an 18.9 percent score, and I'm not ashamed to say it.

ABNORMALITY: 7 STUPIDITY: 8 ENTERTAINMENT: 8

445

The Reflex Tester Game
www.reflexgame.com

Think you're alert? Think you're in a constant state of cat-like readiness? Think that you can pounce from the darkness onto your unsuspecting foe?! OK, I put that last one in for fun, but this web page answers the other two. Here's how it works: you start up the test and a window will pop up, cueing you to press the button when the screen changes colors. Judging on how fast you click the button, this site will give you a rating.

COMMENTS: This is pretty cool. It's kind of addictive, actually. (I don't need practice, do I? One more time!) And if you do get addicted, I can't help you. You've been warned!

ABNORMALITY: 6 STUPIDITY: 7 ENTERTAINMENT: 7

444

The First Church of Shatnerology

www.shatnerology.com

Here's more fun from the Great. Space. Captain. Who. Speaks. Disjointedly.

At the First Church at Shatnerology, you can learn tons of bizarre facts about this fanatical fellowship of followers of William Shatner. They "are transfixed by his almighty toupee and girth!" The site is littered with stupidly senseless quotes such as "Exercise is good for the monkey!" and "Putting a Shatnerologist in a room full of ordinary people is like putting a velociraptor in a room full of wiener dogs." Delve deeper into the church's archives and you'll find the "Shatner Discography," featuring artifacts from Shatner's amazingly bad music career. View cover shots of albums such as *The Transformed Man*, which Paul McCartney called "wrong, but so wrong it's great."

COMMENTS: If there's one album I must order from the site, it's *Spaced Out: The Best of Leonard Nimoy and William Shatner*. Leonard Nimoy actually sings a song called "The Ballad of Bilbo Baggins," among others. Truth be told, however, my favorite section isn't the discography; it's the hate mail. In keeping with the site's stupidity, many of the "hate" letters have nothing to do with the former *T.J. Hooker* and current *Boston Legal* star, but merely consist of personal attacks on the writers.

ABNORMALITY: 8 STUPIDITY: 10 ENTERTAINMENT: 8

443

Random Chicken
www.randomchicken.com

This is a page where "chickens are random, and random is the chicken." It's actually quite simple: you get a random picture of a chicken on the page. Then, if you want another random picture, click your refresh button or a special button on the page and presto! You've got a completely different picture of a completely different chicken! Now, I will say that I find absolutely no appeal in this concept, and I don't think you will either; the chickens aren't even doing anything. I mean, show them being chased by pigs or cows or something entertaining! The only things worth seeing are the chicken jokes and recipes (mmm...chicken recipes; now there's something useful).

COMMENTS: The maker of this site must have spent a long time finding chicken pictures. The question is whether he took the pictures himself or got them off the Internet or some other photo source. I hope the latter is true, because if he did go out all over the country and take pictures of chickens, then he needs help. Serious psychological help.

ABNORMALITY: 6 STUPIDITY: 9 ENTERTAINMENT: 5

442

Stop Dr. Laura.com
www.stopdrlaura.com

This is the home page of a truly righteous cause: stopping the evil that is Dr. Laura Schlessinger. According to the site, the mission has been a success; something that few sites of this kind ever do. Dr. Laura's TV show was cancelled. However, you can still look at the archived Stop Dr. Laura.com site. This contains various articles and news regarding the controversial things Dr. Laura has said and done over the years, which the site recorded in an attempt to make people realize how many extreme opinions Dr. Laura has or has had.

COMMENTS: Dr. Laura's show had the potential to cause major misery for me. Misery as in watching *The View* misery (don't get me started with that hideous show). I had listened to Dr. Laura in my grandmother's car for years, and I just don't like her. Let's thank whatever forces were behind the proverbial roadblock that stopped Dr. Laura from further brainwashing the world.

ABNORMALITY: 6 STUPIDITY: 8 ENTERTAINMENT: 8

441

Riddlenut.com
www.riddlenut.com/show.php

If a man walks up to you and says, "Everything I say to you is a lie," is he lying? I'm not quite sure, to tell the truth. In fact, I know that many people have pondered this question. It might be a paradox. Anyway, you can find this riddle and more at Riddlenut. There are more than five hundred riddles for you to ponder for as long or as little as you want.

COMMENTS: Riddles are often full of stupidity. This site is no exception. Why would anybody think these things up? Why would anybody want to spend their time figuring out something that has absolutely no use in ordinary life? I guess that in itself is a riddle we'll never solve.

ABNORMALITY: 8 STUPIDITY: 7 ENTERTAINMENT: 8

440

Useless Information
Home.nycap.rr.com/useless/index.html

The electronic pickle. The guy who bought twelve thousand pudding containers. Antarctica's Red Light District (don't ask). All strange but true stories you can find here on the Useless Information site. Ever heard about how somebody tricked people into thinking that one part of Manhattan was sinking, and that they could cut the end off the island and spin it around to distribute the weight? It's quite funny when you read it.

COMMENTS: These are some weird stories. I never expected these to be true, but supposedly they are. Whether you want to believe it or not (no reference to Ripley's intended there) is for you to decide. Still, regardless of whether you think these stories are true, you'll like them.

ABNORMALITY: 9 STUPIDITY: 7 ENTERTAINMENT: 7

439

The Dialectizer
Rinkworks.com/dialect

"Ah fo'git mah chile at skoo, an' she's still thar. C'd yo' hoof it git her?" This is Redneck dialect (I like rednecks, in case you haven't noticed) from something I typed in at this website. Just type in text, and the Dialectizer will translate it into the slang of your choice. Jive, Swedish Chef, and Pig Latin are among the others available for your translation pleasure.

COMMENTS: This very amusing site is a good one to bookmark. Try typing in some TV catch phrases, like "Is that your final answer?" Now that's funny! Once again, this is a site where the possibilities are endless, so be sure to stop by often.

ABNORMALITY: 6 STUPIDITY: 8 ENTERTAINMENT: 8

438

Crazy Thoughts
www.crazythoughts.com

When someone with multiple personalities threatens to kill himself, is it a hostage situation? How do you know if you're out of invisible ink? These questions are listed along with many others for your pondering pleasure. There are about one hundred, and some of them are actually quite interesting. Why are there Braille signs on drive-up ATMs? I guess we'll never know.

COMMENTS: This site is cool. Check it out once or twice. You'll get a kick out of a lot of the questions here. Some of them actually make you think. For example, I now wonder why psychics keep their jobs if they know the winning lottery numbers. Hey, I would quit my job if I knew what the Powerball jackpot numbers were going to be.

ABNORMALITY: 7 STUPIDITY: 7 ENTERTAINMENT: 7

437

The Animal Defense Militia
www.animaldefense.org

Can you picture a rabid group of animals terrorizing human citizens? Whether you can or can't, check out this site.

It's the Animal Defense Militia, and they're one bad bunch of critters. In the "about ADM" section, the Animal Defense Militia is defined as "a massive paramilitary underground movement of covert operatives committed to using extreme violence while preserving the autonomy and merriment of non-human vertebrates." The words "extreme violence" alone make this group seem like they're not too nice. You can also check out the articles on the site, examples of which are "the war against PETA," "Chickens traumatized by mass egg abductions," and the cruel, gross, and insensitive (but funny) "Eating Right: Grandpa—The Other White Meat."

COMMENTS: Looking at this site, you wonder what exactly your cute little pooch is capable of. You can't know if he has killer instincts implanted deep in his brain, or if he's just thinking, "I want my tummy scratched." Hey, it could be either one. This is a funny satire site, so go see it. But beware the animals!

ABNORMALITY: 7 STUPIDITY: 8 ENTERTAINMENT: 7

436

LemonadeGame.com
www.lemonadegame.com

Did you ever sell lemonade when you were little? Did you ever make money off of it? If you didn't, you should try this game. The goal is to sell as much lemonade as you can in thirty days. You can select how much you charge, manage supplies, and dictate the amount of sugar, lemons, and ice in each pitcher.

COMMENTS: This game is actually really fun! I didn't expect it to be, but it is. There's just something addictive about it. Hmm, maybe that lemonade is getting to me. Must be the sugar. Anyway, try it out! I think you'll like it.

ABNORMALITY: 6 STUPIDITY: 6 ENTERTAINMENT: 8

435

Virtual Flowers
www.virtualflowers.com

Send a virtual flower bouquet to someone using this site. You can order real flowers too and see information about the company, but the stupid part of the site lies in the virtual-bouquet-sending feature. You just click on the picture of the bouquet you want, type in your email address and the recipient's email address (it can be yours, if you want), a short message, and bingo! You've sent a virtual bouquet!

COMMENTS: This could be serious or stupid, depending on how you use it. I mean, does anybody really need virtual flowers? What do you use flowers for if you can't display them in your house? I'm not sure, but this site doesn't seem to care. Anyway, try adding a humorous message with your bouquet. It makes the flowers worth a little bit.

ABNORMALITY: 3 STUPIDITY: 5 ENTERTAINMENT: 7

434

Chicken or Tuna?
www.chickenortuna.com

"Chicken of the Sea? Is it Chicken or Tuna"? This famous line, brought to us by America's favorite blonde bimbo, Jessica Simpson, inspired this mouth-watering website. It's quite simple: you are shown a picture of a mysterious, processed meat-like substance (usually on a sandwich of some sort), and are asked to vote on whether it's chicken or tuna. The website will give you the real answer, along with some hints on how to actually make the dish in the picture. There are a total of ten sandwiches on the site. See how much you know your chicken from your tuna.

COMMENTS: Ah, the antics of Jessica Simpson. I can understand her confusion, actually. I mean, who can tell whether "Chicken of the Sea" is actually chicken or tuna? It's deceptive advertising! These fishy flimflammers should be ashamed of themselves! Who knows how many people like poor Jessica are confused by their sick scam? Actually, it's pretty obvious that it's tuna. It's just fun to pretend that we're all as dense—but unfortunately not as rich—as Jess.

ABNORMALITY: 8 STUPIDITY: 7 ENTERTAINMENT: 7

433

The First Church of the Last Laugh

www.saintstupid.com

This is a website hosting a church dedicated to supreme stupidity. Everything, and I mean everything, on this website is stupid. Period. You can click on sayings, signs, and pictures of stupidity (and there are plenty of those to go around). You can even dare to take the notorious pledge of stupidity or see the First Church of the Last Laugh FAQ.

COMMENTS: Do you get the impression that this site is stupid? If you don't then I can't help you. The people who don't know stupid are the kind of people who watch MTV's *Yo Momma*, the show with tournaments consisting of two people telling "yo momma" jokes to each other. (For example, "Yo momma's so stupid she watches this show!") On the other hand, a religion based on stupidity can't be that bad. As the old saying goes, ignorance is bliss.

ABNORMALITY: 8 STUPIDITY: 9 ENTERTAINMENT: 6

432

I Know Where Bruce Lee Lives

www.skop.com/brucelee/index.htm

Okay, so Bruce Lee is dead. But still, this is one heck of a page.

In it, you make your own kung-fu action movie, complete with special graphics, Flash fighting scenes, and more. You initiate each effect by clicking one of several buttons. Each one delivers a unique scene that's a few seconds long. You can even turn on a recorder, then click combos to make an action film intro worthy of the real thing.

COMMENTS: This site is great! The action music is pretty cool. Classic Bruce Lee. Anyway, this site is great for kung-fu director wannabes, and it's great fun for nearly anybody else. So get to this website, chop chop.

ABNORMALITY: 7 STUPIDITY: 7 ENTERTAINMENT: 8

431

The Deadly Follies of Stick Figure Warning Man
www.capnwacky.com/warning/

Most of us who see warning signs with stick figures in dangerous poses don't think too much of them. But there is a man behind the signs, according to this site. This is the story of Stick Figure Warning Man, who rants angrily about how his job of posing for warning signs makes him miserable. He recalls the unpleasant experiences he had making the signs, and mocks the stupidity of the people who actually need the signs to know what's dangerous.

COMMENTS: Shouldn't it be pretty obvious we're supposed to stay off the subway tracks? Besides the fact that there's a dangerous high-voltage electric current, aren't there also trains that go on the tracks? Then again, some people are pretty stupid. Maybe Stick Figure Warning Man's job is necessary, if only for the idiots of the world.

ABNORMALITY: 8 STUPIDITY: 8 ENTERTAINMENT: 8

430

The Mel Gibson Drunk Driving Game
www.compfused.com/directlink/3970

This entertaining Flash game pokes fun at the drunk driving incident involving Mel Gibson back in July 2006, in which he allegedly harassed the officers who pulled him over by yelling anti-Semitic remarks. Whether Mel is really anti-Semitic may be debatable, but this game is still fun if you're not obsessed with being politically correct. In the game, you get points for picking up tequila bottles while trying to avoid police officers and dodging Stars of David thrown by rabbis on the side of the road. The more booze Mel chugs, the more points you get, but as a tradeoff your control becomes increasingly erratic. There's no time limit, but turn five officers into roadkill, and it's game over. When you finally do get busted, the game gives you your score along with a comment on your driving abilities, usually using a pun from one of Mel's movies, like "Put away your Lethal Weapon and get your hands on the wheel!"

COMMENTS: If you can get over the fact that this game is a little offensive, it can be pretty fun. See how far you can get before you're busted.

ABNORMALITY: 7 STUPIDITY: 6 ENTERTAINMENT: 9

429

Line Rider
www.official-linerider.com/play.html

This is one strange game. You start off with a blank screen, then use a pencil to draw a line. After that, press play and a little person on a sled (I think it looks more like a monkey, but that's probably just me) rides down the line. You can draw the line in any shape you want, but the rider reacts realistically to the slope of your line. Draw an uphill line that's too steep, and the rider won't be able to go up. Draw a ledge that goes down too fast, and the rider will tumble and fall face down (the red around his neck is a scarf, not blood, so don't worry if this happens). Other things can happen, too. Experiment and see for yourself.

COMMENTS: This is one bizarre game. I don't even know what it's supposed to represent. Perhaps the rider represents our inner child, and the line represents our chaotic lives, and the red scarf represents…a red scarf? Darn, this game makes me think too much. I'm going to go watch an episode of *Dancing with the Stars*. That doesn't require any thinking at all.

ABNORMALITY: 9 STUPIDITY: 6 ENTERTAINMENT: 7

428

Byron's Stuff
glob.com.au/byron

Yet another senseless collection of…stuff. I have no idea whatsoever what its meaning could be. It is, like a ton of the other sites in this book, beyond explanation. There's fiction, such as a comic strip called "Noob" and "The Adventures of Prince Bob" (where the heck did he get the idea for "Prince Bob"?). There's also the collection of words starting with A, great inventions, and a shoe survey.

COMMENTS: Ever reached a point with something where you just give up on understanding it? I'm starting to feel that way with things like this. I just don't get it. Some of the stuff is funny, though, so you might want to take a look. On the other hand, you might just end up disgusted and leave immediately.

ABNORMALITY: 8 STUPIDITY: 9 ENTERTAINMENT: 7

427

Juicy Raoul
www.juicyraoul.com

Want to see some really weird movies? If so, Juicy Raoul is the site to go to. If your computer can play them, these movies are some of the weirdest on the Web. "The Dead Chimp in a Space Helmet," "The Legend of Chess Piece Face," and "The Pregnant Man with the Bad English Accent" are among the movies available for viewing. With bad acting and stupid plot lines, these movies unquestionably qualify as incredibly stupid.

COMMENTS: Despite watching on a broadband connection with a cable modem, the quality of the viewing wasn't great. The colors were washed out and the audio stunk. But even if you only read the synopses you'll be laughing at their stupidity. If you visit this site for a few minutes, it's worth it.

ABNORMALITY: 8   STUPIDITY: 9   ENTERTAINMENT: 7

426

Sims Survivor
www.buten.com/bobopolis/mario/survivor2

Have you ever played *The Sims*? For those of you who haven't, it's a computer game where you control the lives of a number of people. I'll assume that everybody has watched or heard of the *Survivor* TV series, so the concept here is self-explanatory. For a period of time, the creator of the website decided to put in pictures from the Sims and type text along with them. He then grouped them together and made them into "episodes."

COMMENTS: This site is hilarious! I highly recommend seeing it, even if you haven't played the game. It's very creative. Who knew a hybrid game/TV show could be so much fun. Be sure to view them all; they are quite well done.

ABNORMALITY: 6   STUPIDITY: 7   ENTERTAINMENT: 8

425

How Much Is Inside?
www.cockeyed.com/inside/howmuchinside.html

Ever wondered how much cream filling is in a five-dollar pack of Oreos? Ever wondered how much fizz is in a two-liter bottle of cola? These questions and more are answered at this bizarre site. One ingredient or property is chosen in a product, usually an amusing attribute. Then there is an attempt to measure it in some way. Some of the other products are silly string, print cartridges, and Magic Shell ice-cream topping.

COMMENTS: As stupid as this one is, it is funny. I never knew that there was an entire cup of cream filling in one of those Oreo packages! Such useful knowledge, isn't it?

ABNORMALITY: 8 STUPIDITY: 8 ENTERTAINMENT: 7

424

Loyal Nanaimo Bathtub Society
www.bathtubbing.com

This is actually the official—yes, official—site of a water race that uses bathtubs! The site itself is very well done. There is an FAQ, history story, sponsor list, team list, and memorabilia. They also have dates for the event (who on Earth would want to attend a bathtub race?) and specifications for your own bathtub should you choose to enter this bizarre race (I know I won't be entering anytime soon).

COMMENTS: Who knew that bathtubs could go that fast? I am very surprised they made a race out of these things. It's funny to imagine the race…a bunch of bathtubs rocketing their way through the water.

ABNORMALITY: 8 STUPIDITY: 7 ENTERTAINMENT: 6

423

Universe of Bagpipes
www.hotpipes.com

Love bagpipes? If so, this site is for you. Of course, you are also demented, sick, and twisted. Or Scottish. (Wait, I guess there isn't any difference!)

It's a whole universe of bagpipes, and you can see a bunch of stuff related to this fascinating instrument. On the main page, there's links to a history of bagpipes (which, for some reason, really confused me), bagpiper extraordinaire Sean Folsom (you can purchase one of his highly desired albums!), and even lessons on how to play a bagpipe (which I'm sure are in huge popular demand). There's even info on electronic bagpipes. What a concept! There are also articles, interviews, photo essays, and pretty much anything else on bagpipes that you can possibly think of.

COMMENTS: People in Scotland probably think this is a big thing. However, I just don't see the big appeal in it. The instrument just plain sounds weird. I hope this site has some sort of fan base; otherwise the hard work put into this web page will have been wasted. Not that it already hasn't been wasted.

ABNORMALITY: 6 STUPIDITY: 7 ENTERTAINMENT: 5

422

The Pumpkin-Go-Round
www.kuhnewer.com/pumpkins%2005/
PGR_home.htm

Here's something you might not know: "Chicago is home to more pumpkin-go-rounds than all other places in the world…combined!" Wow, who would've thought? This site tells you the story of the pumpkin-go-round, supposedly invented out of necessity ("we needed a pumpkin-go-round"). Well, I know I couldn't survive without my pumpkin-go-round. This site describes the construction of the pumpkin-go-round, complete with pictures of the construction of the cockamamie contraption.

COMMENTS: What use does the world have for a spinning wheel with pumpkins attached to it? Wouldn't it be great if we could take all the weird devices, all the stupid websites, and all the dumb videos you see in this book and direct the effort put into them towards something useful? It's like the monkeys on a typewriter theory: thousands of typing monkeys will eventually produce Shakespeare. People like the inventors of the pumpkin-go-round are close enough to monkeys—maybe not quite as smart, though.

ABNORMALITY: 9 STUPIDITY: 8 ENTERTAINMENT: 6

421

Easy Air Guitar
mirrorimage.com/air

Ever done that air-guitar thing, where you pretend you have a guitar and strum along? Ever wanted to have a genuine, guaranteed-to-work air guitar? Although I sincerely doubt that this is the case with you, head over to this site if you do think along that weird path. This site is actually home to a specific type, er, style of air guitar. It's called the Philson, and this site has all the info on it that you need. They have some cool '80s-style photos, too.

COMMENTS: Rock on with an air guitar! Seriously though, this site is very weird. They even have copyrights (supposedly) on some of their phrases! Now that is the pinnacle of stupid: copyrights on something that isn't real. Go figure.

ABNORMALITY: 8 STUPIDITY: 8 ENTERTAINMENT: 7

420

Don't Click Here!
www.hat.net/abs/noclick/index.html

This site is quite simple to explain. You are presented with a message and a link. The author warns you *not* to click on the link. If you do, another message appears saying something different but with the same general message. This process is repeated over and over and over again, and eventually you will reach the end—after a ton of clicking, that is (your finger will probably be sore; that's how many pages there are).

COMMENTS: I found this site quite amusing as I kept clicking and the creator kept "begging" me to go back. There's just something about irritating something or someone you can't see. This is a page that I *will* recommend seeing for those of you who have a streak of stubbornness in you.

ABNORMALITY: 8 STUPIDITY: 8 ENTERTAINMENT: 7

419

Pip's Web Site!
www.pips-web.co.uk

This is another collection of jokes, games, art, and whatnot. There's one comic page that shows disaster because pigs are flying (OH NO!!!). There's also a funny "what if" sequence in which they describe a deleted scene from *The Empire Strikes Back* after Vader told Luke he was his father. What was it about? Let's just say Vader gives Luke some self-image issues based on his experiences in Episode One.

COMMENTS: This is yet another funny variety website. Check out their archives if you're not satisfied. They have plenty of jokes from the website's history, and it's more than enough to keep you occupied with lots of brain-degrading material.

ABNORMALITY: 7 STUPIDITY: 8 ENTERTAINMENT: 8

418

Ode to Dairy Products
www.ocl.net/projects/poetrycontest/ contests/online_dairy/index.html

All hail the cows!
Well, not if you're lactose intolerant, but still, most people aren't. If you are in the majority of milk chuggers, check this site out. This British site is a collection of bizarre, stupid, and just plain weird poems and songs about dairy products. The site includes a collection of poems, information on contests, links to other literature and dairy websites, and information on the Oxford Public Library.

COMMENTS: Poems celebrating cheese. I have no idea why this is even an officially sponsored event. Maybe it's those British people. They're into weird things. Take fish and chips, for example. If they call french fries "chips," what do they call chips?

ABNORMALITY: 8 STUPIDITY: 7 ENTERTAINMENT: 6

417

The Time Travel Fund
timetravelfund.com

This is an official—yes, official—site of a fund for time traveling. The concept is that if you put your money in now, these people (or their descendants, I guess) will take you back to their future in about five hundred years. What a great investment! Screwing around with time is a wacky enough idea; *Star Trek* and bad B-movies (*Timecop* starring that ultra-talented actor Jean-Claude Van Damme) have shown us that. The website is basically an FAQ. It's even been featured in *USA Today*!

COMMENTS: Once again, I am amazed. Why these things are "official" is beyond me. Can't anyone do something! HELP! Stop the madness! Anyway, if you do decide to go time traveling, keep in mind everything you've learned from the movies. You've been warned.

ABNORMALITY: 9 STUPIDITY: 8 ENTERTAINMENT: 6

416

WatchMeDance.com
www.watchmedance.com

Here's a site where there's a video each week that you can download to watch someone shaking his or her groove thang. They have quite an impressive selection, and each of the videos is about two minutes long. This gives you plenty of time to keep saying to yourself, "Good Lord! These people are absolute morons!"

COMMENTS: These videos are funny, especially when you get to watch a regular person like me who knows absolutely nothing about dancing. I recommend downloading one or two.

ABNORMALITY: 7 STUPIDITY: 8 ENTERTAINMENT: 7

415

PEZ Central
www.pezcentral.com

This is a page dedicated to what may be the world's most popular candy with such cute little candy dispensers. On it, you'll find flavors, polls, a store, and even a forum. From Looney Tunes to the Superhero series to the happy little Christmas elf, this site has thousands of PEZ dispensers for you to view. It's all quite handy if you're a PEZ collector, or even if you're not.

COMMENTS: This site isn't very stupid, but the idea of worshipping plastic candy dispensers is. It has an extensive collection of everything and anything PEZ related. It's very fascinating to take a look at the fun history of one of America's most beloved candies. They even have some stuff from throughout the world (check out the Japanese PEZ packs!).

ABNORMALITY: 5 STUPIDITY: 5 ENTERTAINMENT: 8

414

The Church of Ed Wood
www.edwood.org

"To answer your question, yes, we're serious!" This is a church that worships Ed Wood, creator of some of the worst movies in the history of cinema. The "Church of the Heavenly Wood" is "an internet church that practices Woodism," a pop-culture religion founded in 1996 by the Reverend Steve Galindo. "Woodites" claim that watching the films of Ed Wood and learning about his life helps them "learn to lead happy, positive lives" and "strive for the acceptance of others and of the self." Sounds like a solid belief system, if you can put aside the fact that they worship the director of *Plan 9 from Outer Space*. Articles about Woodism elaborate their beliefs, all with the seriousness of any credible organized religion. But they also have messages from Ed Wood himself—like the one that tells you to go to the site store and "buy strange crap!" Well, at least he's honest. Deranged and dead, but honest.

COMMENTS: I find it hard to believe this site's claim that there are three thousand "legally baptized followers" across the world. How can anybody, after seeing *Plan 9 from Outer Space*, think that Ed Wood is a savior? If you're going to worship somebody, pick somebody talented. Try the "24 Hour Church of Elvis" instead. You won't regret it.

ABNORMALITY: 10 STUPIDITY: 9 ENTERTAINMENT: 8

413

24 Hour Church of Elvis
www.frankwu.com/elvis1.html

Here's a lady who likes Elvis a little bit too much.

This web page is a report from a traveler who visited a very personal shrine to the King. Here you'll find photos and info on her, her friends, and her store. The photos are amusing to say the least, and some of the photos show some very old equipment—old as in 1976 old. The description in the site of "a garish, turgid, jumble of '70s toy store, junk shop, and flea market" fits the 24 Hour Church of Elvis perfectly.

COMMENTS: "Hail to the King!" is a phrase that millions apply to Elvis even today. Just goes to show that the King of Rock and Roll still finds fans today among the smart and stupid alike. I like him, morons like him, and geniuses like him; there are very few people who don't like him.

ABNORMALITY: 7 STUPIDITY: 7 ENTERTAINMENT: 6

412

The Story of Andy's Computer
www.best-marketing-tools.com/lego/lego.html

This is a collection of pictures showing Lego men putting together a computer (supposedly; somehow I doubt Lego men have the ability to put together an entire computer). There's some text along with the pictures, which makes the experience a bit funnier, and at the end of the entire thing there's a picture of a finished computer.

COMMENTS: For some reason, I found this a bit funny. I should have found it really stupid that someone would waste all that time photographing a bunch of Lego men next to costly computer equipment, but I guess that's just me. Stupid, like beauty, is in the eye of the beholder.

ABNORMALITY: 7 STUPIDITY: 8 ENTERTAINMENT: 7

411

Peanut Butter Jelly Time

etrata.home.attbi.com/flash/banana.swf
etrata.home.attbi.com/flash/donkey.swf

This is an animated Flash sequence featuring some music, along with a dancing banana, and a version with a banana and a donkey. I know what you're thinking, and I agree. It makes no sense whatsoever. You get to see this madness all while the banana sings: "It's Peanut Butter Jelly Time! It's Peanut Butter Jelly Time!" The sequence is very funny, though, so you definitely will want to view it. The donkey has a funny smile.

COMMENTS: Time does wonders to strange Internet videos. Since this book was first released, Peanut Butter Jelly Time has become a pop culture legend. Even the recently revived hit cartoon *Family Guy* immortalized PBJT, with Brian Griffin dancing in a banana suit singing the song that still rings stupid four years later. We may now enter this crazy clip into the irreverent annals of history.

ABNORMALITY: 8 STUPIDITY: 10 ENTERTAINMENT: 6

410

The Ugly Toy Contest

www.toughpigs.com/soapboxuglynominees.htm

They're Muppets and they are butt-ugly! That's right. U-G-L-Y, they ain't got no alibi! Now that I'm done using extremely bad English, let's get down to the site itself. The site chronicles several ugly Muppet dolls, figurines, and collectables. There are several to choose from, including Kermit, Miss Piggy, Gonzo, and, of course, all of the *Sesame Street* gang, like Bert, Ernie, Big Bird, and whatever that big brown fuzzy elephant-thing is called.

COMMENTS: This is not very amusing. I mean, sure, they're ugly toys, but for Pete's sake you don't have to make a site out of them! That's almost pure lunacy! That's like making a site for broken computer mice (although there's probably a site for that too). I tell you, people these days have too much time.

ABNORMALITY: 8 STUPIDITY: 8 ENTERTAINMENT: 5

409

2000 Uses for Peanut Butter

members.kconline.com/kerr/pb.htm

This site is exactly what it says it is: a site sharing all the uses of this wonder food. They even have a rating system for the uses and recommend if you should try them or not. For example, two of the ratings are "DO NOT try this under any circumstances" and "It would be cool to do, but it's impossible." Some of the uses include "Plug holes in your paneling," or "Keep a jar in your car because it rhymes."

COMMENTS: Yet another site that is just my type of thing. Naturally, it gets a great rating in my book. Some of the uses are quite funny. Check it out once or twice. And unlike other things, there really are more than two thousand uses for peanut butter. Now that's value!

ABNORMALITY: 8 STUPIDITY: 8 ENTERTAINMENT: 7

408

Institute for Naming Children Humanely

inch.stormpages.com

Ever wondered what not to name your kid? If so, then this page is for you. It includes a bunch of categories listing bad ways to name your kid. One is the "Abstract Quality" category. In this case, they make a point that people named after qualities usually display the opposite quality, and then they list some examples: "Girls named Hope are always gloomy. Girls named Faith are atheistic. Girls named Charity always order Alaskan cod when their boyfriends are paying. And girls named Chastity dress like prostitutes."

COMMENTS: This site is especially relevant today, considering some of the crazy names celebrities are giving their kids. Consider *My Name Is Earl* star Jason Lee. Great show, great actor, but he named his son Pilot Inspektor! What kind of screwed up name is that?! The poor kid is going to be terrorized when he starts going to school! If I won a million dollars, I'd donate the whole thing to this site to stop the neurotic names that parents give unfortunate children. My rant aside, check out this site.

ABNORMALITY: 7 STUPIDITY: 7 ENTERTAINMENT: 7

407 Dust Bunny Facts
www.dustbunnies.com/dust_bunny_facts.htm

Want a pet that's low maintenance and fun, too? No, we're not talking about goldfish here (you can hardly call them pets, anyway; they're more of a high-maintenance decoration). We're talking about dust bunnies! That's right, dust bunnies are your answer! Well, maybe not, but if you do think so, check out this page. It shows how to find and care for dust bunnies in your very own home.

COMMENTS: This is stupid, but I have seen stupider. Dust bunnies for pets?! Come on, you can do better than that. Where are the pink monkeys or the blue-footed boobies (that's a real animal, in case you didn't know)? The search for stupid continues.

ABNORMALITY: 7 STUPIDITY: 8 ENTERTAINMENT: 6

---

406 Origami Boulder Company
www.origamiboulder.com

This is a real, non-joking site selling origami boulders. You may be asking, "Aren't origami boulders just wadded up pieces of paper?" Well, if you think so, you're right; that's essentially what they are. Even though they may just be wadded-up pieces of paper, this guy is charging money for them! You'll find ordering info, pictures, an FAQ, and more.

COMMENTS: Selling wadded-up paper for money…so, you're saying we should pay you for something a street corner bum could do? Oh well. If it's your karma to make money crumpling up paper, more power to you. I'm sure there's some special technique to making paper boulders that makes this site special…right? Decide for yourself, if you really want to find out.

ABNORMALITY: 8 STUPIDITY: 8 ENTERTAINMENT: 6

405

The Great Pop vs. Soda Controversy
www.popvssoda.com

The concept of this page is quite simple. It is a map of the United States showing, with colors, the regions where people call soda pop "pop" and where they call it "soda." Interesting, huh? They also show where they call it "coke" or "other" (what else could you call it?). There's also a brief explanation and examination of the controversy. And, of course, you can vote. What do you call it?

COMMENTS: Being a Southeastern Wisconsinite, I call it "soda." But that's my region. Anyway, it's kind of cool to see this fascinating phenomenon, and it's also quite stupid. How can it be both? Well, stupid stuff can be cool, in case you haven't learned that by now. Homer Simpson is most definitely a classic example of cool and stupid rolled into one. Mmmmm…donuts. By the way, if you call all soda pop "cola," then you're really weird…in the opinion of a Southeastern Wisconsinite.

ABNORMALITY: 7 STUPIDITY: 8 ENTERTAINMENT: 7

404

Cow Abduction
www.cowabduction.com

333,946. That's the number of cows that have been abducted by aliens, according to cowabduction.com By the time you visit this site, that number may be much higher. This site gives all the information you'll need on this deeply disturbing phenomenon. Some questions in the FAQ are simply heartbreaking, like, "I just can't eat or sleep since I lost my beloved cow Isadora, two months ago today. What should I do?" Cow Abductions advised seeking a support group. Fortunately, the site doesn't take itself too seriously, as shown by the question, "Are the aliens Reptilians or Zeta-Reticulians?" "Gary, we have no idea what that means, but we're pretty sure the answer is, 'You need to get out more.'"

COMMENTS: This is an amusing take on the many conspiracy theories that revolve around aliens abducting and mutilating cows. The theory doesn't really make sense to begin with. Why on Earth would aliens want to steal our bovines? Maybe they just need some fast milk. Milk does alien bodies good, too, I guess.

ABNORMALITY: 8 STUPIDITY: 9 ENTERTAINMENT: 6

403

Barney Smith's Toilet Seat Art Museum

www.unusualmuseums.org/toilet

An art gallery dedicated to a little-known art form: the toilet seat. Some people have actually found ways to make art out of these household objects. Creativity at its finest, isn't it? On this site, you'll find a wide variety of seats with unusual properties, such as license plates or even artwork. Is it possible to paint the Mona Lisa on a toilet seat? We may never know; Leonardo Da Vinci is dead. Anyway, there are even toilet seats with coin collections pasted to them.

COMMENTS: Next time you see your toilet seat, just think of how it could be more interesting. Think of how you could spice up your house with a macaroni-encrusted toilet seat (isn't that the kind of stuff Martha Stewart does?). Are you listening to me? Do you even care? No? Neither do I.

ABNORMALITY: 8   STUPIDITY: 9   ENTERTAINMENT: 6

402

The Worldwide I Hate Mayonnaise Club

www.nomayo.com

Well, I hate mayonnaise too, but I'm not stupid enough to dedicate a site to detesting this slimy condiment. It's The Worldwide I Hate Mayonnaise Club, and you're invited in! Step inside and see the history of this club. From its creation by a Honolulu newspaper columnist to its step into cyberspace, you can ponder joining the "revolution against the thick, nasty, spreadable evil junk." If you're still not convinced, you can read letters and testimonials from members who joined due to mayonnaise allergies to the editors at an Air Force magazine who declared "you are God" (that's going way too far).

COMMENTS: Why is there so much hate in this world? Can't we just all get along? Will we never see mayonnaise in harmony with bacon, lettuce, and tomatoes, or creationists getting along with evolutionists (who are apparently all going to hell, regardless of good deeds)? Hopefully, one day, world peace will be possible. On the other hand, some of the best movies are about conflict, like *Godzilla vs. Mothra*! A masterpiece of moviemaking: giant lizard vs. giant moth.

ABNORMALITY: 8   STUPIDITY: 9   ENTERTAINMENT: 7

401 The U.S. National Debt Clock
www.brillig.com/debt_clock

This clock will tell you our exact national debt as of the moment you look at it. Talk about breaking information!

Simply go to the U.S. National Debt Clock page to see how many dollars we are in debt. Now, I won't say how much it is now, but believe me, they need to do something about it. I'll be wishing good luck to the U.S. taxpayers though; the number is phenomenally large. If you want to learn more about the national debt, there are links to articles from various newspapers and magazines regarding the subject.

COMMENTS: Now, whom exactly do we owe the money to? This was always something that I never quite got. I guess it's of some concern; no debt is good debt. Now, people may react differently to this page. For some, they'll get really concerned and start saving for a national financial meltdown. For others, it'll drift into obscurity in their minds, much like the Spice Girls or Boy George.

ABNORMALITY: 5 STUPIDITY: 7 ENTERTAINMENT: 7

400 The Mooses Are Coming
www.expage.com/moosesarecoming

Oh no! They're coming! Help us!

This page gives you information on moose and how they're more dangerous than you think. First off, moose can and will eat your brains out. No, really, it's true! There's a "Never Do This" section to help you avoid this gruesome fate. There are also true facts about moose, most of which actually seem to have some accuracy. The rest of the site, however, is just nonsensical gibberish about how "mooses are evil" and how polka music causes them to dance like a "maniac moose."

COMMENTS: Now, I know that moose can be dangerous if they're provoked, but I sincerely doubt that they will eat your brains. I haven't heard of any animal that preys upon humans in order to consume their brains. Except maybe Howard Stern. Anyway, remember that moose are not evil and that they're just trying to get along like us. Or are they?

ABNORMALITY: 8 STUPIDITY: 8 ENTERTAINMENT: 6

399 Missouri Trailer Trash.com
www.missouritrailertrash.com/index.html

This page exhibits Missouri trailer-park trash at its finest. Redneck habitats! Hicksville! Whatever you want to call it, it's all here. You can see pictures, read comics, and even view trailers for sale. And what great bargains! For $500.00 you can get a trailer with everything (except a living-room wall). You can even take the trailer-trash quiz, with questions like "Did you have to remove a toothpick for your wedding pictures?" There is also a short biography about the author of the site, which is also pretty funny.

COMMENTS: This site sports more rural goodness from the less civilized parts of our society than a family trip to a *Jerry Springer* taping. Maybe Maury Povich could give these folks a trailer-park makeover, where they get a new flour-sack dress, a trip to the dentist, or a car that isn't up on blocks.

ABNORMALITY: 7 STUPIDITY: 8 ENTERTAINMENT: 6

---

398 Captured! By Robots
www.capturedbyrobots.com

This is the official page of a band comprised of malfunctioning robots (now I've seen it all) called Captured! By Robots. Yes, I know that's written as two sentences, but that's the name of the band. You can see the twisted, ridiculous story of this band (which is beyond ridiculous), as well as pictures (which are also way beyond ridiculous), and the fan club (they have a fan club?).

COMMENTS: The story of this band makes no sense. It's like *Toy Story* meets *Rocky Horror Picture Show*, if you can imagine that. I haven't listened to the songs, but I'm sure they also make no sense. In fact, none of the sites in this book make sense, in case you haven't noticed by now.

ABNORMALITY: 9 STUPIDITY: 9 ENTERTAINMENT: 6

397

Engrish.com
www.engrish.com

This site shows Japanese products that are either in English or attempt to be in English. Some examples are soda ("newly tasty"), coffee ("both creaminess and dry coffee taste!"), chocolate ("bourbon pickle chocolate sticks"), snacks ("baked chunk cookies"), and even Engrish building signs ("Pumpkin Poo cake shop"). However, my favorite is a description for using a Sanyo electronic rice cooker: "I hope to play along with the heartiest gadgetry manifesting my sensibility." Um, sure.

COMMENTS: I just want to say that I mean no offense by including this site. I'm just reporting the facts. Anyway, you should check it out. It's worth it.

ABNORMALITY: 7 STUPIDITY: 6 ENTERTAINMENT: 7

396

The World's Largest Catsup Bottle
www.catsupbottle.com

Here's yet another "official" site, this one for the World's Largest Catsup Bottle. Talk about a national landmark! Here, you can see a history, buy merchandise (merchandise relating to a giant catsup bottle...right), read about the restoration effort (why restore something like this?), and keep up with a news archive. Get this: it's 170 feet tall! That's more than half a football field. The Cincinnati Bengals don't even get half a football field worth of yards most games, so why should a catsup bottle get more?

COMMENTS: To see something so ridiculous is funny, and this is a very high-class site, too! I highly recommend checking out the story behind this amazing structure for a laugh or two. By the way, note that they use the word "catsup." This is the *inferior* and stupid spelling of the sweet tomato product properly known as "ketchup."

ABNORMALITY: 8 STUPIDITY: 7 ENTERTAINMENT: 7

395

The Stump Online
www.thestumponline.com

The Stump Online's main attraction is a vast library of mug shots from counties in Idaho, along with the stupid things crooks did to get cuffed. Some of the bigger winners here are a sixty-year-old man who was arrested for "video voyeurism," and another guy who was booked for battery and "excretion of human waste." Aren't we lucky to have guys like these? But it's not just the guys that are stirring up things in Idaho. Check out mug shots from the upstanding female citizen who was charged with DUI driving, assault and battery upon an officer of the law, resisting and obstructing officers, and two counts of injury to children. Who knew Idaho was such a colorful place? Appropriately, there is also a section for pictures of actual tree stumps. Needless to say, Idaho inmate pictures are much more entertaining.

COMMENTS: Pictures of stumps and Idaho mug shots...what a combination! Makes you think about what other odd-but-awesome combinations we could have. How about Simon Cowell and William Shatner? All the eccentricities of the charismatic captain turned insane attorney, combined with the witty, venom-tongued insults of the infamous *American Idol* judge. The only question is who would be the sidekick?

ABNORMALITY: 7 STUPIDITY: 8 ENTERTAINMENT: 8

394

AirlineMeals.net
www.airlinemeals.net

This site is an independent review of airline meals. It classifies itself as "the world's first site dedicated to nothing but airline food." It's probably also the last site of its kind. Here you can find the meal of the week (such vital information, isn't it?), past reviews, info on the organization and its origins, pictures of in-flight meals from the '70s and '80s (very vital information, don't you think?), and more.

COMMENTS: Who knew that there was so much preparation involved in airline meals? I thought they just whipped something together on the plane! I guess I was wrong. This site is good if you want to see something useful or something out of the ordinary.

ABNORMALITY: 8 STUPIDITY: 6 ENTERTAINMENT: 6

393 The Hobbit Name Generator
www.chriswetherell.com/hobbit

This concept is quite simple: you enter a name, and the name generator will generate a name fit for J.R.R. Tolkien's fantasy series. Try any name—Ozzy Osbourne, Britney Spears, Bigfoot, Bill Clinton, Jacko—any name will do. Enter a name and the name generator will assign you a genuine Middle Earth name.

COMMENTS: Did you know Santa Claus's hobbit name is Nob Peatfingers of Brockenborings? Just wanted to let you know that. Call Santa Claus "Nob" the next time you write him. He'll be surprised.

ABNORMALITY: 7 STUPIDITY: 6 ENTERTAINMENT: 7

---

392 Vending Machines of Japan
www.photomann.com/japan/machines/index.htm

The Japanese have brought us some crazy stuff. Digimon, Hello Kitty, Nintendo's Mario, anime—the list goes on. But it turns out that Japanese bizarreness is not confined to weird toys and Italian plumbers in a land of magic mushrooms. It also extends to a fixture of daily urban life across the world: vending machines. "The most common [machines] are drink and cigarette machines, followed by machines with pornography," according to the site. (Porno vending machines? I doubt you'll see those in the U.S. anytime soon.) The site goes on a tour of Japan with its mechanical merchant machines selling everything from rice to eggs, and even fishing supplies for the Japanese angling enthusiast. The most disturbing machine, however, is one that sells "used schoolgirl panties." That's more disturbing than wacko Lisa Nowak wearing an astronaut diaper on her way to kidnap her boyfriend's lover. Just thinking about it makes space travel seem nauseating.

COMMENTS: As weird as Japan's vending machines may seem, you've got to give them kudos for their practicality. There are even vending machines for toilet paper if you need it. Hey, we've all been there, and you don't always have someone nearby to hand you a new roll.

ABNORMALITY: 8 STUPIDITY: 6 ENTERTAINMENT: 7

391

California Astrology Association

www.calastrology.com

This site has info on a stargazing and witchcraft association in California. You have to pay to use its services (and you probably won't want to, unless you believe in that gibberish), but it's just interesting to see what kind of stuff is on these sites. You'll find available for purchase astrology readings, the "love-luck-money spell," good-luck charms, voodoo dolls, "witch doctor spells kits," and more. There's also an FAQ and more info on the association.

COMMENTS: Is this site complete nonsense? Probably. But I guess it's kind of groovy nonsense. There is a certain allure to using a voodoo doll to poke your friends from miles away. I'm not buying the idea of this weird stuff working, but if you decide to try it out, let me know how it goes (without a voodoo doll, please).

ABNORMALITY: 9 STUPIDITY: 8 ENTERTAINMENT: 6

390

Mr. Picasso Head

www.mrpicassohead.com

What would it be like if you took the lovable and versatile Mr. Potato Head and combined him with the artwork of the Cubist movement? The answer lies in Mr. Picasso Head, an abstract, abnormal, but still awesome virtual builder based on the artwork of famous painter Pablo Picasso. Start with a face (most of them are solid black or thin lines), then add eyes, a nose, lips, and more, all with the interpretive weirdness found in Picasso's art. You can even type in your name and get a signature on your masterpiece worthy of Picasso himself. You can also view the gallery with creations by other "artists"; However, both times I tried to open the gallery up on Safari (the Mac browser) it froze, so be careful if you're a Mac user. It does work with Windows computers.

COMMENTS: Mr. Picasso Head is good and all, but where's Mrs. Picasso Head? Poor Mr. Picasso Head. I wonder why he hasn't started dating? Perhaps he has that image of the lonely, rogue artist that he wants to keep up.

ABNORMALITY: 8 STUPIDITY: 5 ENTERTAINMENT: 8

389

Pure Pwnage
www.purepwnage.com

"DooD, I liek Pwning nOObs, dO U?" No, that's not a really bad typo. That's the pathetic pseudo-language of the losers at Pure Pwnage. So, what exactly is this site about? As their barely understandable explanation goes, "I pwn noobs liek hard rite n my roomate has dis camera rite so hes all liek 'we can make a show lol' n im liek dats teh pwnage…" Translation: We're gonna go out and do stupid stuff because we have nothing better to do. For those of you who have no clue what this is about, "pwning" is a highly overused term in online video game communities, used by doltish players to claim that they are doing better than their opponent, when usually they're the ones getting "pwned." These cavemen-like gamers often say this to others they don't like, and also call them "noobs," a term short for "newbie." Ironically, most people who are called noobs are actually those who are best at the games, and intelligent gamers know that being called a noob is really a compliment disguised as an insult. Site videos consist of two guys (who obviously are single) going around making bad attempts at irreverent humor, and talking to random strangers about how they "pwn noobs."

COMMENTS: When I see language like this, I wish that they would all go and take some English classes. I mean, what are they going to put on their job applications? "I pwn teh McDonald's burgr maekers"? God help the employer who hires these guys. Do me a favor: if these guys try talking to you—online or offline—ask them if they "pwned" a grade school spelling bee. The answer is definitely "no."

ABNORMALITY: 7 STUPIDITY: 10 ENTERTAINMENT: 5

388

The Rejection Line
www.rejectionline.com

The concept behind this "service" is quite simple: when somebody asks, "Hey gorgeous, can I have your phone number?" you give him or her a very special phone number. It won't be yours; it will be the Rejection Line—a calling service that basically tells them that they've been rejected as a loser by the giver of the number. Useful, huh? Especially for all of the ladies who are annoyed by those guys who try to get the ladies with dumb pick-up lines.

COMMENTS: This service can produce lots of different results, depending on how you use it. If you don't use it, you can just get more info on the service. I recommend checking it out, whether you want to use it or not.

ABNORMALITY: 7 STUPIDITY: 8 ENTERTAINMENT: 6

387

Guinness World Record Gum Wrapper Chain

www.gumwrapper.com

This page is mind-blowing. It shows the World's Largest Gum Wrapper Chain, which holds the Guinness record. It's made of only Wrigley's gum wrappers (this guy must really like Wrigley's gum), and when spread out, it covers a whole room. The site shows some incredible statistics regarding this chain. It is nearly eight miles long and contains more than $50,000 worth of gum. There's also a picture of this mammoth accomplishment. It is truly something to behold.

COMMENTS: This guy has wasted a good chunk of his life already making the chain, so why shouldn't his stupidity have a place on the Web? Why someone would think of doing this is beyond me. Stupid beyond recognition. Go see it. You'll laugh. You'll cry. You'll be amazed.

ABNORMALITY: 9 STUPIDITY: 9 ENTERTAINMENT: 7

386

Top 10 Creepiest Fast Food Mascots

www.fanpop.com/spots/legendary-ads/soapbox/56

We all know that most fast food mascots are a little weird. When you go to a restaurant and see a guy with a giant Styrofoam head, or some big purple thing eating a hamburger, it makes you wonder what their marketing departments were thinking (or smoking) when they created these freaks. This site has conveniently organized the top ten nightmarish mascots ever seen in America's fast food joints. Domino's Noid, McDonald's Grimace, and "Quizno's Rat/Hamster Thing" (who needs those real names anyway?) are just a few of the entries on the list. Ronald McDonald holds the honor of having two places on the list—one for his "modern" incarnation, and another for the "old" Ronald (see for yourself which is creepier).

COMMENTS: Top ten lists are always cool, and this one is no exception. The pictures chosen for each mascot do even more to convince you of the creepiness of these icky icons. I do, however, disagree with the number one choice (visit the website to find out who it is), mainly because there were some cool video games starring that particular mascot (any Xbox game that only costs four dollars has to be good).

ABNORMALITY: 9 STUPIDITY: 7 ENTERTAINMENT: 8

385

McChicken Head
www.breakthechain.org/exclusives/mcchicken.html

This page tells the story of how some lady bought some McDonald's food one day to take to her kids. Upon opening the Chicken McNuggets box, she found a grotesque chicken head! Really, it happened! This page tells the full story, as well as a scary (kinda) picture of the offending foreign object.

COMMENTS: This is a weird story. It doesn't say if she sued Mickey Ds, but she could have. She certainly had a better reason than the lady who spilled hot coffee on her lap and sued for big bucks. Remember that? That was just ridiculous. Enough soapbox preaching, though.

ABNORMALITY: 8 STUPIDITY: 7 ENTERTAINMENT: 7

384

The Phobia List
www.phobialist.com/index.html

This site shows you a plethora of phobias for almost anything imaginable. They range from the common (claustrophobia) to the bizarre (Anglophobia, fear of England and/or English culture). Some of the phobias are very odd indeed, such as the fear of gold (aurophobia). There is an alphabetical list of phobias. In the "G" category alone you'll find gamophobia (fear of marriage), geniophobia (fear of chins), and even genuphobia (fear of knees). There are also ways to conquer your phobias, phobia links, and quotes.

COMMENTS: It was Franklin Roosevelt who said, "The only thing we have to fear is fear itself." Obviously, he didn't factor stupidity into that quote. I tell you, stupid people will be the downfall of humanity! Heed my warning now, before it's too late! Or we may all go insane and become victims of dementophobia. Seriously, though, this page is very entertaining. I highly recommend it.

ABNORMALITY: 8 STUPIDITY: 7 ENTERTAINMENT: 8

383

Monkey Kick-Off

www.rubytooth.com/media/50817

Most games starring monkeys are more than a little weird—Sega's Super Monkey Ball, for example, in which the player rolls plastic balls with monkeys inside around strange obstacles—and Monkey Kick-Off is no exception. In it, a monkey can be seen bouncing what appears to be a volleyball. Click anywhere on the screen or press a key, and the ball will go launching across the screen. The distance the ball goes is measured in "Monkey Meters." I'm not sure how (or if) a Monkey Meter is different from a regular meter. How far the ball goes varies (I'm still not sure how it works). It can go only a few Monkey Meters, or it can go several thousand. The goal is the "Monkey Village," which is about 4,000 Monkey Meters away. The strangest part about the game is the look. It's hard to describe, but the monkey looks like he belongs in a Mr. Picasso Head painting (see number 390).

COMMENTS: This game is a fun one, if only to figure out how it works. Interestingly, every aspect of the game has the word "Monkey" in it. You can even send it to your "Monkey Friends" (which accurately describes most of my friends—no offense, guys). For some reason, I was able to get 3,059 Monkey Meters on my first try, but the next time I tried I was lucky to get 100 Monkey Meters. Try getting the ball to the Monkey Village. I don't know what happens when it gets there, but I'm betting monkeys live there.

ABNORMALITY: 8 STUPIDITY: 7 ENTERTAINMENT: 8

382

Name That Candybar

www.smm.org/sln/tf/c/crosssection/namethatbar.html

Here, you are shown a cross section of a certain candy bar, such as a Kit-Kat, a Butterfinger (mmm…Butterfinger), or a Mr. Goodbar. Based on that cross section, you try to identify it. Some are easy and some are hard, but they all look delicious! I've never even heard of some of the candy bars, like the Coffee Crisp candy bar. There are more than twenty of these cross sections available for your viewing pleasure.

COMMENTS: *Delicious.* I don't know why, but when you say that word in a sinister way, like that guy from the James Bond film *Tomorrow Never Dies*, it sounds really funny. "Delicious!" Anyway, this site is fun to visit and a must for candy aficionados.

ABNORMALITY: 8 STUPIDITY: 7 ENTERTAINMENT: 7

381

When you have a big emotional issue, or a deep philosophical question, do you turn to a trusted friend, family member, or teacher? Of course not! Head over to Ask a Ninja instead! You can ask the Ninja just about any question, such as, "Do Ninjas like poetry?" or "What Ninja Tips do you have for when I go to college?" The Ninja answers these questions in brief, (sometimes) concise videos on the site. The Ninja gives the answers in a very dramatic, senseless, fast-paced, irreverent manner, mixing rants on everyday life with descriptions of deadly ninja methods (poisoned darts, cutting off arms, etc.). The videos range from pretty stupid to mildly amusing.

COMMENTS: I wonder why the Ninja hangs out with these Douglas and Kent guys. Maybe they stumbled across his Ninja Fortress and the Ninja must supervise them to make sure they don't reveal special Ninja secrets. Or, maybe the Ninja is just one of them in a black shirt and ski mask. Anyway, the videos are kind of dumb, but this site is still entertaining just because he's a Ninja. And like the site says, "Ninjas are cool."

ABNORMALITY: 9 STUPIDITY: 9 ENTERTAINMENT: 5

380

CornCam
www.iowafarmer.com/corncam/corn.html

This official website features the CornCam, a camera whose sole job is to monitor the cornfields twenty-four hours a day, seven days a week. Nothing else. Not the weather, not cars, just corn. All day, every day. You can see info on the CornCam's host, the Iowa Farmer's Association, or you can just stare at the corn. Of course, those tricky farmers don't let you off the hook by merely having you watch corn. You will also feel compelled to gaze at the SoybeanCam and the "continuously updated" DairyCam, where you can see live lactation from an automatic milking parlor.

COMMENTS: Why would someone want to watch corn? Maybe something will come out of the cornfields…or not. Anyway, like I said earlier, I have no idea why an organization like this would want to waste their money and time on a site like this. Check the CornCam if you're really, really bored.

ABNORMALITY: 8 STUPIDITY: 7 ENTERTAINMENT: 2

379

Underwear Boy
www.geocities.com/SouthBeach/Surf/5847/home

This is the home page of a superhero who, apart from wearing underpants on the outside of his pants, has no real powers. Zip. Zero. Despite this fact, you can learn all about him here or check out the underwear links and enter a contest. (Contest? There's an underpants contest? Now that's disturbing.)

COMMENTS: I don't know what to make of this one. Anybody who wears underwear on the outside of his or her pants is kind of nutty. Besides, it's already been done! Hasn't anybody ever heard of Captain Underpants? He's the best superhero in the world! He could beat up Spiderman! Okay, maybe not.

ABNORMALITY: 8 STUPIDITY: 8 ENTERTAINMENT: 6

378

Sillydude.com
www.sillydude.com

Here's another collection of hilarious jokes, stories, and other things of stupidity. And honestly, isn't that what we all need more of? This site includes a picture where you can click on Louise the Cow for a virtual milkshake. Now that's useful! Or you can watch videos in "Silly Cinema" like "My Life as a Penguin." There's a wealth of information (if you can call it that) on the site, so if you intend to see it all, I recommend bookmarking the page.

COMMENTS: These sites are always funny because of their variety. Some of the jokes are very funny, much funnier than the comedy series *'Til Death*. Don't ask me why, but I hate that show. Anyway, I would definitely recommend checking out this page. Check out the IRS jokes!

ABNORMALITY: 7 STUPIDITY: 8 ENTERTAINMENT: 9

377 Antique Washing Machines
www.oldewash.com

This site is about what it says: antique washing machines from many, many years ago. There are washing-machine articles and a database that can be scanned by brand name or model number. There are animations and photos of models such as the Black and Decker Cinderella or the one-time Eversafe machine. There's even a museum tour available for your viewing pleasure.

COMMENTS: I know antiques are nice to learn about…but a site that specializes specifically in washing machines? That seems a little wishy-washy (no pun intended…I think) to me. What are we gonna be seeing next? Antique microwaves? Hmm. I guess all appliances aren't created equal.

ABNORMALITY: 7 STUPIDITY: 7 ENTERTAINMENT: 5

---

376 Cheddar Vision
www.cheddarvision.tv

This site is pretty simple: cheddar cheese. Taped by a camera. Twenty-four hours a day, seven days a week. The block never moves, and nobody ever does anything with the cheese, and the camera never moves. All this adds up to a show that's just as boring as watching grass grow. (Oh yeah, there's a camera for that too. See number 343.) You can also buy cheese from the West Country Farmhouse Cheesemakers, who apparently run Cheddar Vision. There's a timer on the website which tells how long the cheddar cam has been running, from days right down to milliseconds.

COMMENTS: Who on Earth would want to watch this senseless show? It's like watching paint dry, or C-SPAN. In fact, it's worse than C-SPAN. And that's saying a lot. If you're really, really bored, you can try Cheddar Vision. Otherwise, anything else is better. Like nearly all the other sites in this book. Heck, Pylon of the Month (number 96) is more entertaining than this. At least it has something more than cheese.

ABNORMALITY: 6 STUPIDITY: 9 ENTERTAINMENT: 1

375

Das Keyboard
www.daskeyboard.com

This enterprising site promotes and sells its specialty keyboards. At first, this sounds pretty normal. That is, until we find out that the keyboard is completely blank. No letters, no numbers, no special signs, no Ctrl, no Alt, no Delete (a combination Windows users know all too well)—just blank keys. And it's not a joke either. The site has information on how Das Keyboard is more "efficient," claiming its users type up to "100 percent faster." As with any uncannily crazy product, testimonials are included to make you think that people are satisfied with it. The reasoning for this asinine accessory is that it works like a piano. Pianos don't have letters on them, right? So why does a highly advanced tool that needs a 101-button interface need them?

COMMENTS: I can see getting used to the Das Keyboard in some ways. But since experienced computer users don't look at the keyboard when they're typing anyway, why is Das Keyboard so special? On top of all that, the keyboard costs ninety bucks! What a complete rip-off! The only reason I recommend this site is to laugh at its insane impracticality.

ABNORMALITY: 7 STUPIDITY: 8 ENTERTAINMENT: 4

374

The MegaPenny Project
www.kokogiak.com/megapenny

This page attempts to answer a few questions regarding gargantuan amounts of pennies. How tall would a cube of one billion pennies be? Ever wanted to know how much money in pennies the Sears Tower is worth? This site has the answer to these questions and more. There are even a few that answer how many pennies would be needed to rebuild famous landmarks.

COMMENTS: It would be cool if somebody could stack pennies as high as, oh say, the Empire State Building. Think of the image: a huge tower of pennies, reigning over all of us. They wouldn't be chump change then! I guess it remains a dream…

ABNORMALITY: 8 STUPIDITY: 7 ENTERTAINMENT: 7

373

The McDonald's Employee Simulator

conceptlab.com/simulator

Here's a simulation of a job most of the world takes for granted: the common McDonald's employee. This simulator...well, simulates the life of a typical McDonald's employee. From dawn until dusk, you make the decisions that dictate how your McDonald's employee will live his life. In actuality, though, it is nothing more than button clicking, and most of it has nothing at all to do with McDonald's.

COMMENTS: This sim is a load of crap! I'm disgusted! I guess there's nothing left to do but abandon this page and never, ever look back. Take that, you processed heap of trash! No McJob for me!

ABNORMALITY: 8   STUPIDITY: 9   ENTERTAINMENT: 3

372

Blanks on a Blank

www.originalalamo.com/sites/2blanks/default.aspx

Snakes on a Plane bombed horribly at the box office. But that hasn't stopped people from parodying it more times than a decapitated head appears in a Quentin Tarantino movie, and that's what Blanks on a Blank is about. Aspiring filmmakers signed up to participate in the Blanks on a Blank challenge. A random generator provided each team with an animal and a vehicle, from which they made a movie. *Aardvarks on a Surfboard* and *Roosters on a Moped* are just a few of these ridiculous flicks. As a warning, some of the films have quite a bit of profanity and violence in them, so if you don't want the kiddies seeing a mouse crushed by a stone door, keep them away from this one.

COMMENTS: The irony in this site is that some of the films actually seem more fully thought out than *Snakes on a Plane*. Why pay to see SOAP when you can watch *Dinocroc, Mansquito, Raptor Island,* and *Chupacabra 2* back to back? I rest my case.

ABNORMALITY: 9   STUPIDITY: 8   ENTERTAINMENT: 8

371

The Really Big Button That Doesn't Do Anything

www.pixelscapes.com/spatulacity/button.htm

Another page that is exactly what it makes itself out to be: a big button that, when pressed, does nothing at all. Many a Web surfer has tried their hand at pushing it, according to the "legend," and you can see their interesting comments on the site. What is this object of mystery? What is its purpose? Why does it not do anything? Or does it secretly do something somewhere else, maybe in another dimension? We may never know. We may never care.

COMMENTS: I found this site to be quite interesting. I mean, sure, it's just a really big button that does nothing, but it's a cool button! Still, the comments are what make the site great, like the comments that say the big button does do something (one person testified that it made his stereo fall down). Another person said, "I laughed. I cried. It was beautiful. I pity people who don't understand." Now that person has problems. I pity him or her.

ABNORMALITY: 9 STUPIDITY: 10 ENTERTAINMENT: 7

370

I AM BORED

www.expage.com/page/ndpbored

This web-page maker is bored. Plain and simple. She was (or is?) so bored she made a site about being bored. Now that's really boring. I would do something different if I were bored. You can check out what she wrote on the subject of being bored, as well as some of her personal thoughts on boredom, which are quite...boring.

COMMENTS: Does this explanation bore you? Did you buy this book because you were bored? Is your life boring? OK, I'm gonna stop right there. Anyway, this site is strangely a tiny bit of fun, in a, well, boring sort of way. You don't understand, do you? I don't either. Did I mention that this site is about being bored?

ABNORMALITY: 8 STUPIDITY: 8 ENTERTAINMENT: 6

369

Ninja Burger
www.ninjaburger.com

This is the site of a burger restaurant and delivery service comprised of ninjas. No, not samurai or centurions or Vikings. Ninjas. Those dangerous people in black pajamas. Here, you can see Ninja Burger policies, research employment opportunities (Are you a ninja in need of work? This may be the place for you.), and you can even order Ninja Burgers online! Now that's service!

COMMENTS: This website is very weird. Nevertheless, it is a very funny site, and also very well done. You must visit Ninja Burger; your honor demands it. And remember, you must order wasabi: "To not order wasabi would be to insult our honor." *Hei-ya!*

ABNORMALITY: 8 STUPIDITY: 8 ENTERTAINMENT: 8

368

Yucfu, Inc.
www.geocities.com/yucfu_inc

Here's a site that's very hard to describe. It has a winged spatula for a logo. It's mostly indecipherable gibberish thrown together, like "The story of a little fly named Ezekiel." First of all, why would you want to read the story of a fly, and second of all, why on Earth is the fly named Ezekiel? Why not Bob or Joe or Martin? There are also various miscellaneous articles, as well as info on Yucfu, Inc. And just what is up with the antique picture of "Girl and Chickens," or "I Smell Yams"?

COMMENTS: I have no clue what the meaning of this site might be. And I probably will think about this for a while writhing in mental agony, then quit and forget about it.

ABNORMALITY: 9 STUPIDITY: 10 ENTERTAINMENT: 5

367

Mario Question Blocks
www.bladediary.com/questionblocks

Anybody who's played a Mario video game is familiar with the question blocks that give the player power-ups. Well, these guys like them as well—maybe a little bit too much. So much that they want to create blocks and string them up around town. Here, you'll find instructions on how to make your own Mario question blocks. Their construction is fairly simple, using only cardboard, wrapping paper, and string. The instructions are very thorough, so most people shouldn't have trouble if they choose to make them. After you're done, the site encourages you to put them up in random places in the town or city where you live. You might want to consider this, though: On this same site, they imply that somebody got into trouble for putting up these blocks and that there were some nasty legal issues. Doesn't exactly motivate the block making, does it?

COMMENTS: I like the Mario blocks as much as any video game fanatic. I will also say that the blocks in the photos are very well made. But risking a criminal record just to express your inner nerd is a little too extreme. If you really want to make the question blocks, go ahead, but be sure it's just for interior decoration. Unless the town sheriff is a Mario fan, you might get yourself a game over—in the form of jail time and a hefty fine.

ABNORMALITY: 8 STUPIDITY: 7 ENTERTAINMENT: 7

366

Mr.Winkle.com
www.mrwinkle.com/index2.htm

This is the official homepage of Mr. Winkle, the cutest dog in the world! Okay, maybe he's not a *real* dog, but he still is the cutest dog in the world. Here, you can view the Mr. Winkle doll, see general info, watch videos, visit the Mr. Winkle store, and much more. There's even a fun-facts section, which is actually more like an FAQ.

COMMENTS: Aw, isn't he cute! Look at him! Even though he's just a stuffed, weird-looking Japanese dog, he's still cute. Still, that cuteness doesn't overcome the site's stupidity. Not even a cute puppy will spare this site from my vengeful wrath! HA HA HA HA HA!

ABNORMALITY: 7 STUPIDITY: 8 ENTERTAINMENT: 7

365

Zamboni

www.zamboni.com/welcome.html

It's the official website of hockey's famous arena cleaner: the Zamboni! Here, you can see old Zamboni models, check out info on the Zamboni company, shop the Zamboni Pro Shop, and more. Whatever you desire for anything related to Zambonis, this site has more than enough information and items to stoke your admiration of the machine that cleans the ice rink. Check out the video of the Model F Zamboni in action!

COMMENTS: This site struck a chord with me, my family being into hockey and all. Anyway, this site is not really stupid, but rather amusing. Hockey fans will like this one. So will Canadians. And remember, according to the copyright section, "Zamboni" is a trademark, not the name of the machine. The proper name for this contraption is "Zamboni Ice Resurfacing Machine." The name must be capitalized and spelled correctly and should never even remotely be used in a generic sense. You have been warned. Improper usage will result in being dragged around an ice rink in your underwear.

ABNORMALITY: 6 STUPIDITY: 4 ENTERTAINMENT: 7

364

Goatlover.com

www.goatlover.com

There's not much to this website except a picture of a goat and an email address to correspond with those who are interested in goats. It's the pinnacle of stupidity. This site captures everything that this book stands for.

COMMENTS: Ever seen the "Goat Boy" skit on *Saturday Night Live*? "Goat Boy" was one of the best skits ever…back in the '90s, when the show was going somewhere for the first time in a while!

ABNORMALITY: 8 STUPIDITY: 8 ENTERTAINMENT: 6

363

Parrot's Playground
jackmacaw.tripod.com

This is a biography page about a parrot named Jack. It was obviously created by someone who has way too much time on his or her hands. Here, you can learn more than you'd ever want to know about Jack in particular and parrots in general. Jack has some unusual hobbies and favorite foods. There was one thing that really blew my mind: Jack eats chili. Who ever heard of a parrot that likes chili?

COMMENTS: You'll probably get a little kick out of the parrot's favorite foods, but other than that there's really nothing to see here. Go find a cracker somewhere else.

ABNORMALITY: 7 STUPIDITY: 7 ENTERTAINMENT: 5

362

Bake Your Own Internet Cookie
www.cookiedemo.com

This is an interesting site where you can learn a little bit about cookies. I can't explain exactly what they are, but this site lets you visit and tell what kind of cookie you like. Choose chocolate chip or Oreo. With milk or without. The next time you visit the site, your cookie will be there! Amazing! It's even funnier because the technology that makes this possible is in your browser, and the little bookmarks the Internet makes on your personal browser are actually called "cookies"!

COMMENTS: This is an educational page, but the concept of the cookie makes it eligible to include in this book. How much amusement can you get out of a cookie appearing on your screen? Right? Still, the cookie does look good.

ABNORMALITY: 8 STUPIDITY: 8 ENTERTAINMENT: 6

361

Bin Punched
mistupid.com/stuff/binpunched.htm

Here's a game that's quite simple. A hand appears, you move it over Osama bin Laden's face, click, and you'll punch him! You can repeat this over and over again. It sounds so stupid and useless, but it's *soooo* fun! On top of that, he makes weird sounds as you sock him in the face. For some reason, I just can't get enough of it. It's addicting!

COMMENTS: I couldn't stop laughing as I spent several minutes straight punching bin Laden in the face! I highly recommend this page. I thought it was hilarious; you might, you might not. All I know is it shouldn't be addicting, but it is. Kind of like the smell of coffee. Oh sure, you say you're not addicted to caffeine, but we both know you are.

ABNORMALITY: 7 STUPIDITY: 8 ENTERTAINMENT: 8

360

Switcheroo Zoo
www.switcheroozoo.com

Here's a website where you can take an animal and mix and match body parts from other animals. You can create a pig with the tail of a monkey, the head of a bison, and the feet of a cheetah, along with hundreds of other possibilities. You may think that this sounds silly, but in practice it's actually quite fun. It's great to mix up the rear portion of a rhinoceros, the torso of a monkey, and the head of a dog. It's a dinokey!

COMMENTS: A silly, fun site that everybody can enjoy. It's one of the most fun things you can do, playing God with animals. Those people down at the medical laboratories do it with mice; when's our turn? Now, apparently.

ABNORMALITY: 8 STUPIDITY: 7 ENTERTAINMENT: 8

359

Jim's Streetlighting Homepage
www.eskimo.com/~jrterry/splash.html

This website is about those lights that illuminate the streets at night. Here, you can find out almost everything about them, direct from a guy who's had an obsession with them since he was a small child. There are photos, articles, comments, and more available for viewing. You can even join the streetlighting mailing list, if you're so inclined. Articles on streetlights. Now if that's not odd, I don't know what is (although I've said that before and I will say it again).

COMMENTS: This guy says at five he could tell the difference between a high-pressure sodium streetlight and a mercury vapor streetlight. Does that scare you? It should. I, for one, am very intelligent and I cannot tell the first difference between high-pressure sodium streetlights and mercury vapor streetlights or incandescent lights. They all shine when you turn on the switch, so who cares? I find this site highly disturbing, yet funny, too.

ABNORMALITY: 8 STUPIDITY: 7 ENTERTAINMENT: 6

358

Paper Airplanes
www.paperplane.org

This is the official website of a man who holds the Guinness world record for time aloft with a paper airplane. You can find info on him and his books. He has written three books, including *Aviation Legends Paper Airplane Book* and *The World Record Paper Airplane Book*. Wow, I didn't know they had world records for paper airplanes!

COMMENTS: Who knew this guy could make such a career out of paper airplanes? I'm sure you're asking how I can make a living from listing stupid websites, too. Well, it just goes to show you that capitalism is the world's greatest invention, next to paper airplanes.

ABNORMALITY: 7 STUPIDITY: 7 ENTERTAINMENT: 5

357

The Duct Tape Guy's Wall Taping Gallery

www.octanecreative.com/ducttape/walltapings/index.html

On this site, you can see people who have been duct-taped to walls and ceilings, for various purposes. Yes, I know there are not many good purposes, but still, they say it's a purpose. My personal favorite was the photo entitled "Why Duct Tape Pros Are Not Allowed to Babysit." Never have I seen something as weird as people being duct-taped to a wall. In some cases, the tape covers 95 percent of their body! Now that's thorough!

COMMENTS: This site is funny on so many levels. I love duct tape. We should all love duct tape. Let's have three cheers for duct tape! This is an all-around fun site to visit, and I'd recommend it if you're looking for something out of the ordinary. Just remember, duct-taping people to walls can be and is dangerous "unless you know what you are doing."

ABNORMALITY: 8 STUPIDITY: 8 ENTERTAINMENT: 7

356

The Way of the Exploding Stick

www.stickpage.com/wayoftheexplodingstick.shtml

Here's a fun little game where you are a stick figure trying to beat up other stick figures. Well, if that isn't entertainment at its finest, then I don't know what is. A triple scissors kick, a quick jab, a spin kick, and many other moves are at your disposal. You can even climb up a ladder and deliver justice from above! At the end of the level, you fight the dojo master in a dramatic final showdown. Judo chop!

COMMENTS: I found myself laughing and playing this game for a long time. Stick Master Sensei would be proud. Maybe. In any case, I highly recommend this site for anyone!

ABNORMALITY: 7 STUPIDITY: 8 ENTERTAINMENT: 8

355

Emo Darth Vader
emodarthvader.ytmnd.com

This site shows us an even darker, more depressing side of Darth Vader. Not only is the Sith Lord a tyrant with a sadistic penchant for psychically choking people, he's also a singer…an emo singer. For those who aren't up with the times (myself included; I had to research this stuff), "emo" is a slang term short for "emotional," describing people who are depressed, lonely, heartbroken, confused, and so on, further exacerbated by their belief that the world just doesn't understand their pessimistic plight. Emo is also a style of music which describes popular bands such as Death Cab for Cutie and Dashboard Confessional (even the names sound depressing, don't they?). Anyway, this page has Darth Vader singing "How Could This Happen to Me" by Simple Plan, and it's painful, in more ways than one. His voice is horrible, and I can barely understand the words, but I was able to make out "I'm sick of this life" through the ear-wrenching vocals. Woe to the tragic life of Darth Vader. The song is complete with depressing, melancholic instrumentals to further add to the misery.

COMMENTS: Emo people really need to lighten up. Get some sunlight. Listen to some more energetic music. Get some friends who aren't constantly depressed. Laugh a lot more. Life isn't that bad. Maybe it's harder to become un-emo than I think it is. But at least emo nerds (is there such a thing?) have Lord Vader to relate to now. Just thinking about all this makes me depressed. I'm going to go write a sad poem now. Sigh…

ABNORMALITY: 8 STUPIDITY: 8 ENTERTAINMENT: 6

354

RubberFaces.com
www.rubberfaces.com

This is a website where you can take the faces of celebrities and stretch them out as if they were rubber. This is another instance where technology really pulls off a miracle. A number of celebrities are available for your stretching pleasure, including Kelly Ripa, George W. Bush, Kathie Lee Gifford (she actually looks better with her face stretched out), and more.

COMMENTS: This is still a great site, especially considering recent additions. There are new faces to stretch from popular shows like *Dancing with the Stars* and *Grey's Anatomy*. (Dr. McDreamy won't be so dreamy when you're through with him.) Besides, it's still fun to pull William Shatner's *Star Trek* uniform over his head. I took great pleasure in doing that for some reason. Don't ask me why. Anyway, this is a very entertaining site, and I highly recommend visiting it.

ABNORMALITY: 8 STUPIDITY: 8 ENTERTAINMENT: 8

353

This site is about something called asdf. What exactly this is, I'm not entirely sure. All I know is that they tell you what it is, but it makes no sense. For example, asdf is a "significant difference," but at the same time it's "aoeu's cousin." This site has a number of other weird text messages all relating to this mysterious thing.

COMMENTS: There is not a shred of logic, sense, or meaning in this site. It is stupidity and meaninglessness in its purest form. Period. This site makes absolutely, positively no sense at all, and nobody but the person who made it up can understand it. And I doubt even that person can understand it.

ABNORMALITY: 10 STUPIDITY: 10 ENTERTAINMENT: 3

352

Chessboxing
www/chessbase.com/newsdetail.asp?newsid=3208

Move over, football and baseball. There's a new sports craze sweeping the nation (or at least this website): chessboxing! "This unusual sport, in which two competitors face each other in eleven alternating rounds, six of chess, five of boxing, is rapidly gaining popularity. You know that is the case when you see chessboxing on the front page of a leading sports website, and as a major story in a number of men's magazines." A typical chessboxing match begins with a four-minute round of chess, with the board placed directly in the middle of a boxing ring. After each round of chess, the bell sounds and the chessboard is removed from the ring. Two minutes of boxing follow, and then it all repeats for another nine rounds. The site has profiles of supposedly popular chessboxers (I find it hard to believe that the sport itself is at all popular), as well as pictures and videos of chessboxing rounds.

COMMENTS: What a concept. Take two of the most boring spectator sports in existence (besides soccer, which by now you know I don't like at all), then combine them and promote them in dirty magazines. I know I find that exciting. Seriously, though, I'd rather go see another *Saw* movie than watch chessboxing.

ABNORMALITY: 7 STUPIDITY: 8 ENTERTAINMENT: 4

351

The Prank Institute
www.prank.org

This website contains more than ten thousand pranks, all available for viewing! They're divided into categories, including home pranks, one of which is to make a solution out of habanero peppers and other ingredients to make your Christmas tree stink really bad! Talk about useful information! Office pranks, Halloween pranks, and more are also on the site. The collection is extensive, so if you find yourself liking this site, you'll be spending a lot of time there.

COMMENTS: Very entertaining. A must-see for anybody with even a slight sense of humor. If you have a sense of humor that's above average or average, then you'll really dig this site. If you have no sense of humor, I pity you.

ABNORMALITY: 8 STUPIDITY: 8 ENTERTAINMENT: 8

350

The Insanity Test
funny-funny-pictures.com/insanity

The concept behind this page is simple: look at a picture of a race car without laughing. How hard could it be? I know what you're thinking, what's the catch? Well, my friend, let's just say that you'll be surprised. Just be sure to have your speakers turned up. That's a key part of this experience.

COMMENTS: I found myself howling with laughter over this site! I almost laughed as much as when I saw a pay-per-view event from WWE. I recommend visiting it once in a while when you need a pick-me-up. It's very uplifting and it will make you laugh.

ABNORMALITY: 8 STUPIDITY: 8 ENTERTAINMENT: 7

349

The Ultimate Build
Your Own Cow Page
members.tripod.com/~spows/cow.html

On this page, you are given a cow, and you can select from a number of options to customize it in any way you desire. From extra tails to polka dots, you can create your very own cow so that you can say, "I made that!" Sure, you may have made a cow that's extremely ugly and something you'd never want to be seen, but still, you made it!

COMMENTS: You can make some weird cows with this page—some cows that could not possibly exist in real life. Still, it is somewhat entertaining. I recommend it...kind of. You be the judge.

ABNORMALITY: 8 STUPIDITY: 8 ENTERTAINMENT: 6

348

Punk Kittens
www.rathergood.com/punk_kittens

This is a page where you can see some kittens rocking out to some sweet tunes. There is a guitar player, a drummer, and some admiring kittens in the crowd. It's an unusual site and one that is definitely quite amusing to see. After all, it's not only humans who like to rock and roll. Kittens like music, too, don't they? Although, if I would have guessed first, I wouldn't have guessed rock and roll.

COMMENTS: I liked this site. Kittens jamming on guitars are somehow amusing to me. Sure they're not quite like the Rolling Stones or Pink Floyd, but still, they sound better than Justin Timberlake. (Not surprisingly, he's just as horrible as a solo artist as he was when he was in *NSYNC.) Anyway, if you want to rock out with some gnarly kittens, drop by this site.

ABNORMALITY: 8 STUPIDITY: 7 ENTERTAINMENT: 6

347

Give Me a Name
www.givemeaname.com

Could you use an easy $25,000 right now? If so, this is the place to do it. This guy is going to give a big twenty-five grand (or so he says) to anybody who will give him a new name. "My name is Aaron Schwarz and I've decided to change my name," he says. The process for giving Aaron a new name is outlined in five steps. The first is probably the hardest and most agonizing: you have to actually get to know this weirdo. The "About Me" section has a very boring life story along with completely useless "facts." (He claims to have dated Meg Ryan, Jessica Alba, and Mila Kunis—which, he admits, was "in my imagination and not actually in real life." Creepy.) The sad part, however, is that he has already chosen a name (so much for that $25,000...). Out of the many names voted on, Aaron has selected "Sunshine Megatron." And, that's better than Aaron Schwarz how?

COMMENTS: Ol' Sunshine Megatron here can have fun spending the rest of his life wondering why he would let a complete stranger change his name. I can only imagine the awkwardness and/or shame of introducing myself to a stranger as "Sunshine Megatron." Luckily, this guy did that before I could think about it too much. Isn't it great when other people do stupid stuff so we don't have to?

ABNORMALITY: 9 STUPIDITY: 10 ENTERTAINMENT: 8

346

The World Carrot Museum
www.carrotmuseum.co.uk

It's called The World Carrot Museum, and you can learn all about carrots. From origins to types to fun games, this site has it all. You can wander freely throughout the site, or take a guided tour of the museum by clicking on the picture. (Talk about luxury, a guided tour!) Test your knowledge of carrot trivia. Learn what the ancient Greeks and Romans thought of carrots. How can you resist this wonderful site?

COMMENTS: This site's headline reads "Discover the power of Carrots." What power? I've never heard of carrots imbuing anybody with special powers, except for turning orange from eating too many. That does, in fact, happen, in case you were wondering. No joke. Since this site has no pictures of that happening, it is quite useless.

ABNORMALITY: 8 STUPIDITY: 8 ENTERTAINMENT: 6

345

101 Uses for Duct Tape
thezac.com/ducttape

What?! I've neglected to include a page on how to properly use the world's greatest resource? Shame on me! Duct tape is most assuredly the world's greatest invention ever. It can do anything and everything. Anyway, this page is self-explanatory; 101 uses for the greatest household tool on Earth. Some uses include "toilet paper" (ouch, that's gotta hurt!) and "lawn furniture."

COMMENTS: Some of the uses on this page are actually quite practical. Others are complete lunacy. You decide which ones you want to use. For those you use, do so at your own risk. There could be serious consequences, like using duct tape for unsightly hair removal. In fact, if you use some of the ways on these pages, your story may end up among the many stupid tales on the Internet that we've seen. You've been warned.

ABNORMALITY: 8 STUPIDITY: 8 ENTERTAINMENT: 7

344

LEGO Crossbow
www.makezine.com/blog/archive/
2006/05/lego_crossbow.html

We've seen LEGOs in just about every form. We've seen LEGO castles, mansions, island fortresses, the White House, the Taj Mahal, and Mount Everest. The one LEGO thing I have not seen, however, is right here—a crossbow! According to this site, some guy named Alexei wanted an elastic gun that would shoot LEGO blocks. Some three hundred hours later (he admits it would have been better spent on some charitable works), he completed the LEGO Crossbow, pictured here. The crossbow is extremely elaborate, and supposedly fires LEGO blocks about 20 yards.

COMMENTS: This guy obviously needs something more productive to keep him occupied. Here's an idea: have him build a life-size house made out of LEGOs. Some underprivileged family could go live in it. If he can build a crossbow out of LEGOs, he should be able to build something that has a shred of practical use. This oversized toy weapon is certainly lacking in that department.

ABNORMALITY: 9 STUPIDITY: 7 ENTERTAINMENT: 6

343

Watching Grass Grow
www.watching-grass-grow.com

Like Cheddar Vision (see number 376), this one is pretty self-explanatory. It's a camera fixed on a field of grass. You watch it grow. The backdrop for this spectacle appears to be the front lawn of a suburban house—simply amazing, isn't it? There's only one other thing to do on this site: a time-lapse, year-long video of grass growing (nine months longer than Cheddar Vision's—amazing!). That's 365 times better than watching grass growing at normal speed! And 365 times better is…still boring. There's also some horrid music on this site. It's the kind of music that will make you clinically insane if you listen to it for more than fifteen minutes.

COMMENTS: Haven't we gone down this road before? To relate how incredibly boring this site is, I use an exaggerated simile to compare it to something I really don't like (professional outdoor soccer, Carrot Top, MTV, *American Idol*, etc.), and I indicate how this site is a last resort when you've completely run out of things to do. So, if you're really that desperately bored, the question is: Grass Growing or Cheddar Vision?

ABNORMALITY: 5 STUPIDITY: 9 ENTERTAINMENT: 1

342

Streetmattresses.com
www.streetmattress.com/sm.php

On this site, you can view photographs of mattresses. Mattresses? Everyone has one, so why is this unusual? Mattresses aren't stupid or abnormal; in fact, they are really useful. Except for one special thing about these mattresses: they've been abandoned on the streets! Submitting your own photos and viewing the locations where these mattresses have been found are options available on this site. You'll find "amazing" photos of abandoned mattresses from many countries, including the U.S., Canada, New Zealand, Belgium, and Nepal. You'll even find six, yes six, submissions from Malaysia.

COMMENTS: A lot of people throw out old mattresses. Some even abandon their mattresses on the street. Who would have thought someone would feel a burning desire to photograph them? Maybe their intent was to have some local hobos see the photos and flock to the mattresses for a softer place to sleep. Of course, most hobos don't have access to the Internet…do they?

ABNORMALITY: 8 STUPIDITY: 8 ENTERTAINMENT: 6

341

Lobster Magnet
www.savethegoldfish.co.uk/fun/lobster.php

This is a very, um…unique cartoon movie sequence. It's about lobsters, magnets, and some hard-rock tunes. Now if those aren't three things that have absolutely nothing in common, I don't know what three things do. I actually spaced out while watching it, pondering its stupidity. You can take my word for it. Other than that, the only thing is to see it for yourself.

COMMENTS: Are rabbits made of metal? Can lobsters use magnets to avoid being eaten? What does a lobster have to do with a sinking ship? And how do you prove the song's refrain of "lobster sticks to magnet"? This site answers all of those questions and more. Actually, I think it just makes those questions a whole lot harder to answer. Once again, you decide. Also, a warning: this video is quite loud. Prepare your eardrums for a beating if your computer's volume is up.

ABNORMALITY: 9 STUPIDITY: 9 ENTERTAINMENT: 7

340

Useless Fact of the Day
www.ufotd.com

On this page, you can see facts that have absolutely no use at all. One useless fact is that "the odds of getting a royal flush in a regular game of five-card stud poker are 365,000,000 to 1." Now that's useless! Well, actually, that could help if you're a big gambler…but still, very few people can make use of it. Of course, those fitness freaks looking for the latest exercise craze will be pleased to note that banging your head against a wall uses 150 calories an hour. Even more importantly, Homer Simpson would be delighted to know that beer is less fattening than milk.

COMMENTS: This is a very well-done page that deserves a place in your bookmarks. The facts you see on this page are almost utterly useless and amazingly stupid. However, be warned! You might learn something. And I know you didn't have that in mind when you purchased this book.

ABNORMALITY: 9 STUPIDITY: 8 ENTERTAINMENT: 9

339

Museum of Soviet Calculators

www.taswegian.com/MOSCOW/soviet.html

This is definitely an odd site: a museum of Cold War–era calculators made by the Reds. Here, you can learn a little about each featured calculator, as well as how it works and when it was made. There are a number of different types of calculators, including manual and electronic ones.

COMMENTS: Sure, the site is sort of educational…but why calculators? Why not weapons or cars or clothes or hair combs? OK, not hair combs, but why not the rest? This site is very bizarre indeed. Nevertheless, it is kind of interesting.

ABNORMALITY: 6 STUPIDITY: 7 ENTERTAINMENT: 6

338

The Head Shop

users.rcn.com/cocopug

This is a collection of unusual faces created from graphic animations and drawings. From a toenail head to an insanely deformed head, this site has a lot to see.

One thing's for sure: this is definitely one of the odder sites on the Internet. In fact, it is so weird that you would probably believe in alien hippie ninja rappers before you'd believe these things are real.

COMMENTS: This is probably *the* most unusual page I've come across; therefore it receives my highest abnormality rating. It defies explanation. Still, it is definitely worth checking out.

ABNORMALITY: 10 STUPIDITY: 7 ENTERTAINMENT: 7

337 The Center for Prevention of Shopping Cart Abuse
www.shoppingcartabuse.com

This is the official headquarters of an organization attempting to stop a horrible crime: shopping cart abuse. Each day, thousands of shopping carts are subject to being climbed on, rammed against objects, and other acts of atrocity. Here, you can see the top offenders, case studies, and more. The site even features an article that "proves" Bob Crane, the late actor who starred in *Hogan's Heroes*, really faked his death so that he would be "free to operate unfettered in the seedy underworld of Shopping Cart abuse."

COMMENTS: What awful crimes these are! Whoever abuses these things should be ashamed. Shopping carts have feelings, too! Seriously, though, this is a hilarious site that's great to visit. It combines an unfathomable amount of abnormality and stupidity—a rare thing; or not, depending on how much time you spend on the Internet. Check out the photos; they're quite well done.

ABNORMALITY: 9 STUPIDITY: 10 ENTERTAINMENT: 7

336 The American Spy Cow
www.fmp.com/rodent/spycow

On this website, you can learn about a program called the Military Farm Animal Operations Program, or MFAOP. Sounds serious....I wonder if this is classified information? Anyway, according to this demented page, robotic farm animals, mainly cows, are equipped with explosives, guns, and spy tools that would be the envy of James Bond. Then these bovine beauties are put into the field to go after criminals and/or wartime enemies. Talk about creativity!

COMMENTS: Kudos to the mind who thought this twisted idea up. You're creative! You have a gift! You could make some money! Just think: together, my friend, we could rule this town. OK, enough with the Donald Trump speeches. Twisted idea, but good site.

ABNORMALITY: 9 STUPIDITY: 9 ENTERTAINMENT: 8

335 The Blenderphone
www.cycoactive.com/blender

Here is the homepage for an ingenious device: the blenderphone! Part blender, part phone, all radically cool. (Who wouldn't want a drink mixer for a telephone?) It gives info on the phone, as well as an FAQ and ordering info. Now, I have one question: Is this thing for real? If it is, it may be one of the signs of the apocalypse.

COMMENTS: Seriously, though, could somebody please tell me if this thing is for real? I mean, sure, it looks cool, but could such an absurd product possibly exist? This requires further investigation, although not by me. You do it. No, really. Go. Go now. Anyway, just keep in mind that the price probably isn't worth it; this thing costs $300! Yes, you heard me right.

ABNORMALITY: 9 STUPIDITY: 7 ENTERTAINMENT: 6

334 The Complete and Utter Idiot's Guide to Making a Baloney Sandwich
www.brunching.com/idiotsandwich.html

Don't know how to make a baloney sandwich? Visit this site, and all your questions will be answered. Here, you'll find a step-by-step guide to making a baloney sandwich. The one thing, though, is that this guy thinks you're a complete idiot. And if you need to visit this website for its educational appeal, you probably are an idiot. Hey, come on. If you don't know how to make a baloney sandwich, there's something wrong with you.

COMMENTS: Anybody could understand this page. Well, almost anybody. The point is that none of us need to know how to make a sandwich. Since this site offers little other humor, it is useless.

ABNORMALITY: 6 STUPIDITY: 10 ENTERTAINMENT: 3

333

U.S. Lawn Mower
Racing Association
www.letsmow.com

Go Lawn Mower Racer, go! Okay, maybe they don't deserve a cartoon series like *Speed Racer* (that cartoon was crazy…everybody talked so fast!), but this site does deserve some attention for its inventive use of a common item found in many a suburban garage. Here, you'll find lots of stuff on lawn mower racing, including rules, a schedule, an FAQ, and more. There is even information on the Lawn Mower Races, including rules about what kinds of models can enter.

COMMENTS: Once again, I'm wondering, is this site for real? I think so, but I'm not sure. Check this page out; it's definitely worth a look. You might find yourself laughing at how absurd the thought of it is. Lawn mower racing! Absolutely insane!

ABNORMALITY: 10 STUPIDITY: 8 ENTERTAINMENT: 7

332

Bros. Grim Side Shows
www.brothersgrimsideshow.com

"Freaks, wonders, and human curiosities" await you at the Bros. Grim Side Shows. Although it may seem creepy at first (especially with the drawing of a demented clown among various demons on the greeting page), this is actually a fairly generic circus sideshow. This site actually promotes a real circus act formed in 1995 by a "circus historian." It claims to be one of the world's last "authentic remaining side shows." Bros. Grim has standard circus attractions such as fire breathers, wolf people, bearded ladies, shrunken heads, and many exotic artifacts from Middle and Far Eastern locales. You can accompany the attractions with a calliope playing old-fashioned circus music. Just makes you want to join the circus, doesn't it?

COMMENTS: Whatever happened to circus sideshows? They used to be all over the place in the old days. Now this appears to be one of the only ones left. Maybe people got desensitized to the sideshows' weirdness after a while. Now all you have to do is go to a goth rock concert or a heavy metal hair band concert to see sideshow freaks. Still, Bros. Grim is a nostalgic reminder of the days when our world seemed so much larger, and we weren't quite so jaded.

ABNORMALITY: 9 STUPIDITY: 8 ENTERTAINMENT: 8

331

Send Me a Dollar.com
www.sendmeadollar.com/welcome/welcome.html

The concept of this site is deceptively simple; the creator wants you to send him a dollar. That's it. Nothing more. In exchange, you can post a short message. Now, if you ask me, that doesn't seem like a very fair exchange; you can post messages on tons of other websites for free. But if you enjoy spending stupidly, you might like this. Anyway, you can see other messages, an FAQ, and mailing info.

COMMENTS: Who does this guy think he is? Does he think we're his bank or something? Does he expect us to just send him our hard-earned cash so he can do who-knows-what with it? If you're stupid enough to actually send this loser money, you should consider therapy. Your urge to indulge complete strangers with money could be signs of a deeper problem. Don't worry, it's okay. You're going to get through this.

ABNORMALITY: 6 STUPIDITY: 5 ENTERTAINMENT: 4

330

Museum of Burnt Food
www.burntfoodmuseum.com

The Web address says it all: this is a museum specializing in burnt food. Here, you'll find a comprehensive list of burnt food, complete with pictures and an interesting history of the museum and its origins. There's even info on how you, yes you, can start your very own burnt-food museum. It's great that the site offers information on how you can start your own museum, but I have one problem with that: who would want to burn food, at least intentionally?

COMMENTS: I never thought burnt food had any use whatsoever, other than to be tossed in the trash. And guess what? I still don't. This site is ridiculous! Stay away. Stay far, far away.

ABNORMALITY: 9 STUPIDITY: 8 ENTERTAINMENT: 4

329

Virtual Church of the Blind Chihuahua
www.dogchurch.org

This is a site that is full of useless, ridiculous information. As the introduction states: "Welcome to this sacred place in cyberspace named after a little old dog with cataracts, who barked sideways at strangers, because he couldn't see where they were." Here, you'll find jokes, office activities, quotes, and other random items that don't belong in any particular place in this world. Features include an FAQ that says that the Virtual Church of the Blind Chihuahua is "part of a miniscule conspiracy to help virtues like civility, honesty, kindness, and common sense achieve world domination." Sounds noble enough, but it has the word "conspiracy" in it! That can't be good.

COMMENTS: Beware false idols! This heathen canine is attempting to lure you into Satan's grasp! Worship this dog, and you are doomed to an eternity of pain! On the other hand, he is pretty cute. I suppose I'd worship him if I already didn't have my own idol. Who is my false idol, you ask? It is none other than the divine Texas Ranger himself: Chuck Norris. He is better than any deity imaginable. Almighty Chuck could roundhouse kick you into hell if you defy him. You have been warned.

ABNORMALITY: 9 STUPIDITY: 10 ENTERTAINMENT: 6

328

The Flying Cow
www.funhills.com/g/38.html

Here is a game where you try to fling a cow into the center of a target. Hmm… seems ordinary enough. You click and hold the left mouse button on the catapult, release it, and depending on how long you hold the click, the cow will go a certain distance. The closer to the bull's-eye, the more points you get. See if you can get the high score! If you can, you might be able to post a message on the website.

COMMENTS: Yeah, you know when you put the cow on the catapult, and then you fling it, and then it goes flying, and then it lands, and then you get points? Yeah, that's cool. I don't know why, and there is no reason at all that it should be cool, but it just is.

ABNORMALITY: 8 STUPIDITY: 9 ENTERTAINMENT: 8

327

Lip Balm Anonymous
www.kevdo.com/lipbalm/home.html

Is Carmex an insatiable daily need that has you hooked? Do you get the shakes when you run out of Chap Stick? Do you need help for your addiction? If you do, or even if you don't (you may be in denial!), head on down to this page. Here, you'll learn all about lip balm, its addicting properties, and how you can cope if you have an addiction.

COMMENTS: I am proud (or perhaps ashamed) to say that as of this edition, LBA has honored me and this book: "Lip Balm Anonymous was # 327 out of 505 in the new book *505 Unbelievably Stupid Web Pages*. LBA is considering legal action against the author and publisher." Oh no! I will be sued for every penny I'm worth! Save me Jeebus! Hopefully, Kevin C. of LBA will reconsider his decision...please?

ABNORMALITY: 9 STUPIDITY: 8 ENTERTAINMENT: 7

326

Eric Conveys an Emotion
www.emotioneric.com

Here's a site with a relatively simple concept: viewers name a situation or emotion, and this guy, Eric, will try to recreate it. It sounds stupid, but some of the pictures are quite funny. Examples include "suspicious," "finding dead body in the trunk," and my favorite, "Emotion is illogical, Captain." It's funny to see what his expressions are for the more...unusual circumstances.

COMMENTS: This guy is funny! Check out the picture he put on the site for if he had "found Cameron Diaz in his closet." Very funny! A site I'd highly recommend seeing, along with the other meaningless sites in this book.

ABNORMALITY: 7 STUPIDITY: 7 ENTERTAINMENT: 9

325

The Dancing Paul Page
www.dancingpaul.com

Probably a cousin to the Dancing Bush (see number 467), Dancing Paul is where you can select a number of dance-move options for Paul. You can add various music pieces, like "Shake Your Booty" and "Staying Alive," choose backup dancers who are horribly ordinary, select a ton of different dance moves, and display various backgrounds, like the Taj Mahal.

COMMENTS: I found myself strangely attracted to this site. No! It's…too…stupid! Must…pull…away from…computer screen! Agh! Seriously though, this is a pretty funny site, although pretty darn stupid. Check it out, but don't count on wanting to come back a second time.

ABNORMALITY: 8 STUPIDITY: 9 ENTERTAINMENT: 7

324

Wacky Zoo
www.wackyzoo.com

This site contains mostly abnormal pictures and a few jokes and links to other humorous sites. Some of the photos are very, very odd. There are a few containing cars that you definitely don't see every day, a few others that are quite amusing, and a number of pictures that you just *don't* want to see, among which are a school bus doing a wheelie and "Osama bin Laden's SUV." Geez!

COMMENTS: Just exactly where do people get their stupidity? Did they inherit a stupid gene from their parents? Or is it a learned behavior? The great nature vs. nurture debate now extends into stupidity. Someone should do a documentary on stupidity. Leonard Nimoy should host it. Why? Two reasons: Leonard Nimoy is great at hosting documentaries (*Ancient Mysteries with Leonard Nimoy*, of which I have seen just about every episode, is my favorite), and…SPOCK RULES!

ABNORMALITY: 10 STUPIDITY: 8 ENTERTAINMENT: 9

323   Online Slang Dictionaries

www.uwasa.fi/comm/termino/collect/slang.html

That lil' ankle biter will be apples at the barbie tonight! For a translation of that rather unusual phrase, head on over to the Online Slang Dictionaries page. It has several dictionaries of various dialects of different languages, including English dialects from, well…England, English dialects from Australia (my personal favorite), and even the alternative French dictionary. *Sacre bleu!* There's even a dictionary for Esperanto. Esperanto slang? Now I've really seen it all!

COMMENTS: This website gives you some interesting perspectives on how other people speak. An interesting activity for this site I suggest would be researching a dialect and trying it out for a day. It's worth it when you say something and everybody just stares at you with dumbfounded looks on their faces.

ABNORMALITY: 7   STUPIDITY: 6   ENTERTAINMENT: 8

322

AllCamels.com
www.allcamels.com

Here is a site dedicated to those hump-backed animals you find in the desert. You can find articles on camels, camel pictures, and info on—get this—camel races! Camel races?! What have professional sports sunk to? Of all of the weird types of racing I've heard of, camel racing is way up there. There are also links to other sites, as well as some other camel information tidbits.

COMMENTS: Maybe when I travel the world someday, I'll go to a camel race. Then I'll just stand there and gape at the oddity on the racetrack. Or I could just download the video…it's a heck of a lot faster. Anyway, this site is quite funny because camels are funny. They look like llamas, except lumpier.

ABNORMALITY: 9   STUPIDITY: 7   ENTERTAINMENT: 6

321 The Chameleon Conspiracy

www.angelfire.com/mi/slackertrash/mychameleon.html

This site is going to be hard to sum up. Oh well, here it goes...this person believes his pet chameleon was kidnapped in an attempt to influence a presidential election as part of a secret United States government conspiracy! (Huff...puff...) You can see pictures that "prove" this conspiracy theorist's supposed theory.

COMMENTS: Wow. It's so silent here I can almost hear a pin drop. Truly a bizarre website that deserves the highest of honors in terms of abnormality. As such, you should go see it. It's actually pretty funny if you read it. Still, you do kind of feel pity for the guy. His chameleon was kidnapped...or so he says.

ABNORMALITY: 10 STUPIDITY: 9 ENTERTAINMENT: 7

---

320 Born Rich.org

www.bornrich.org

We've all met them: the spoiled little rich girls (and boys) who have everything they could ever want just because their daddies are totally loaded. Unless you're one of them, you probably despise them for their laziness and greed (I know I do). Unfortunately, there are many people in today's society that encourage these little leeches—and Born Rich.org has a good number of them. This site's sole purpose is to advertise fancy, expensive (as in, "more than your family's combined yearly salaries"), completely useless and impractical widgets that these people can waste their excessive wealth on. Examples include an armored sports car, a $4,100 stereo that can automatically play music depending on your current mood (funny, I didn't know they could make telepathic stereo systems), and a pumpkin-shaped swing worth 18,000 British pounds—which translates into even more American dollars. You know, UNICEF or Red Cross could really use a donation of an expensive pumpkin-shaped swing.

COMMENTS: Wouldn't this world be a lot better if people would stop spending ridiculous sums of money on stupid pieces of junk like these (that usually only make them happy for a few days, at which point they need to spend even more) and donate that money to worthy charities? Shame on you, Born Rich.org. If you're not going to donate even a little bit from your bottomless bank account to charity, donate it to some other worthy cause—like me. I'm not picky. I'll take a two-year-old Lexus. After all, you're not using it anymore.

ABNORMALITY: 6 STUPIDITY: 9 ENTERTAINMENT: 5

319

Crying While Eating
www.cryingwhileeating.com

Crying is (usually) a very unpleasant experience. Eating is (hopefully) a pleasant experience. So why would you want to combine the two? That is a question that Crying While Eating attempts to answer. It's quite simple: there are hundreds of pictures and videos of people crying about something while eating various food products. You are told what is being eaten and what they are crying about. While this may sound boring at first, some of the entries are fairly amusing. A shirtless guy named Mike eats grilled salmon fillet and chile con queso while crying about his "punctured ego." "Hank and Earl" eat pudding, peaches in a cup, and whiskey while crying because "NASCAR was preempted." Why would that be a reason for crying? That's a reason for celebration!

COMMENTS: It is kind of fun to go through all these videos, although some of the "crying" is just pathetically bad acting. On the plus side, there is one classic among these pedestrian actors: Homer Simpson crying about Pinchy the Lobster while eating…Pinchy the Lobster. When Homer cries, we all cry.

ABNORMALITY: 8   STUPIDITY: 8   ENTERTAINMENT: 8

318

Dog Judo
www.dogjudo.co.uk

Spot knows something you might not know: martial arts! Fortunately, this site doesn't try to teach your dog martial arts. Instead, it's a humorous blog and video series about two talking dogs named Rexley and Roy, who are both roommates and judo practitioners. Perhaps what makes these videos so distinct from others of their ilk is their British-style humor—and there's a lot of British humor. Not that that's a bad thing. This site also has a link to a store where you can buy merchandise—unfortunately, it hasn't been updated in a while, as there are only sold-out Christmas cards on the page. Come on, where are the dog judo suits?

COMMENTS: There's something that is laudably laughable about two talking British dogs in an Odd Couple relationship practicing martial arts. None of the videos are particularly outstanding, but somehow they make me laugh, or at the very least amuse me.

ABNORMALITY: 9   STUPIDITY: 8   ENTERTAINMENT: 8

317 Kennedy's Used Shoes
www.geocities.com/mkennedy64/shoes.html

No, these are *not* any of "the" Kennedy family's shoes. These are the shoes of Mark A. Kennedy, an average, well-to-do American. He wants to give away his shoes. No, not sell them away; *give* them away. He'll even pay for shipping and handling! Just go there and present your case by filling out the request form. If he decides you can provide the right home for the shoes, he'll deliver them right to you.

COMMENTS: I found the fact that this guy was willing to dedicate an entire website to his shoes really and truly kind of odd. Why not go to a used clothing store and try to sell them or just give them to charity? Well, I guess some people just think differently. Maybe he feels sorry for his old shoes and wants them to have a good home. Shoe adoption. Yeah, that's probably it.

ABNORMALITY: 8 STUPIDITY: 9 ENTERTAINMENT: 5

---

316 Sound Effects for Your Cat
www.yuckles.com/catsounds.htm

Here are a multitude of sound effects having to do with cats. I don't exactly know what they're for, but a few of them don't sound too real. There's also something called the "Cat Commandments," which include: "THOU SHALT not projectile vomit from the top of the refrigerator" (gross), "THOU SHALT not walk in on a dinner party and commence licking thy butt" (very gross), and "THOU SHALT not jump onto thy sleeping human's bladder at 4 a.m." (now that's just disturbing!).

COMMENTS: Cat sounds! What an original concept! Why hadn't I thought of that? If only I had made a fake cat sound website…I can only dream. Anyway, this site is rather stupid, but if you want some cat sounds, head over to this site. Perhaps you can figure out some use for them. I sure couldn't.

ABNORMALITY: 6 STUPIDITY: 9 ENTERTAINMENT: 3

315

The Traffic Cone Preservation Society

www.trafficcone.com

This site is dedicated to the preservation of traffic cones. The "evolution" section tracks the "conus" genus from prehistoric times to today. You have your standard "orange conecone," or "Conus traficus." Also included are the rare "Blue conecone," or "Conus smurficus" (this cone was hunted to near extinction due to the "mistaken belief that melting it would produce gold"). Most cones are harmless, but beware the extremely dangerous "Esther's Cone," or "Conus estheris." Remember the old rhyme about this cone: "Orange stripe around, death abound. No stripe in sight, all is right."

COMMENTS: This site is simple, yet ingenious. It's obvious that this site is "art." At least that's what I would have said before I discovered that they actually charge money for "traffic cone adoption kits." This greedy exploitation of orphaned traffic cones makes this worthy of being one of this book's stupidest.

ABNORMALITY: 9 STUPIDITY: 10 ENTERTAINMENT: 9

314

Survive 2012

www.survive2012.com

Ever heard somebody say that the world is going to end in 2012? This crackpot theory is mostly based on a misunderstood claim that the ancient Mayan calendar "ends" on December 21, 2012. According to the "Survive 2012" introduction, there was a highly advanced civilization ten thousand years ago that was wiped out in a cataclysmic event, and there will be another such event in 2012. This site goes on wild tangents citing many sources—besides the Mayan calendar, there's also "evidence" from fractal time theories, the I Ching, and unstable stars that will explode in—yep, 2012.

COMMENTS: The sad thing is that there are hundreds of other theories like this, all centering around the Mayan calendar "ending" in 2012. While it is true a baktun (a period lasting about four hundred years on the Mayan calendar) will be ending in 2012, it's just like a century or millennium ending: significant, but not the end of the world.

ABNORMALITY: 10 STUPIDITY: 10 ENTERTAINMENT: 7

313
The T.W.I.N.K.I.E.S. Project
www.twinkiesproject.com/index.html

This is a site related to the Marshmallow Bunny Survival Tests (see number 497). It's just like it, in fact, except with Twinkies. Because Twinkies are the superior dessert, this site is better (come on, which would you rather have?). The twisted creators of this site have exposed the wonderful gooey goodness of Twinkies to all sorts of unmentionable experiments, many of which have left the Twinkies in a...not-so-good condition, shall we say (surprise, surprise).

COMMENTS: A very well-done site, especially since it's strictly about torturing Twinkies. That still doesn't answer some questions: Why torture food? Why not eat it? Twinkies are delicious, for goodness' sake! Some people just don't appreciate what they have. Kids in China would love a Twinkie! And they had to go ruin those perfectly good treats.

ABNORMALITY: 8 STUPIDITY: 9 ENTERTAINMENT: 6

312
Gregology
www.gregology.net

"Abraham, Moses, Jesus, Muhammad, and now Greg, the fifth and final apostle of God." Is it even possible to take that statement seriously? According to Gregology, it is. Here, you'll learn how you can save yourself from the apocalypse by selling your soul to some guy named Greg. There are four simple requirements for becoming a Gregologist: "Dedicate your life to the study of Greg," "Bestow your soul to Greg," "Donate 55 percent of your earnings to Greg," and "Learn everything on this site (there is an exam!)." An exam? The first three, maybe, but Greg expects us to take a freakin' exam? This guy is nuts! On the plus side, once you become a Gregologist, you are "promised a place by his side in the afterlife as well as a fridge magnet and ceremonial brick which will be used to grant you access to the afterlife in the yearly sacrament ritual." There's still that exam, though....

COMMENTS: I never understood cults that well. Are people's lives so crappy that they're willing to worship some guy as their god, without questioning his sanity at all? Fortunately, the mild sarcasm here implies that this site is a joke, so at least we know Greg isn't planning anything horrible...yet.

ABNORMALITY: 9 STUPIDITY: 9 ENTERTAINMENT: 6

311

RallyMonkey.com
www.rallymonkey.com

Here is the homepage of the Rally Monkey. What exactly is the Rally Monkey, you ask? Legend has it that on June 6, 2000, the Anaheim Angels were losing to the San Francisco Giants. The stadium's film team started playing video clips to encourage the crowd. Most had no effect, but when the monkey from *Ace Ventura: Pet Detective* appeared on the video screen, the crowd went wild! Thus was born the legend of the Rally Monkey.

COMMENTS: Very creative introduction. This site also has a wealth of info on this real-life mascot, including photos and an FAQ. I think it's a great mascot, personally. Why? Because it's a monkey! Monkeys are naturally cool. Check it out; it's worth a quick look.

ABNORMALITY: 9 STUPIDITY: 7 ENTERTAINMENT: 6

310

Random.org
www.random.org

With a name like Random.org, you may expect random humor, right? Random.org is not about random humor, but about random generators. Coin flippers, dice rollers, list randomizers, and jazz scale generators are just a few "random" generators on this site. You can select the number of items and the type of item used (there are hundreds of types just for coins). After that, click on the randomize button and you'll automatically get a random result for dice, coins, or whatever you choose. There are even testimonials that confirm random.org is indeed…random. The statistics and explanations are elaborate enough to make nerds drool, but if you just want randomness you can go straight to the generators.

COMMENTS: This site is actually pretty practical. Flipping coins or rolling dice can sometimes be sketchy when you're dealing with someone who does it the wrong way. The generators do indeed seem to be random if you use them enough. Sometimes it's fun just to play around with them. Try doing weird stuff with them, like testing your non-existent psychic powers. It would be cool if we did have psychic powers, though. Wouldn't it be nice to telekinetically grab a soda from the fridge? I'd use that power all the time.

ABNORMALITY: 8 STUPIDITY: 9 ENTERTAINMENT: 5

309 Star Wars: Endor Holocaust
www.theforce.net/swtc/holocaust.html

Here's some documentation on how the explosion of the second Death Star caused a nuclear holocaust on Endor. The site answers the "burning" question: *"What happens when you detonate a spherical metal honeycomb over five hundred miles wide just above the atmosphere of a habitable world?"* The answer is simple: "Regardless of specifics, the world won't remain habitable for long." So that's why we never heard anything more from those furry little Ewoks! Anyway, you can see full evidence of this, including works from unfilmed, yet "official" *Star Wars* documentation.

COMMENTS: When you put together what happened at the end of *Return of the Jedi* with the stuff in the *X-Wing Trilogy* and that little incident in *Dark Forces Rising*, well, what do we get? The answer is a bunch of geeks who have way too much time on their hands, as well as a bunch of useless literature. Of course, a lot of people would consider this book to be useless literature, so I can't complain.

ABNORMALITY: 9 STUPIDITY: 7 ENTERTAINMENT: 7

---

308 Mojo the Monkey
www.mojothemonkey.net

"Mojo is a monkey. Mojo likes typing." Mojo likes typing, all right—typing gibberish. Here's how the site is meant to work: Mojo types random stuff in a box. If you see a real word, highlight it and tag it. The website then considers it "your" word. The only problem is that Mojo never types any real words. You can sit here for ten minutes and Mojo will not type even one real word. Maybe if you wait an hour, or five hours, he'll type a word. But if you're patient enough to sit at a computer for hours on end for a virtual monkey to type one real word, you should do something useful with that patience. Like becoming a teacher, or a therapist. God knows they need patience.

COMMENTS: What a boring site! Who thought that somebody would find this site to be fun? I might even be persuaded to watch the Lifetime movie channel instead of visiting this site. Actually, scratch that one. Besides the cheesy and generic plots, Lifetime movies have men as bad guys 99.9999 percent of the time. Why do Lifetime producers have such hatred towards men? Maybe man-hating gets ratings for Lifetime. After all, who would want to watch a movie about a man who's actually a decent person? I know I wouldn't. Anyway, there is one thing that men and women can both agree on: that Mojo the Monkey is unbearably boring.

ABNORMALITY: 9 STUPIDITY: 9 ENTERTAINMENT: 6

Unicycling.org
www.unicycling.org

There are, apparently, many thriving unicycle communities across the world. "Unicycling is a recreational sport that has many diverse disciplines. Traditional activities include freestyle, touring, racing, riding in parades, and team sports such as hockey and basketball." Unicycling hockey? On the plus side, players smacking each other with sticks and getting in fist fights would look really funny on unicycles. France, Spain, Germany, England, and New Zealand all have large communities dedicated to this one-wheeled transportation medium. There is an archive of unicycling events, both past, present, and future, as well as links to other unicycling organizations, including the International Unicycling Federation and the Deutschen Einradhockeyliga, which is a German unicycling organization. Guten Tag, Unicyclers!

COMMENTS: Who knew unicycling was so popular? Maybe the Tour de France should have a unicycle division. It'd be like the circus, only with much more competition and doping controversies.

ABNORMALITY: 8 STUPIDITY: 7 ENTERTAINMENT: 5

Flea Circus.com
www.flea-circus.com

Flea Circus.com: "Where the Secrets of the Fleas Are Revealed!" What secrets? We like to stay on things and make them itch? This site is literally about a flea circus, and some guy in a lab coat who "runs" it. "First of all, if you've watched the sample video, you MUST know by now that YES, the fleas are real and real fleas can and are trained to do real stunts. (Some people cannot accept this even after seeing it done! So strong is the humbug associated with fleas!)" The only video on the site shows the poor fleas shoved onto metal strings and being pulled around into various positions, which are supposedly "tricks." What a sadistic flea circus ringleader! There are "histories" of fleas as well as "fleas for sale" and the opportunity to "book" this crazy guy.

COMMENTS: Maybe you won't see any people ranting about the torture and mistreatment of fleas (except the Insect Rights Activists—number 27). But even if you don't care what's happening to them in these videos, you have to admit that these are hardly "tricks."

ABNORMALITY: 8 STUPIDITY: 8 ENTERTAINMENT: 4

305

The Internet Shredder
www.potatoland.org/shredder

Simply type in a website address, and you'll be presented with the "shredded" version of that site, courtesy of the Internet Shredder. It's actually quite interesting to see what Britneyspears.com looks like when it's been "shredded" by the Internet shredder. No damage will actually occur to the website or your computer, but it's still fun.

COMMENTS: An Internet Shredder instead of a browser? Now that, my friends, is the most worthless "device" I've ever seen. Websites are meant to be viewed, not shredded. Most of the sites in this book would be good candidates for shredding, though.

ABNORMALITY: 8 STUPIDITY: 9 ENTERTAINMENT: 6

304

Adopt a Useless Blob
www.spacefem.com/blobs

Here is a page that is home to some useless blobs. That's right, they're useless, and they're blobs. Fairly simple concept, huh? The adopting procedure is simple: copy the URL and paste it on your web page, desktop, or wherever. More detailed instructions can be found at the site. There are a variety of different colors to choose from, including green, blue, and pink.

COMMENTS: Now this is one that I can understand. Who wouldn't want a worthless blob to put on their computer? Of course! They just have an appeal that makes your computer kind of different from all of those "other" computers. Adopt these blobs; they deserve good homes.

ABNORMALITY: 9 STUPIDITY: 8 ENTERTAINMENT: 6

303

Acts of Gord
www.actsofgord.com

This site is a Bible-type spoof relating to someone named Gord. Now who or what Gord is and what he does, I'm not entirely sure. It appears that he's a game retailer of some kind. Parts of the site include the Book of Annoyances, the Book of Victory, and the Book of Justice. Query: does a game retailer really need his own bible? As Gord says: "Let us come forth and continue the violent repelling of the intellectually challenged from our centers of commerce." No, wait, don't! If we reject the intellectually challenged from our stores, I'll never get anyone to buy this book!

COMMENTS: I have no idea who or what this Gord is. And to tell you the truth, I don't really want to know. All I know is that this site is, like the others in this book, stupid. Still, it is fun to see what kind of misadventures this "Gord" has been through.

ABNORMALITY: 10 STUPIDITY: 9 ENTERTAINMENT: 8

302

Beaterz
www.beaterz.com

This is a site containing a lot of automobiles with unusual properties. You can browse the extensive archives through four categories, including "It Still Runs" and "Urban Oddities." Some of the cars look quite unusual and don't look like they're in much of a condition to drive (even the ones under "It Still Runs"). The "Leper Truck" has a body that is falling apart, while an aging Ford Taurus sports a uniquely hand-crafted wooden bumper.

COMMENTS: These autos are kind of unusual. You may have even seen some of these "past their prime" vehicles. Heck, you may have even driven them. However, that doesn't mean that this site isn't worth visiting once or twice. It is a fairly good website. It just demonstrates some bad taste in car decoration and design, which isn't really a crime (although with some of these cars it should be).

ABNORMALITY: 7 STUPIDITY: 7 ENTERTAINMENT: 5

301

CrashBonsai
www.crashbonsai.com

Ever seen a car crash into a tree? Usually, the tree is much bigger than the car, in terms of height and width. Usually the tree weighs more, too. Unless you crash into a tiny little baby tree; then you might just get a dent. This site features small toy cars that crash into even *smaller* bonsai trees! Cars crashing into bonsai trees; imagine that! Here, you can see the crashed-car gallery, along with prices of crashed cars available to buy.

COMMENTS: Earth to website maker: Who would want a crashed car?! Nobody! Except for freaks that buy weird stuff. But they don't count! Stupid! Absolutely stupid! I tell ya, some people just don't get it.

ABNORMALITY: 9 STUPIDITY: 9 ENTERTAINMENT: 7

300

Pets in Uniform
www.petsinuniform.com

Like Dog Judo (number 318), this is another site putting pets in weird outfits and making them look like total idiots. The only difference is that Dog Judo was actually humorous. This site is not meant to be funny—it's a service. You actually pay money to have your pet's head juxtaposed onto a uniform. There are testimonials from "Corporate clients" (only one from a small-time newspaper), and an FAQ that basically says, "Yes, we're serious" and "No, we're not crazy." I highly doubt that second one. The pictures shown are extremely tacky and look like an amateur Photoshop job. The cost is twenty dollars, the same cost as a dinner for two, tickets to a movie, or any number of other things that are actually useful.

COMMENTS: Why would I want to pay twenty bucks to have a crappy picture of my pet in an astronaut suit or marine uniform? Sometimes it's nice to put outfits on pets to make them even more adorable, but even pets need a shred of dignity. Don't take it away with this stupid service.

ABNORMALITY: 8 STUPIDITY: 9 ENTERTAINMENT: 6

Machina Dynamica
www.machinadynamica.com

In spite of my best efforts, I still can't figure out what this site is selling. It has something to do with TV and music sound systems, but the technical jargon makes it harder to understand than a quantum physics textbook. They claim to be "specialists in Vibration Isolation and Resonance Control." Their products include "Brilliant Pebbles," which appear to be pebbles in a very shiny white bottle. It's described as a "unique room and system tuning device for audio systems and satellite TV," and acts as "both a vibration 'node damper' and EMI/RFI absorber, depending on application, via atomic mechanisms in the crystal structures." In English, please?

COMMENTS: Even if I could figure out what these things are for, the prices are so ridiculous that their purchase can't be justified. Does your music really need to be that loud and that good?

ABNORMALITY: 9   STUPIDITY: 6   ENTERTAINMENT: 4

Save Karyn
www.savekaryn.com

Save Karyn was dedicated to the cause of having everybody who visited this site help pay off Karyn's credit card bill. Running up your credit card bill happens to a lot of people, Karyn. You don't see them putting up websites begging people for money, now do you? Karyn, here's a tip: SPEND LESS! The worst part of this is that since this book's first edition, Karyn's devious scheme actually worked! In fact, this site is now dedicated to promoting her book, which will earn her even more money she doesn't deserve! She's even been on a number of talk shows! Come on!

COMMENTS: Let me get one thing across to you: going online and asking people to pay off your credit bill is not—I repeat, not—a good way to get out of debt. It may have worked for Karyn, but it won't work for you. As the old saying goes: "Fool me once, shame on you. Fool me twice, shame on me." Bottom line: kids, don't try this at home! Call the law offices of Richen and Poorer to file Chapter 13 or whatever. They can help you get out of debt better than a website can. Or maybe it's just time for some plastic surgery: take a scissors and cut up that plastic!

ABNORMALITY: 8   STUPIDITY: 8   ENTERTAINMENT: 7

297

The Web's First Japanese Pizza Page
www.chachich.com/mdchachi/jpizza.html

This is the home page of a joint in Japan that makes pizza!

That's right, here you can find all the info on the pizzas this Japanese restaurant makes, including prices and ingredients. There are some pictures that are not so appetizing and pictures that are just plain weird.

COMMENTS: Japanese pizza! What a unique concept. Actually, it's just another culture's spin on a popular dish. Still, it's quite odd to see pizza made in Japan. Check it out once or twice.

ABNORMALITY: 9 STUPIDITY: 7 ENTERTAINMENT: 7

296

Monobrow.com
www.monobrow.com

This is a site that, weird as it sounds, is dedicated to people who have only one huge eyebrow.

That's right; it's Monobrow.com. Here, you can see all of the latest and finest examples of the famed united eyebrow that so many people exhibit. "We don't view having one eyebrow as a grotesque, freakish human deformity. On the contrary. We think you are special." You can see monobrow movies, which of course make no sense at all (consider this quote: "we've had many clients over the years, from Burt Reynolds to Bert from Sesame Street"). You can also play "Monopoly," which is actually not *Monopoly*, but more a memory game, a "mono-match" of sorts.

COMMENTS: Why somebody would so cherish having a "monobrow" is beyond me. Why somebody would want to make a web page out of it confuses me even more. You'll like this site if you have a monobrow or if you just appreciate them. If not, just go to the page and laugh at its stupidity. Oh, and if you value your separate brows, don't forget to shave or wax every once in a while.

ABNORMALITY: 8 STUPIDITY: 9 ENTERTAINMENT: 8

295

This is a little movie of the most unusual type I have ever seen in my life. It has the head of former British Prime Minister Margaret Thatcher on the body of a cat; she's riding a saucer in outer space while a cartoon rabbit is trampling London (which is at the same time burning). It also features flying fish being shot by lasers and the head of a deer superimposed on the body of a dancing fat lady. And to top it off, all the while there is a jaunty little song sung in Swedish that's playing in the background. However, my mere words don't do this site justice. It's even stranger than it sounds. View this mini-movie; you'll see what I mean.

COMMENTS: Wow. That's all I have to say. If I could give this a 100 for abnormality and stupidity, I wouldn't hesitate. It's beyond belief! I was so shocked when I saw this, I was paralyzed with laughter by its stupidity. It *must* be the oddest thing (and probably close to the stupidest) on the Internet. One thing's for sure: you must see this site.

ABNORMALITY: 10 STUPIDITY: 10 ENTERTAINMENT: 8

294

Connecticut Extreme Croquet Society
www.extremecroquet.org

It's the lovely game of croquet…TO THE EXTREME!

Croquet has gone extreme! In Connecticut. And you can see it on this site. "Extreme croquet is croquet on steroids." It's played on a field laid out like regular croquet, except in the wilds or in the woods. "Gone are the manicured lawns of turf grass. Here is where the gullies, rocks and chiggers provide the crucible for champions."

Of course, the demanding conditions call for beefed-up mallets and equipment. No wooden mallets or balls survive; extreme croquet calls for precision playing pieces of polymer or polycarbonate (think bulletproof glass) and wickets made of steel pipes.

COMMENTS: Halfway through reading this, when I realized the site wasn't fake, I thought of how ridiculous the notion of "extreme croquet" is. I mean, croquet is a wimp's sport! I guess you can't blame them for trying to "beef it up" a bit.

ABNORMALITY: 6 STUPIDITY: 8 ENTERTAINMENT: 5

293

Molecules with Silly or Unusual Names

www.chm.bris.ac.uk/sillymolecules/sillymols.htm

The molecules listed here all are real, yet they have very unusual or funny names. Some of them are pretty funny, and you can be sure that whoever thought them up was either crazy or didn't foresee what meaning it would have. Adamantine (like British rocker Adam Ant), megaphone (really!), and, oh yummy, spamol are a few examples. However, probably the best-named substance is moronic acid. In fact, I think most of the designers of the sites you'll find in this book are very, very familiar with moronic acid.

COMMENTS: This is a very interesting site. It's funny to see all the info on these molecules and how they are, in many weird ways, related to everyday life. Who knew that molecular science and '80s pop music shared such a common bond?

ABNORMALITY: 8   STUPIDITY: 6   ENTERTAINMENT: 8

292

Keeping Ken

www.manbehindthedoll.com

Any educated person knows that Ken and Barbie were history a long time ago. This site, though, insists on keeping the memory of Barbie's ex alive. There's a "Ken 101" section, which has all the information you'll ever need (probably more than you want) on Ken. There's also information on Barbie Conventions and value guides if you ever get your hands on a rare Ken doll you want to pawn for some cash (my family actually did that with an old Barbie doll we found—made a few extra bucks selling her on eBay). The most disturbing section is "Ask Keeping Ken," with questions covering topics like the classification of lower torso parts—you know, the area where Ken's shortcomings appear. Maybe that's why Barbie broke up with him.

COMMENTS: I wonder what made Barbie and Ken go their separate ways after decades in a relationship? Maybe Ken was flirting around with Skipper a bit too much. Barbie can't be happy when kids decide to put Ken and Skipper together after Skipper gets a new hat.

ABNORMALITY: 9   STUPIDITY: 8   ENTERTAINMENT: 8

Women in Packaging
www.womeninpackaging.org

When you hear the phrase "Women in Packaging," do you think of a bunch of women being stuck into boxes? If so, you're sorely mistaken. This site is actually for women who want to get into the packaging industry. "Women in Packaging [is] the #1 branded resource for women and men in the packaging industry." Men? I thought this site was about women? They cite the fact that they are at the top when "women in packaging" is searched in Google as proof that they are "number one." There's an FAQ outlining the extensive benefits for belonging to Women in Packaging: "leadership skills," "packaging education," "networking," and "packaging conferences," just to name a few.

COMMENTS: Why would anybody want to get into packaging? Sure, there's more to it than working in a box factory (you can major in "Packaging Science" at several universities), but of all the exciting career paths out there, why packaging? Maybe it's the free boxes.

ABNORMALITY: 7 STUPIDITY: 8 ENTERTAINMENT: 4

Sock Muffin the Elf
www.sockmuffin.com

What is Sock Muffin the Elf about? "Santa Claus's Chief Elf is one of the best-known icons within Christmas Town lore… While there have been many tales of Santa's adventures, we still haven't learned—WHO IS THIS CHIEF ELF?" The answer, of course, is the deeply disturbing Sock Muffin. The synopsis of the book tells how Sock Muffin gets angry when Santa doesn't want him to make toys anymore. He gets so angry that he builds an army of robots to go on "a toy-busting rampage through Santa's Castle." Santa has a castle? I always thought it was some cozy log cabin compound. You can also make your own creepy Christmas story, which is just as far-out and senseless as the real book.

COMMENTS: This is like Christmas on drugs. What do pirates, robots, and an "Octopus Acrobats Team" have to do with Christmas? Even trying to understand is uncannily unsettling. The fact that Sock Muffin burns toys and looks like a demented little weasel doesn't help much either. If you want a weird Christmas story, try Tim Burton or Dr. Seuss, not this slimy little guy.

ABNORMALITY: 9 STUPIDITY: 8 ENTERTAINMENT: 7

The Human Dog Years Calculator

www.onlineconversion.com/dogyears.htm

Here, you can calculate how old you are in dog years. Once again, the wonders of technology have allowed us to gain another incredibly stupid experience. Go figure. The Internet is really a place of magical wonders when you can find such incredibly valuable information right at your fingertips.

COMMENTS: Wow, this site is Coolio! OK, maybe the "talented" rapper's moniker is not the right word to describe this site. Still, you can have some fun getting dog-year and people-year conversions. I recommend you visit it once or twice.

ABNORMALITY: 8 STUPIDITY: 8 ENTERTAINMENT: 7

The Toaster Oracle

www.ruffwork.com/toaster.htm

This site is a "toaster oracle" that, depending on the type of bread product you choose, will predict the type of day you will have. Useful, eh? I should have used this a long time ago to predict when I'd have bad days. After all, who couldn't use such valuable advice as "Do not go walking in thunderstorms," or "Stay away from electrical devices"? After clicking on this "oracle" a number of times, though, you start to wonder whether the process is a bit fixed from the results that you get.

COMMENTS: The oracle knows all! Well, maybe not. This site offers little in terms of originality. In fact, it's about as innovative as yet another prime-time sitcom with the ditzy mom and the wiseacre ten-year-old who knows everything. If I see another one of those on primetime television, I'm going to puke.

ABNORMALITY: 8 STUPIDITY: 9 ENTERTAINMENT: 5

287

World of Mank
www.angelfire.com/sd/mank

This website describes a strange, foreign substance called Mank. I'm not exactly sure what Mank is, except that it is the product of a gross, stupid mind. This website has the full "story" of the creation and existence of Mank. Mank is very mysterious. It began with pudding, "pudding, in other words, so vicious, so bent on harm, so stupendously and malevolently evil." Evil pudding? Well, whatever it is, I can say that it does *not* sound very good. Or very smart.

COMMENTS: Good gracious, this Mank is scary! Everything that is good and righteous in this world is now less so due to Mank. Mank is the devil! Mank is evil! God, please help us all! Please save us from Mank. Stop the stupidity, please! Anyway, this site is very stupid. I am sincerely worried about the mental state of the people who created this site.

ABNORMALITY: 9 STUPIDITY: 9 ENTERTAINMENT: 7

286

Digital Landfill
www.potatoland.org/landfill

Tired of getting spam and junk email? Mail filters and the trash bin are fine for that, but if you want a more novel method of disposal, try the Digital Landfill. This site allows you to "dispose of your unwanted email, obsolete data, HTML, SPAM, or any other digital debris by just clicking the 'Add to Landfill' button." After you've trashed your stuff, you can view the landfill to see what other junk has been thrown in this digital dumpster. There are literally hundreds of junk emails, all piled on top of each other in this virtual dumpster. Most of the trash emails are ads for "male enhancement," naughty sites, and illegal medication. At least I know where I can get some Vicodin if I need it.

COMMENTS: The Digital Landfill is a sign of hope in a way. It shows that most people don't want this stuff, and will gladly throw it where it can't hurt anybody. And this landfill doesn't smell funny.

ABNORMALITY: 7 STUPIDITY: 7 ENTERTAINMENT: 7

285 Psychic Chicken Network
www.ruprecht.com

This is yet another weird assortment of games, stories, and miscellaneous stuff that is just stupid as heck. You can try the psychic test (or psycho test if you don't dig that kind of thing) or read stories by a wannabe sci-fi writer. The stories are about time travel, a knight, a magic pendant in a museum, and other occurrences, although what those subjects have to do with psychic chickens is beyond me. There's also Ruprecht's (what kind of a name is Ruprecht, anyway?) haunted house game, which seems like a demented version of the *Clue* board game.

COMMENTS: This site sure does have a lot of stupid stuff. Even its presentation is pure idiocy, and that says a lot. The psychic test is kind of addictive, though.

ABNORMALITY: 9 STUPIDITY: 9 ENTERTAINMENT: 8

---

284 Fish Posters of the World
www.winword.nodalpoint.net/doc/media/likenne.swf

Many different types of posters exist—concert posters, movie or TV posters, game posters, promotional posters—most worthy of being collected in some way. But some posters are a little less desirable. "Fish Posters of the World" has a niche in this category. This site's only purpose is to find posters with different types of fish and archive them for viewing. If, for whatever demented reason, you want to buy one of these posters, there are links to other sites where they are available for purchase. I would rather spend my money to go see an Uwe Boll film.

COMMENTS: Am I the only one who thinks this is crazy? Maybe it's just because I really don't like fishing. Besides the fact that I find it incredibly boring, those poor fish can't like having hooks shoved through their mouths. I guess some outdoorsmen would gladly spend their money on these things. If you're a fishing fan, maybe these posters have some appeal. But I'd rather have a cold sore than spend my time or money on these.

ABNORMALITY: 6 STUPIDITY: 8 ENTERTAINMENT: 3

283

The Evil Sock Monkey Conspiracy

www.angelfire.com/mo2/evilsockmonkey

This page is another one describing a government plot to steal our socks and do hideously evil deeds with them. Ever wonder where your socks go when they just "vanish" mysteriously? Apparently, this site has the answer: aliens slip into our dryers and snatch them from under our noses! Aliens? That must be why the sock monkey has a disturbing resemblance to Mr. Spock from the *Star Trek* series. Once all the socks are taken, they will be made into the giant sock-monkey ruler, "Sockrates," who is destined to enslave us all in evil sock-making camps. Hmm, these people must be some overactive conspiracy theorists.

COMMENTS: This is a site that is most definitely stupid and could have been thought up by a six-year-old. But it is funny nonetheless. There are plenty of sections, so you'll be kept busy for a long time. Yes, I know I should have mentioned this earlier, but it's too late now, you've been hooked! One final note: check out the *Mission: Impossible* music!

ABNORMALITY: 9 STUPIDITY: 9 ENTERTAINMENT: 7

282

Star Wars Gangsta Rap

wiac.shockwave.com/af/content/atom_1403

It's *Star Wars* meets Jay-Z, as you view this hilariously moronic filmette. Luke is supa fly, Darth Vader and the Emperor say they aren't East side or West side (you can see where this is going), and Yoda is one hip playa (well, not really)! The clever, yet stupid rap verses will captivate you as they take you on a trip through a portion of the *Star Wars* story. "Hey why'd you slice off my hand? It's imperative that you understand." It's all quite interesting, in a stupid, geeky sort of way. I am really having a hard time remembering exactly where I heard the phrase "Vader hater" in the original film.

COMMENTS: This site is funny, and it's pretty well done, even though the rapping would sound hideous to real rap fans. I was even more surprised to learn that this video won an award at the *Star Wars* Fan Film Festival! It's true! And I thought geeks couldn't rap.

ABNORMALITY: 8 STUPIDITY: 9 ENTERTAINMENT: 8

281

Muffin Films
www.muffinfilms.com

This site is home to twelve amusing, albeit odd, animated films on muffins. Click on the muffin tin to make your selection and you are good to go. Films include one where a muffin pleads with somebody to not eat it. Another film shows a person eating a muffin, and then a bigger muffin eats her. They're all in pretty good taste (pun intended), and even though they're not overly clever, they're sure to inspire a laugh or two.

COMMENTS: Oh, just thinking of those scrumptious, tasty muffins. Blueberry. Cinnamon. Mmmmm. Oops, sorry. Anyway, these are pretty good movies, and you'll get a kick out of some of them. I'd recommend visiting this site, although you might be a bit hungry afterwards.

ABNORMALITY: 7 STUPIDITY: 8 ENTERTAINMENT: 7

280

Which Sesame Street Muppet Are You?
www.powersugoi.net/quiz/ssm.php

This is a good concept. It's simple, but creative: you take a short quiz asking a few questions about your personality. Afterward, you click a button and the quiz tells you which Muppet you are. It may sound weird, but it's actually pretty accurate in determining which Muppet is closest to your persona.

COMMENTS: I found this to be a funny site, yet very true to life and accurate. If you do the quiz the right way, it does really lead to the Muppet you most resemble. Anyway, I recommend taking it; you may discover something surprising. I'm Kermit; who are you? Take the quiz and find out.

ABNORMALITY: 5 STUPIDITY: 4 ENTERTAINMENT: 8

279

A real website about totally fake numbers.

This is an interesting site listing a ton of fictional 555 numbers from TV and movies. Here, you can view the extensive archive of numbers, or you can find the owner's email and contribute your own. It's funny to see all the different films and shows where these fictional numbers come from. It is sure to bring back some fond memories for TV fanatics. Here you can find really valuable and incredibly useful phone numbers from the *Brady Bunch* residence to Fred Sanford from *Sanford and Son* to Mr. Burns from *The Simpsons*. You can find them all. The real question is: why would you want to find them?

COMMENTS: Interesting. I had no idea there were so many 555 numbers. My favorite, though, is still from a favorite video game of mine. The number was Cinco-Cinco-Cinco-Nueve-Dos-Nueve-Dos (555-9292), the number for "Fernando's New Beginnings," a rather unique type of "marriage counseling service."

ABNORMALITY: 7 STUPIDITY: 7 ENTERTAINMENT: 7

278

Bad Fads Museum
www.badfads.com/home.html

This is a museum of all of the outrageous fads throughout the years that, in hindsight, were in extremely bad taste. From fashion fads such as platform shoes to events such as streaking and toga parties, this site has them all. There are several categories, so if you're looking for something in particular, you'll have little trouble finding it. Gee, this site really made me sad that I was born after such wonderful fads as Pet Rocks, telephone-booth stuffing, and 3-D movies.

COMMENTS: Unlike these hideous fads, it's cool to look back and see how stupid so many of us were back in the day. Older people will tend to appreciate this more, as they can remember the days of Pet Rocks, Rubik's Cubes, and go-go boots. So if you are looking for a good dose of some warm-hearted nostalgia, I'd recommend this site in a pinch.

ABNORMALITY: 7 STUPIDITY: 7 ENTERTAINMENT: 8

277

Ninja Lesson
www.penny-arcade.com/docs/ninjalesson.jpg

More info on how to be a mysteriously stealthy butt-kicking machine.

This is a simple page, consisting of seven pictures and descriptions of seven steps that you can follow to be a ninja. It's quite easy; all you need are some black clothes and an additional black T-shirt. Follow the steps given on the site, and voila! You're a genuine ninja and automatically an expert killer (well, not really).

COMMENTS: Notice how certain themes, such as rednecks and ninjas, appear repeatedly throughout this book? The Internet is full of them. They may ultimately be stupid, but in case you haven't gotten it yet, I also think they're cool! Who doesn't like mysterious warriors and uneducated hicks? Sure they have nothing in common, but still!

ABNORMALITY: 7 STUPIDITY: 8 ENTERTAINMENT: 6

276

Karsten's Loincloth Site
www.karstensloinclothsite.com

This site belongs to someone named Karsten. Karsten likes big, half-naked, muscular men, but apparently men in loincloths are what really do it for Karsten. To this end, Karsten has dedicated this entire site to anything and everything about loincloths. DVDs, images, films, and links featuring men in loincloths are bountiful, and there's even a link to loincloth vendors ("aka: 'Where can I buy a loincloth?'"). Surprisingly, there are a large number of vendors, including custom loincloth vendor "Leather Rush." Well, I definitely know a lot of people who would want a custom-made loincloth, don't you?

COMMENTS: What is it about cavemen, Tarzan, and bad western movies that's so attractive? Is Karsten a man or a woman? Do we really want to know the answer? What is the meaning of life? Why is Ryan Seacrest a celebrity? Anyway, if you're a fan of men in loincloths, this site is a dream come true. Otherwise, don't waste your time.

ABNORMALITY: 8 STUPIDITY: 7 ENTERTAINMENT: 6

275

The Society to Prevent My Employment

egomania.nu/causes/indexsoc.html

This is someone who wants money for free. It's kind of like Karyn (see number 298), except Princess Natalie is just too lazy to work. She claims that she is a princess, and that actually working for a living is beneath her. As Natalie says, "If I worked I might ruin my manicure, that in itself would be an extreme travesty!" Natalie even gives such helpful suggestions as if you're broke, you should sell your blood to send money to her. It even gives an address for you to send money!

COMMENTS: So, who's worse out there in the universe of Internet begging…a moronic credit-card user or a naïve, spoiled brat? This website is home to another lazy lady. I can't believe how stupid this site is (actually, after seeing all of the stuff in this book, it's not hard at all to fathom). Yet it is pretty funny! If you do send money, you'll have the satisfaction of knowing that when Natalie is "purchasing overpriced lingerie or firearms," she'll be thinking of you.

ABNORMALITY: 8 STUPIDITY: 8 ENTERTAINMENT: 7

274

Jesus Christ Superstore

www.jesuschristsuperstore.net

The Jesus Christ Superstore, which "[puts] the fun back into fundamentalism and the laughter into sectarian slaughter," is your one-stop shop for sacrilegious spiritual products. You can buy action figures of Jesus, the Pope, and God himself, as well as T-shirts with witty phrases describing Jesus. But don't let the name fool you. This site isn't just for offensive Christian products—there are unholy products for other religions, too! Buddha, Krishna, Shiva, the Dalai Lama, and rabbi action figures are all available. There's also the unbelievably un-PC "Islamic Jihad" action figure, which has a Middle-Eastern man dressed in white with an assault rifle.

COMMENTS: For being a religious store, this site is incredibly offensive! Any devout religious person wouldn't buy these products for any reason, save to burn them. But if you're not a religious person and/or aren't easily offended, and you're in need of a politically incorrect gag gift, the Jesus Christ Superstore should definitely be considered.

ABNORMALITY: 9 STUPIDITY: 8 ENTERTAINMENT: 8

273

Quest for the McDonald's Fried Apple Pie

www.ce.berkeley.edu/~ccytsao/friedapplepie.htm

According to this site, in 1992 McDonald's changed their fried-apple-pie formula to a baked version. This organization (or person, whatever) has made it their quest to find the McDonald's restaurants that still serve the *fried* apple pie. This site has a comprehensive database showing which restaurants still serve this pastry.

COMMENTS: Is there really a difference between the fried apple pie and the baked apple pie? Does it matter? Should I even be looking at the site? The answers to all of these questions are unknown, but I'm guessing the answers are no. It doesn't really matter at all whether a rectangular pastry is fried or baked, unless you're this obsessive person. My advice: settle for a nice McFlurry.

ABNORMALITY: 7 STUPIDITY: 8 ENTERTAINMENT: 5

272

Handcuffs.org

www.handcuffs.org

If you're a budding handcuff enthusiast, head straight to Handcuffs.org. "These pages present a guide to collecting handcuffs and related restraints. An emphasis is given to vintage American handcuffs, defined roughly as those made "from the time of the American Civil war through the 1970s." The description goes on to say how handcuffs "have captured the imagination of many" (I can only guess what they're alluding to), and cites Houdini as proof that handcuffs can have an "entertainment side." There are galleries for dozens of historical handcuff models, as well as value guides and a "puzzle for the experts" that challenges you to see if "you know your handcuffs." I don't know handcuffs, and I'm proud of it.

COMMENTS: The one thing that surprised me was that there are actually such things as "thumbcuffs." Why would you want to cuff somebody's thumbs when you can just cuff their hands? Maybe thumbcuffs were invented for when the police knew the criminal wasn't dangerous and they just wanted a good laugh.

ABNORMALITY: 8 STUPIDITY: 6 ENTERTAINMENT: 7

POPO

www.geocities.com/power_popo/home

This page is about POPO, the "Self-Contained Revolutionary Presentation Device," and its creators. Now like a lot of these sites, I'm having a hard time determining exactly what POPO is. The page has a story on it that naturally makes no sense. A nifty feature, however, is that there are hidden links to other sites, such as a hot dog site and Milksucks.com (see Number 270). If you have any comments regarding the site, there is a notation that "hate mail is always welcome."

COMMENTS: This site makes no sense at all. One page has a fighter pilot riding a gorilla, and another page has hot dog wallpaper. The hidden links are a nifty feature, and finding them is fun. Contrary to popular belief that nifty features can make bad content acceptable, that just isn't the case. Like the movie *Dude, Where's My Car?* this site has stupid, meaningless, and useless plastered all over it. By the way, who was the genius who decided to make a sequel to that movie? I wonder.

ABNORMALITY: 9 STUPIDITY: 9 ENTERTAINMENT: 6

Milksucks.com

www.milksucks.com

These people just hate milk.

This site has a bunch of information on how milk is bad for you. It says that milk can cause osteoporosis, not prevent it, and that cows suffer because of milk. Or, like Haley Smith from *American Dad* once said, "Do you know how many cows were raped to get that milk?!" Now that's a good show. Anyway, there are also PETA brochures available at this website, as well as information on how to start a vegan diet. They also have links to newspaper articles to prove that their ideas are real.

COMMENTS: For being a serious effort, the name of the site is very blatant. I mean, do politicians' campaign ads call each other idiots and morons and other unspeakable insults? Well, yes. Maybe indirectly, but still. Milksucks.com is a bad way to start presenting your cause on a website. Try an important-sounding organization name. Those always work. The Society for the Prevention of Milk Consumption would work. Which one would you pay more serious attention to, spmc.com or Milksucks.com? I rest my case.

ABNORMALITY: 6 STUPIDITY: 8 ENTERTAINMENT: 5

269   Vegetable Liberation Front

www.geocities.com/RainForest/Vines/3652

The Vegetable Liberation Front is a "society" devoted to the cause of preventing the consumption of vegetables, much like Milksucks.com. They say that vegetables are "defenseless," and that "all animals, including humans" must stop eating them. They call vegetarians and the like "brutal plant killers," and they practically beg for everybody to stop consuming veggies and start eating meat. To support their cause, they have steak wallpaper and some appetizing pictures. Mmmmm, steak!

COMMENTS: Talk about PETA's worst nightmare. Consuming all meat and no plants? If this were an actual organization, they wouldn't last a day in the political arena. Then again, who says plants aren't people, too? At least plants will never bite you (except for the carnivorous ones in the rainforest; those are scary).

ABNORMALITY: 7   STUPIDITY: 8   ENTERTAINMENT: 4

---

268   The Keanu Report

www.geocities.com/Hollywood/6608/keanu.html

There are many people, recent and historical, who have been accused of being the Antichrist: Adolf Hitler, Napoleon Bonaparte, and George W. Bush, just to name a few. But this site believes they have at last found the true identity of the spawn of Satan: Keanu Reeves? Keanu's filmography, his fashion sense (he has a goatee, therefore he must be Satan), and the fact that he plays guitar right-handed even though he's left-handed are just some of the pieces of "proof" that Keanu is the Antichrist. People are encouraged to boycott Keanu's movies, as well as Cheez-Its, because of a picture in which Keanu is shown eating some. I don't care if Keanu Reeves is the Antichrist—I'm not gonna stop eating Cheez-Its!

COMMENTS: Is Keanu really cunning and clever enough to be the Antichrist? If you're going to deceive all mankind into going to Hell, you've got to be smart, charismatic, and powerful. Keanu doesn't strike me as any of those. Sorry, guys, but The Keanu Report hasn't convinced me. Still, you'll have a good laugh reading this one.

ABNORMALITY: 5   STUPIDITY: 6   ENTERTAINMENT: 7

267 Bonsai Potato
www.bonsaipotato.com

With the Bonsai Potato, you can "quickly and efficiently reach an inner peace that can take monks an entire lifetime to achieve." Wow. According to the site, "Bonsai Potato is the art of nurturing the artistic vision of a potato through various forms of encouragement and manipulation." This site has a gallery featuring pictures of Bonsai Potato followers, as well as the potatoes themselves. There's also an FAQ, which doesn't really answer anything, and a section where you can get your own Bonsai Potato Kit, should you want one for some reason.

COMMENTS: Is the Bonsai Potato merely a tentacled tuber, or is it something more metaphysical, some sort of supernatural spud? This site makes no sense at all, so it's kind of hard to tell. If you are curious about the Bonsai Potato movement, visit this site. You'll either come out extremely enlightened about the universe or you'll come out extremely baffled. My guess is that you'll share my experience: complete confusion.

ABNORMALITY: 10 STUPIDITY: 9 ENTERTAINMENT: 7

---

266 Miss Cleo Soundboard
www.albinoblacksheep.com/flash/misscleo.html

Ever heard of Miss Cleo's psychic hotline (which, for your information, is one of my favorite psychic hotlines, even though I've never called one)? Well, this site has a bunch of sound clips spoken by Miss Cleo. Miss Cleo promoted her site in TV ads featuring her heavy Jamaican accent. She endlessly shilled her site until she was sued by the Federal Trade Commission for fraud. Imagine that, a psychic hotline that's fraudulent! From the wonderful "Is he incarcerated?" to "You're a Libra, ain'tcha darlin'" to "Yeah, dat's da Daddress," this site has all of Cleo's best sound clips.

COMMENTS: Miss Cleo was one of my favorite fake gimmicks a year or two back. It always amazes me when I see what people will believe, from psychics to those countless "easy" weight-loss infomercials. By the way, if Miss Cleo could really see the future, why didn't she predict that nasty federal lawsuit? Well, my prediction is that you will find this site quite stupid, but entertaining.

ABNORMALITY: 7 STUPIDITY: 7 ENTERTAINMENT: 6

265

The Ultimate Loch Ness Monster Site
www.nessie.co.uk

What exactly is lurking below the depths of Loch Ness? Is it a surviving dinosaur, a giant eel, a really big fish, a floating log, or nothing at all? Whatever your belief, if you need to know something about Scotland's mythical monster, this is the place to go. The "official" site of Nessie herself "brings you facts, pictures, and sightings of this most elusive of creatures and Loch Ness technical information." Technical information? I didn't know Loch Ness was computerized. Film evidence, a list of sightings, information on Nessie Hunters, and the geology of the loch are just a few tidbits of the vast amount of information on this site.

COMMENTS: Whenever I think of Loch Ness, I think of a commercial I saw when I was a kid for a show called *Happy Ness: The Secret of the Loch*. Nessie and her friends all had different colors, and the voiceover work was creepier than a psychotic clown's laugh. Maybe it's a good thing I never actually saw the show. Anyway, whether you're a believer or a skeptic, if you're curious about Nessie, give this site a visit.

ABNORMALITY: 9 STUPIDITY: 7 ENTERTAINMENT: 8

264

Psychedelic Republicans
www.psychedelicrepublicans.com

Do you think George W. Bush is groovy? Is Trent Lott your hero? If you're a Republican or conservative with a little bit of hippie in you, or someone who couldn't care less about politics, this site may be for you. Here, you can find out about these funky politicians, including fun facts, personal information (some of which is in serious question as to whether it's true or not), and a mailing list you can subscribe to if the cards need to be restocked (hard to believe they could run out of stock).

COMMENTS: Although Republicans may be going out of fashion these days, this site is still good for a lighter look at American politics. Perhaps it's human nature for us to argue with each other...but maybe tie-dye shirts are human nature too. Groovy, dude.

ABNORMALITY: 8 STUPIDITY: 7 ENTERTAINMENT: 7

Drop Squad
www.dropsquad.com

These computer-geek college students decided to drop objects down a very tall stairwell. It was fun, and so they decided to do it again. And again. And again. This site has tons of tales about how they gathered various objects and just threw them down the stairwell. From "Smashing Pumpkins" (the Thanksgiving treat, not the band) to videotapes to an old manual typewriter, numerous items met their tragic end in the stairwell of death. Ah, college fun. Once again, through the magic of the Web, we lucky surfers can share in the Drop Squad's chronicle of chaotic and senselessly stupid acts.

COMMENTS: Some of the drops were really plain. Others were, well, unique, and others were just plain messy, like when they dropped 125 McDonald's cheeseburgers down the stairwell. Yes, 125! Isn't that amazing? From the pictures, though, you could tell it was a pretty big mess. They had to call environmental services to clean it up, supposedly, because it smelled so horrible.

ABNORMALITY: 7 STUPIDITY: 8 ENTERTAINMENT: 7

262

Grocery Store Wars
www.storewars.org/flash

Cue the Imperial march music: it's *Star Wars* meets the supermarket in *Grocery Store Wars*. This movie begins with "Not so long ago in a supermarket not so far away," and quickly jumps into the ways of "The Farm" and introduces "Obi-Wan Cannoli" and "Cuc Skywalker" (short for "Cucumber"). Cuc must rescue "Princess Lettuce," and enlists the help of "Ham Solo" and "Chewbroccoli" to assist him and Obi-Wan (the puns are starting to become nauseating). The movie is mostly humorous, but it's also a political statement in disguise, promoting organic foods and protesting against mass-manufactured, chemical-enhanced foods. Those sneaky little organic rebels....

COMMENTS: What a way to spread a political message: hide it in a movie parody involving talking food products. Whether or not you agree with the politics of the movie, you owe it to yourself to see it if you're a *Star Wars* fan—or even if you're just fond of food.

ABNORMALITY: 8 STUPIDITY: 8 ENTERTAINMENT: 9

261

What would you say if there was a sport where people fight dressed like pirates, knights, wizards, and samurais in costumes made of boxes? Anybody who wants to do that is insane, right? Well, I agree, but that doesn't make Box Wars any less funny. The videos here show events where people with weapons and armor made out of boxes battle in a pathetic yet amusing test of…stupidity? Is there any other word to describe these people? There appear to be no rules for box battles, and the fights last as long as twenty minutes. Why would you want to spend twenty minutes bouncing and bumbling like a buffoon in the burning sun with boxes on your back? Too many Bs and too many boxes. You can also take a look at the schedule and see when the next box war is coming up.

COMMENTS: I would never participate in a Box War—too much trouble and time, not to mention that I'd make a complete fool out of myself. But as stupid as the concept may be, there is a certain appeal to watching people covered in boxes awkwardly fighting each other. Isn't it great that people act like morons so we don't have to? One thing that may shed some light on this is that the whole thing takes place in Australia. Those crazy Aussies...

ABNORMALITY: 9 STUPIDITY: 9 ENTERTAINMENT: 8

260

Skeletor and Gang
www.skeletorandgang.tk

Another weird set of live-action movies for your viewing pleasure.

This site chronicles the "adventures" of Skeletor, an action figure, and his rowdy gang of friends and enemies. Of course, these live-action movies are anything but adventures. They are, in actuality, just a bunch of figures zipping across the screen due to some delayed filming techniques.

COMMENTS: Viewing one adventure was more than enough; I didn't find it necessary to subject myself to any further torture. This is pure idiocy in film-making, and it is, in my opinion, something that should not be seen by normal people. Well, then again, exactly what is "normal"? Everybody's got some freaky thing going on in his or her life, so maybe you'd want to take a look at this. Or not. You decide.

ABNORMALITY: 9 STUPIDITY: 9 ENTERTAINMENT: 6

259   Enron Code of Ethics
www.thesmokinggun.com/enron/enronethics1.shtml

This document has probably never been read up until now, considering what happened to Enron. Here, you can see Enron's book containing its "Code of Ethics." Now, this site seems pretty serious. It appears to be the actual Enron Code. In any normal company, it would exist to guide workers in exactly what moral attributes are expected from an employee. But with Enron, a company that was destroyed due to bad morals, I'm not so sure about this one. Particularly interesting is the passage stating: "Ruthlessness, callousness, and arrogance don't belong" at Enron. Also, "relations with stockholders…employees…and bankers will be conducted in honesty, candor, and fairness." Yeah, right. Tell that to the workers without pensions.

COMMENTS: This site says on its cover page, "Below you'll find some selected pages from the guide, which was aggressively ignored by many of the Texas [executives] who drove the firm—and its workers—into the ground." In my opinion, this is true for the most part. Enron was, by most accounts, destroyed because corrupt Enron executives disregarded this document as a useless waste of paper. They put dishonesty and greed above virtue and ethics. Okay, now I'm done rambling on about business ethics.

ABNORMALITY: 6 STUPIDITY: 7 ENTERTAINMENT: 5

---

258   Britney Underground
www.britneyunderground.com

This site has a bunch of posters of the defaced diva, mainly from the "Live from Las Vegas" HBO posters hung up in the New York City subways, only to have goatees, thick-rimmed glasses, and God knows what else drawn on them. There is also a little bit about the site's origins and purpose. Hey Brit, the beard looks good. Have you considered keeping it?

COMMENTS: Most of these pictures are pretty funny and have a humorous sort of art to them. Others just have some bad scribbling. The ones with the funny faces are worth looking at; they make Britney Spears look like a total idiot. Wait a minute…was I supposed to say look *more* like a total idiot? Hmm.

ABNORMALITY: 7 STUPIDITY: 8 ENTERTAINMENT: 7

The 47 Society
www.47.net/47society/main.html

This site is, appropriately, about the number forty-seven: "the quintessential random number." Here, you'll find all sorts of info, stories, and various other materials all having to do with this mysterious number, from a plane that crashed killing forty-seven people to a man born in 1947 who lived in a house with the street number forty-seven. Coincidence? I think not. Perhaps a Communist plot with Nazi overtones! I think forty-seven is just some random number that these makers used to create a website just for this book. But who knows?

COMMENTS: Once again, I don't know and I couldn't really care less. I have no idea who thought it up or why it exists. I suppose we can blame human stupidity for that, as we did for "reality" shows like *Love Cruise: The Maiden Voyage* or *Celebrity Fit Club* (any show where Wendy the Snapple Lady tries to lose weight has to be pathetic).

ABNORMALITY: 8 STUPIDITY: 8 ENTERTAINMENT: 6

256

Homestar Runner
www.homestarrunner.com

Before I started on this book, I had no idea what Homestar Runner even was. Now I know that this site's weirdness goes beyond Strongbad Email, which was the original subject of this entry. For those who don't remember, Strongbad Email is about a weird-looking guy named Strongbad who answers email questions from people. The answers to these questions, of course, are extremely stupid and senseless. One part of the site that is pretty cool, though, is the games section, especially Trogdor, a game about a medieval dragon that, although crude, is still fun. The instructions are simple: "Use the arrow keys to control Trogdor. Stomp ten peasants to achieve burnination. Burn all cottages to advance a level. Avoid knights and archers!"

COMMENTS: This is another one of those sites that I didn't realize would be so big when I put it in the original book. Trogdor was even immortalized in Guitar Hero 2; "Trogdor" was one of the bonus tracks, and was definitely the best song in the whole game. So, I take back my initial judgment that Homestar Runner is completely useless. Still mostly useless, but not completely.

ABNORMALITY: 8 STUPIDITY: 9 ENTERTAINMENT: 8

Cheese Racing
www.cheeseracing.org

This site is home to a unique sport (if you can call it anything near a sport) known only as cheese racing. The concept is a little odd: a number of people throw individually wrapped cheese slices, still in the plastic wrapping, onto a barbeque grill. The one whose cheese wrapper inflates and bursts first wins. What a unique concept.

COMMENTS: I must admit, I would never have thought of this in a million years. I would compute the currently nonexistent dynamics of perpetual motion before I'd think of cheese racing. And the stranger thing is that they actually call this a sport! In the news section of the website, there are highlights from cheese races in such diverse places as England, Florida, and Australia. Good Lord, what is this world coming to?

ABNORMALITY: 9 STUPIDITY: 8 ENTERTAINMENT: 7

YETI @ Home
www.phobe.com/yeti/index.html

This site aids you in expanding the search for Bigfoot into your own backyard. You are encouraged to set up a digital camera linked to your computer, particularly if you live in the Pacific Northwest. The goal is to film your backyard in order to capture Bigfoot (or Bigfeet) on film. The site has info on this project and also some well-placed, witty comments.

COMMENTS: More madness by a bunch of weirdos. However, this site is obviously humorous in nature, so I'm inclined to give it a slightly lower rating for stupidity. When things that are super serious are super stupid, *that* is the ultimate in stupidity. But this is all in good humor, so I'll take off one point. I can't be *that* lenient.

ABNORMALITY: 8 STUPIDITY: 8 ENTERTAINMENT: 6

Lost in Translation
www.tashian.com/multibabel

Do you remember playing telephone? You know, the game where you pass along a message and then another person passes it along, altering it slightly, until it comes back to you? Well, this site does the same thing, except with languages.

Here, you can type in a message, and the website will translate it into a ton of different languages. Eventually you'll get the message back and with it the many alterations that had to be made due to language limitations.

COMMENTS: This is an interesting website. I love these interactive sites, where you actually do something. You can make it more or less stupid, but it's funnier when you make it even stupider, like Jackie Chan does with bad comedy movies. The only difference is that he makes it stupider, but not funnier.

ABNORMALITY: 7 STUPIDITY: 7 ENTERTAINMENT: 7

Foxy Felon Mug Shots
www.thesmokinggun.com/archive/
morehotfelons1.shtml

For all you male readers, this site is home to pictures of some hot chicks. Too bad all of them are doing time in the jailhouse.

That's right! They may be hot, but their rap sheet is hotter! Here, you can see mug shots of the girls, along with their name, age, hometown, and the crime they're doing time for. Most of these criminal chickadees are actually pretty attractive. Most also seem to be blonde. A lot of them are doing time for theft. Well, I'd sure let them steal my heart!

COMMENTS: These are some hot girls. It's sad they're all jailbirds. Otherwise, they'd be good dates. Or not. Of course, the environment they grew up in determines a lot, but I'm not a profiler; I'm a writer. Still, there are probably a bunch of guys who couldn't give a crap whether they're criminals or not; those guys are so desperate. Also be sure to check out the archive for the "Mug Shots of the Not So Rich and Infamous." It's a real hoot, guaranteed to make you laugh out loud.

ABNORMALITY: 7 STUPIDITY: 7 ENTERTAINMENT: 6

251

My Cat Hates You.com
www.mycathatesyou.com

Cats seem to have a bad rep on the Internet, if My Cat Hates You.com is any indication. "Started in 2000, we proudly present you the largest collection of sour-faced, indignant felines on the Internet." Once you see the pictures for yourself, though, "sour-faced" and "indignant" seem like compliments. These cats are downright nasty. The "About" section gives a few pictures of cats along with explanations for their hatred. For example, a black cat with a paranoid look is shown, "This is Lulu 'Jive Turkey Jones.' She hates you because you're a pathetic loser." You can even submit your own callous and crabby cat if you're so inclined.

COMMENTS: It fascinates me how much some people hate cats. I don't hate cats that much anymore, but I know plenty of people who do. Maybe cats just know that humans like to pet them excessively and talk in weird baby voices to them. Is that why these cats hate us so much? I don't know, but I am going to steer clear of these critters.

ABNORMALITY: 8 STUPIDITY: 8 ENTERTAINMENT: 7

250

Tomatoes Are Evil.com
www.tomatoesareevil.com

"WELCOME HOME TOMATO HATERS, and the perverted tomato lovers among you! Prepare to be educated." "Education" on Tomatoes Are Evil.com translates into an extended sermon on how tomatoes are more sinister than a Satanic baby-killer. The Evil Facts section is the most fervent of the anti-tomato propaganda. It has a table of the word "tomato" translated into different languages, followed by, "in all languages: tomato = evil." The Facts section also claims that tomatoes are full of poison. Tomatoes can also "re-trigger cigarette addiction" and are "fatal for cats." Which tomatoes are the worst, then? Beefsteak? Roma? "There are more than 10,000 varieties of tomatoes. All are evil."

COMMENTS: I'd like to see some backup for these "facts." If tomatoes are poisonous, how come people aren't keeling over from tomatoes in salads, or on burgers and sandwiches? Well, nobody said propaganda has to be logical.

ABNORMALITY: 8 STUPIDITY: 9 ENTERTAINMENT: 8

249 Boy the Bear's Age Gauge
www.frontiernet.net/~cdm/age1.html

This is a cool game if you want to have some fun with your birth date. You start by typing in the day, month, and year of a birthday, be it yours or another person's birthday. The Age Gauge then gives you a plethora of birthdays and dates of famous people and events, along with how old you were when they happened. For example, I am fifty-three years and five months younger than Yoko Ono (guess she's too old to break up any band I'd have), sixteen years and three months younger than Mariah Carey (fortunately, it doesn't tell me how old I was when *Glitter* was made), and four years and seven months younger than Britney Spears (that's ten years too little when I consider that bimbo is part of my generation).

COMMENTS: This site is a blast! It's pretty cool seeing all the different pop culture and historical events that happened during my lifetime. It also brings back memories, some fond and some shameful. One shameful event was the O.J. Simpson trial. It's even more shameful that I remember that debacle of due process. But he was innocent, wasn't he? Only an innocent person would try and publish a book about how he would have killed his victims…right?

ABNORMALITY: 6 STUPIDITY: 6 ENTERTAINMENT: 9

248 On the Hoof
members.hometown.aol.com/_ht_a/ porfle/myhomepage/profile.html

This is another downright odd story from the twisted mind of some overly imaginative individual. A Harvard English professor with a PhD in literature analysis couldn't make any sense of the plot. This is a story about cows, vampire bats, a World War II veteran, and a whole lot more. So what if the story elements have nothing to do with each other? This story has cows!

COMMENTS: I love cows. I can't explain why, but the sight of a big, beefy Holstein cow just makes me want to laugh until I hurl. Cows just have that funny look to them, like monkeys, squirrels, and leprechauns. So this one gets a good rating in my book.

ABNORMALITY: 8 STUPIDITY: 9 ENTERTAINMENT: 8

247

Lame Life.com
lamelife.com

Here, you can view a bunch of lame lives, sorted by rating. Each time you click a number on the rating scale, one of many random photos corresponding to that rating will appear. There are lame pictures and lame summaries, which you can blame on the website itself. On the other hand, some of the pictures display lives that are actually quite…lame. An added bonus is the site's offer to accept emails about *your* lame life. "Unemployment, breakups, unexplainable rashes, embarrassing situations"— send in your lame life stories and become part of this site.

COMMENTS: These lame pictures range from dull to hilarious. Keep clicking on one rating and see what happens. You might just see a picture that makes you realize how fortunate you are to be semi-cool (that was *not* intended to be an insult toward you!).

ABNORMALITY: 7 STUPIDITY: 9 ENTERTAINMENT: 7

246

Not Mensa
www.mockery.org/notmensa

We all know Mensa is the official club for know-it-alls and smarty-pants bragging about how their IQs are ten times higher than mine or yours. Not Mensa is also a club for bragging about IQs—incredibly low ones. Also known as the "interplanetary society for the stupid," Not Mensa invites you to see if you're stupid enough to join their "dim-witted mindless exchange between our low-IQ members." You can take the Not Mensa IQ Test, with questions like, "the word 'dumb' can be created using letters from the alphabet: true or false?" or "if you divide 100 by 25, what will you eat for dinner?" There's also information on joining Not Mensa, and a section to find out if your pet is smarter than you.

COMMENTS: I took the Not Mensa test, and was quite disappointed with myself. According to the test results, I am "far, far too intelligent to join Not Mensa." Darn it! Why did I have to be born smart?

ABNORMALITY: 7 STUPIDITY: 10 ENTERTAINMENT: 9

245

WeaselCircus.com
www.weaselcircus.com

This is another variety site with a whole ton of photos, games, and cartoons. There's a funny sequence of photos showing some dogs trying to change a light bulb (which, of course, are regular photos with witty subtitles). You'll also find "Ozzy attacks," a photo showing Ozzy Osbourne about to devour Kermit the Frog, and much, much, more.

COMMENTS: This is by far one of the most fun sites I've visited. All of the photos make you laugh, and one of the games, "Survivor Fishing," kept me occupied for a good fifteen minutes. This one gets a top rating for entertainment in my book (this book, more specifically).

ABNORMALITY: 7 STUPIDITY: 8 ENTERTAINMENT: 10

244

Dog Food for the Soul
www.peds.8m.com/humor

This site is about "cures" for common problems affecting people, such as irritability, fear, and short attention spans. The cures are written as medicinal prescriptions, even though they contain emotions or social properties, such as common sense and sensitivity, as ingredients. One of the less intelligent ones is a cure for your hospital bill. However, if you are reading this book, you might want to check out the "cerebral synaptic enhancer," with the trade name of the "anti-stupidity pill," "to be taken as needed for deficiency of grey matter." Now there is something that should be prescribed for the creators of all the sites in this book. Finally, something useful.

COMMENTS: This site is kind of stupid, yet much of the advice actually makes sense. The cure for these problems should be taken to heart and used in real life. But I didn't put this site in the book for philosophical discussion; I put it in for stupidity.

ABNORMALITY: 7 STUPIDITY: 8 ENTERTAINMENT: 7

243

Weird But True

www.geocities.com/mikey_wbt/wbt.html

These are some pretty darn weird, but at the same time completely true, facts.

Here, you'll find a bunch of strange, interesting, and downright nutty facts about people, animals, and the rest of the world. One of the facts is that "Michael Jordan makes more money from Nike every year than all the Nike factory workers in Malaysia combined." Another is that "the Fourth Railway Bridge in Scotland is a meter longer in the summer than it is in the winter" due to heat expansion. Another fact with no relevance whatsoever is "a cockroach can live several weeks with its head cut off." From the stuff I've seen on the Web, I would guess that applies to many website creators, too.

COMMENTS: Once again, I am not surprised that all of this useless knowledge is floating around on the Internet. Who knew that a certain bridge grew and shrank in between seasons? Not me, that's for sure. Now I do, and you do, too. Anyway, this site is for anybody who likes the out of the ordinary.

ABNORMALITY: 9 STUPIDITY: 7 ENTERTAINMENT: 8

242

Spot the Duck Webcam

www.dotcomscotland.co.uk/weirdsites/spottheduck0.htm

This Scottish webcam appears at first to be another boring webcam. But at least this one has an amusingly pathetic story behind it. "Spot was first spotted at Loch Lomond way back in August 2001 and has been sighted several times since. Scientists studying pictures of Spot are totally bewildered as to what type of duck Spot can possibly be—there are no known ducks of this type anywhere in the world!!" Patience and luck are needed to catch him, according to the site. In reality, it's actually quite easy to catch him. Simply hit the "click to refresh" button and Spot will miraculously appear. See if you can take a guess as to what "mysterious" species Spot is.

COMMENTS: Besides being a good one-time gag, the Spot the Duck Webcam is pretty average as weird sites go. Not great, not horrible; just average. Kind of like what *Wife Swap* is to reality TV. You'll get a good laugh the first time you visit Spot the Duck, but don't count on coming back.

ABNORMALITY: 7 STUPIDITY: 9 ENTERTAINMENT: 7

241

Animal Communication with Joanne Hull
www.joannehull.com

If you went up to some stranger and said to him, "I can communicate with animals," he'd stare at you like you were nuts, right? Well, that's what Joanne Hull is trying to sell to us on this site. Joanne tells the story of how her love for animals caused her to drop out of school and start working for a horse dealer. This dealer specialized in reselling battered and abused horses. Sounds like a noble, but still normal, success story—until Joanne claims that this was when she developed the ability to psychically communicate with the horses. She doesn't tell how she got the ability on this site, but instead tells you to buy her book. Hmm…

COMMENTS: Don't get me wrong; working with abused animals is undoubtedly a noble cause. If you think that you have some unspoken bond with the animals, that's great. But to claim you use psychic powers to communicate with animals, and then try to teach that to other people—that's a little off the rocker.

ABNORMALITY: 9 STUPIDITY: 7 ENTERTAINMENT: 6

240

Fly Powered Airplanes
www.flypower.com

We've all heard about flower power—but what about fly power? "In case you are interested, you have now entered the only site on the Internet totally devoted to the intricacies and pursuit of fly powered avionics." What could possibly be "intricate" about airplanes flown by bugs? If you're crazy enough to want to learn more, this site won't let you down. The Fly Power in History section claims that the concept dates back to ancient Babylon and Egypt. If you're sold on the idea, you can buy your own fly airplane kit, which includes wing components and "engine mounts" for two aircraft, as well as "tips for modifications" and "handling instructions."

COMMENTS: The strangest part about this site is that there is a "No Smoking" style icon over a picture of a fly. Shouldn't this site exalt flies instead? Flies have rights too, you know! Well, not really. But this contradiction further proves that this site makes no sense whatsoever.

ABNORMALITY: 9 STUPIDITY: 8 ENTERTAINMENT: 7

239

Theories on Grimace
www.angelfire.com/mo/jogrimace/

This site attempts to answer a mystery that has plagued mankind for years: just what the heck is that McDonald's Grimace character?

The site offers some theories on what this creature of mystery is. And while the site is rather brief, it's likely that it will tickle your funny bone somewhat. The comments about how the Hamburglar and the Fry Guys stealing food provided bad role models for little kids are kind of funny, as is the speculation about how the definition of the word "grimace" may provide some clues to the "benign, steroid-inflated, pre-Barney lookalike's" true nature.

COMMENTS: I've often wondered myself what on Earth Grimace is supposed to be and why he's called Grimace for that matter. This site is sure to strike a chord with anybody who enjoys burgers, fat purple blobs, and/or creatures that have appeared in a TV commercial with Donald Trump.

ABNORMALITY: 7 STUPIDITY: 7 ENTERTAINMENT: 7

238

The Outhouses of America Tour
www.jldr.com/ohindex.shtml

This site is about the outhouses that still exist in some parts of the United States and how they are used today.

Here, you can find all sorts of stuff on outhouses, including pictures and information on outhouse racing. There are tons of photos of outhouses, some of which are actually quite nice and are attached to or near mansions. Hmm, must just be some odd millionaires. Browse the literature section and see a copy of "the most wanted book" among outhouse collectors: *Flushed with Pride: The Story of Thomas Crapper*. You can even hear outhouse songs like "That Little Old Shack Out Back." Yes, outhouse songs!

COMMENTS: Who knew there was so much to outhouses? I mean, I can see dedicating a page to their past history, but the ones that currently exist? And I still wonder what on Earth outhouse racing is. We can only guess.

ABNORMALITY: 8 STUPIDITY: 8 ENTERTAINMENT: 7

237

Leonard Nimoy Should Eat More Salsa Foundation

web.tampabay.com/lnsemsf

These people believe Leonard Nimoy should eat more salsa. It's that simple. "Leonard Nimoy is excellent, and salsa is excellent, and if Leonard Nimoy would eat more salsa, he would become an unstoppable force of excellence." On this page, you'll find "research" that states how great Leonard Nimoy would be if he consumed more of this delicious Mexican condiment. The site also contains irrefutable evidence such as "shocking photos of Leonard Nimoy's past avoidance of salsa." This site strives to find out the cause of Nimoy's "problem" and "correct" it. Some useful salsa recipes and some entertaining games are also featured here.

COMMENTS: It doesn't take a Vulcan to realize that the premise of this site makes about as much sense as constructing a "mnemonic memory circuit using stone knives and bearskins." (*Star Trek* fans will undoubtedly remember this classic Spock line.) Do yourself a favor and take nothing that this site says seriously. It is kind of funny, though. Enjoy it for what it is.

ABNORMALITY: 8 STUPIDITY: 9 ENTERTAINMENT: 8

236

John Ashcroft Sings!

www.cnn.com/video/us/2002/02/25/ ashcroft.sings.wbtv.med.html

This is a CNN video of former senator and Bush attorney general John Ashcroft ending one of his meetings with a song that would make William Shatner scowl. The song, "Let the Eagle Soar," is an off-key, semi-religious attempt at a patriotic song. It is also a total travesty and an affront to serious musicians. It hurts your ears like heck. While some people may disagree with Ashcroft's politics, we can all agree on one thing: please don't sing anymore! In the name of all that is decent, don't sing!

COMMENTS: Nobody deserves the punishment of hearing people like Ashcroft sing. It should be a felony for politicians to consider music careers. First Bill Clinton blowing a saxophone, now this. Of course, it could have been worse. It could have been "Janet Reno sings!" God help us all if that ever happened.

ABNORMALITY: 7 STUPIDITY: 8 ENTERTAINMENT: 2

235

Scott Pakin's Automatic Complaint-Letter Generator

www.pakin.org/complaint

This is for people who like to complain in style, but are either too lazy or not skilled enough in writing to write an elaborate complaint letter.

Here, you'll find a brief form with blank spaces. Simply fill out the form, and the complaint generator will generate a letter to complain about whatever activities your friend, nemesis, or other associate may be doing. The letter is a long and rambling string of gibberish that sounds impressive, but really doesn't say too much.

COMMENTS: This is a somewhat funny letter generator, but, in my opinion, there aren't enough blank lines to create stuff that's really random and funny. The less variables there are, the worse it is. It's because of this that a hick could write a better letter suited to the specific situation than this letter generator does. This site takes a kind of stupid but funny concept and makes it just plain stupid.

ABNORMALITY: 7 STUPIDITY: 8 ENTERTAINMENT: 5

234

Fainting Goats

www-personal.umich.edu/~jimknapp/goats.html

And I thought I had seen it all.

This site is home to information on a breed of goat known as "the fainting goat." "Thanks to a genetic condition called myotonia congenita, [the goats] actually seem to faint when they are startled." Interesting, isn't it? Well, sorta. You can learn all about these swooning goats, including their history, where the breed is often found, pictures of the goats, and pictures of the goats as they are actually fainting! However, this site had me wondering a lot about the pictures of the guy hugging and kissing the goats. Goat hugging? Disturbing. Goat kissing? *Very* disturbing.

COMMENTS: Fainting goats. Wow. I never thought that I'd see such bizarre farm animals. The scenario of a fainting goat is pretty funny when you think about it. Unless you're a goat. Anyway, this site is proof that truth is stranger than fiction. If you don't believe me, you just might want to check this site out.

ABNORMALITY: 9 STUPIDITY: 6 ENTERTAINMENT: 7

233

Purple.com
www.purple.com

The point of this site is quite simple: the color purple. When you first visit, that's all you see. No pictures, no text, no fancy graphics. Just a purple screen. The only other thing on this site is a "Purple FAQ," with questions like, "Can I buy or lease purple?" "Buy, no. Lease, maybe," with the word "lease" linking to a section where you can advertise on Purple.com. Be prepared, though. Advertising goes for a whopping five thousand bucks a month. The questionable advertising policies aren't the only controversial thing about this site. A question in the FAQ makes the accusation that the main page is, in fact, not purple, but lilac, pink, or another color entirely! Those deceivers!

COMMENTS: It doesn't appear that much effort was put into this site. This site's simplicity is both its biggest asset and its biggest weakness. But at least now if you have an urgent need to see the color purple, you know where to go.

ABNORMALITY: 8   STUPIDITY: 8   ENTERTAINMENT: 7

232

Bureau of Atomic Tourism
www.atomictourist.com

Are you a fan of nuclear bombs? If you are, the Bureau of Atomic Tourism can help you in your radioactive research efforts. According to the intro, the Bureau is "dedicated to the promotion of tourist locations around the world that have either been the site of atomic explosions, display exhibits on the development of atomic devices, or contain vehicles that were designed to deliver atomic weapons." Atomic explosion sites are tourist destinations? Isn't there a little thing called radiation to worry about? Besides the Atomic Museums and the explosion sites, there's also a catalog of nuclear explosions, as well as a link to "Todd's Atomic Homepage," who is "just a lowly student entangled in Nuke E." Right…

COMMENTS: I still don't get why people would want to visit a nuclear explosion site. Maybe they want to be exposed to the radiation so they'll develop superpowers like those guys in tights you see in comic books. It worked for Radioactive Man and Fallout Boy (the famous *Simpsons* superheroes), didn't it?

ABNORMALITY: 9   STUPIDITY: 7   ENTERTAINMENT: 7

231

Coffee Stirrer Central
www.rubbermullet.co.uk

This site is the only place on the Internet dedicated to the study of "Stirrectomology"—the science of coffee stirrers. This site has been building up for the past ten years, and "now contains in excess of seven extremely rare coffee stirrers for your delight, amusement, and delight." Did they just say "delight" twice when talking about coffee stirrers? Types of Stirrers, Stirrer History, and Classified Ads for coffee stirrers are just a few sections offered on this caffeinated cornucopia. There is also a news section—albeit an outdated one—with an article from 2005 about a "Blockbuster Movie" planned about "a serial killer whose victims are found stabbed through the spleen with sharpened coffee stirrers."

COMMENTS: My favorite stirrer was the "John F. Kidney-Mousectomy" stirrer, which was "a breakthrough in safety: only 112 fatalities in the last forty years can be attributed to this design."

ABNORMALITY: 8 STUPIDITY: 8 ENTERTAINMENT: 8

230

Bureau of Missing Socks
www.funbureau.com

If you do your own laundry often, you know that sometimes socks get lost in the process. So, where the heck do they go? "The Bureau of Missing Socks is the first organization solely devoted to solving the question of what happens to missing single socks. It explores all aspects of the phenomena including the occult, conspiracy theories, and extraterrestrial." The most entertaining part is the Sock Talk section, where users exchange their various opinions on why socks disappear. Theories range from bizarre—extraterrestrials destroying socks as part of their religion, sock cannibalism, Bill Gates as an alien bent on reducing pairs of socks to singles—to mundane and stupid, including one guy who believes he is so attractive to women that they want to steal his socks. I'm sure he's a regular Fabio.

COMMENTS: This site is entertaining just for the weird forum posts. The Bill Gates theories and the conspiracy theories are especially amusing. Anyway, if you're curious about missing socks or just looking for a good laugh, give this one a look.

ABNORMALITY: 9 STUPIDITY: 8 ENTERTAINMENT: 9

229

Super Friends Page
seanbaby.com/superfriends/old/super.htm

This is a page that remembers the *Superfriends* cartoon show. The *bad* version. Sure, there was the *Superfriends vs. The Legion of Doom* series. That was good. However, there was also a much lamer *Superfriends* series. Actually, I'm not quite sure of the order, but somewhere in the different versions of this superhero show was one featuring the characters "Marvin, Wendy, and Wonder Dog." These dorks were a couple of teenagers and a canine, all with no superpowers whatsoever. The preachy Superfriends kept trying to teach these mindless kids namby-pamby lessons about the value of life, the environment, and all that crap. In fact, half of the time the episodes centered around the boring activities of these losers.

COMMENTS: This shows that *Superfriends* was a good show until this monstrosity happened. Or that it changed for the better later on. Either way, this is a funny site that deserves to be seen by all of you who dislike and/or joke about funny people who wear underwear on the outside of their pants.

ABNORMALITY: 7 STUPIDITY: 7 ENTERTAINMENT: 7

228

No More AOL CDs.com
www.nomoreaolcds.com

One of my previous sites (number 495) discussed uses of those omnipresent AOL disks. This site wants to eradicate them. Here, you'll find, in one convenient place, all the information needed on the cause to purge the Earth of AOL CDs. Their mission: to gather one million AOL CDs and send them back to AOL, proving that nobody wants them. There is the "10 Things We Hate about AOL CDs" section, an FAQ, AOL CD experiments, and much more on these annoying objects.

COMMENTS: Not to put a damper on your efforts guys (I hate the infernal things as much as you do), but I don't think one million will be enough. Ten million, possibly, but one million is just too few. Think of it this way: Would it have taken only one million people to keep Bill Clinton out of office? No, and we know where that went. The reality is that there are more than 250 million people in the U.S. Think about it.

ABNORMALITY: 7 STUPIDITY: 8 ENTERTAINMENT: 7

227

This is an unusual website about a group of fat geeks. Except they're not that fat. They may not be in great shape, but most of these guys barely have beer bellies.

Here, you'll find more information than you want or need to know about these losers and some information you really wish that they'd keep to themselves. This vanity site doesn't make much sense and is supremely stupid. But, in a way, the Fat Geeks do sorta make up for it. How, you ask? Pictures of women! Yeah, baby! A click on the "Hotties" button finds the only socially redeeming value on the Fat Geeks page. Although, even the "Hotties" label is misleading, with some hot and some not.

COMMENTS: Any group who would call themselves Fat Geeks on a website really are geeks, whether they are fat or not. You're only as good as you make yourself out to be. Or, as good as other people think you are, to a "large" extent. Okay, maybe that wasn't such a good lesson.

ABNORMALITY: 8 STUPIDITY: 9 ENTERTAINMENT: 6

226

Die Screaming with Sharp Things in Your Head
www.bifrost.com.au/hosting/gnomes

It's not as bad as it sounds. Unless you're a garden gnome.

Once again, those poor abused gnomes are at the center of hate here at this website. Disturbing pictures of garden gnomes with sharp sticks, stakes, and whatnot stuck through their heads are graphically (well, not really) featured on this website. Oh the horror! Abuse of vertically challenged garden decorations! Once you've viewed all of these disturbing photos, there are T-shirts, hats, and mugs available. Not that you'd want to buy any of it, of course.

COMMENTS: Whoever did this was a very sick person. Think of what those poor, innocent little garden gnomes thought of when those sharp objects went through their heads. Do you feel guilty now? You'd better! I should start a website that's home to the Anti-Cruelty to Garden Gnomes Society. I should, but I'm too lazy.

ABNORMALITY: 9 STUPIDITY: 8 ENTERTAINMENT: 7

225

HampsterDance.com
www.hampsterdance.com

If you know its history, you'll know this one's a classic.

It is a prime example of the stupidity on the World Wide Web. Not *the* most stupid thing, but a model after which millions of stupid sites are modeled. Basically it's hamsters dancing with some extra bells and whistles to make it a cool site. It's accompanied by some funny hamster-type music, the kind that sounds like a bad version of Alvin and the Chipmunks.

COMMENTS: This was one of the first stupid sites out there, so it gets a top rating in that category. I mean, hamsters dancing? That's even more far out than the movie *Attack of the Killer Tomatoes*. Killer tomatoes. Dancing hamsters.

ABNORMALITY: 7 STUPIDITY: 9 ENTERTAINMENT: 8

224

X-Ball
xballonline.com

This is one weird site. I'm not sure exactly how to describe it, but it has something to do with an imaginary sport, monkeys, rabbits picking flowers, and extreme-sports athletes who are snowmen. What they all have to do with each other is not something I'm not quite sure of. The site features the convoluted rules of X-Ball, a diagram of the playing field, and some weird commentary on the "game."

COMMENTS: This is obviously a site that was made by a couple of over-imaginative guys who have no jobs, too much time on their hands, and no lives. They took a bunch of weird concepts, tossed them in a blender, and came out with…this. I tell ya, it makes less sense than the "plot" for the Troma films movie *Surf Nazis Must Die* (yeah, you've probably never heard of it; but it's a real movie, seriously).

ABNORMALITY: 9 STUPIDITY: 9 ENTERTAINMENT: 8

Voluntary Human Extinction Movement
www.vhemt.org

We hear a lot about organizations dedicated to saving humanity from nuclear war, global warming, and so on. But what about an organization that *doesn't* want to save humanity, but let it die instead? That's exactly what the Voluntary Human Extinction Movement is. "Phasing out the human race by voluntarily ceasing to breed will allow Earth's biosphere to return to good health. Crowded conditions and resource shortages will improve as we become less dense." But what good is a healthy Earth if there aren't any humans around? The Movement anticipated this question, and says that humans are too "collectively centered" on our own species. "It took a long time for people to accept that our planet is just one of many orbiting a star, which is also just one of many in a galaxy, which is also just one of many in the universe." And there's also the whole multiple universes thing, and string theory, M-theory, quantum physics, black holes, super-massive black holes…my head is hurting.

COMMENTS: I wonder if there's an alien race somewhere else that's going through this dilemma. Is there a Voluntary Zeta-Reticulian Extinction Movement, or a Voluntary Reptilian Extinction Movement?

ABNORMALITY: 10 STUPIDITY: 9 ENTERTAINMENT: 8

The Beer Monkey
www.angelfire.com/pa3/beermonkey

This site is about an unusual topic: a group of college students that adopted a monkey. Sounds like something out of a bad comedy show. These are their tales of a monkey named Phonics: a monkey who constantly poops, gets drunk, and does various other stupid acts. Why, Phonics is so smart he even takes his own beer out of the refrigerator! In addition to monkey humor, there are rambling writings about Palestinians, Pamela Anderson, and Molson Ice Beer, as well as other stupid stuff.

COMMENTS: I have an extremely hard time believing this is a real story. Then again, wacky college kids can do anything, right? But I still have doubts. If it is true, it just goes to show that there should be no interaction between drunken college students and monkeys. Monkeys are infinitely smarter and better behaved.

ABNORMALITY: 8 STUPIDITY: 9 ENTERTAINMENT: 7

221 The Pillow Fight League
www.gopfl.com

Although not as pathetic as Finger Jousting (number 133) or Chessboxing (number 352), the Pillow Fight League is another example of some oddball game masquerading as a sport. It opens with a picture of Boozy Suzy, the current Pillow Fighting "World Champion," and proceeds to name the "Top Ten Contenders" who dare to challenge Suzy for her title. There is a set of rules for pillow fighting, chief of which is "female fighters only. No exceptions." Unfortunately, the PFL also requires "good sportswomanship" and no "rude, lewd, or suggestive behavior." Well, what's the point then?

COMMENTS: The saddest part about this is that you can actually pay fifteen dollars (eighteen dollars at the door—better reserve them quickly) to see these Pillow Fighting events. Who would pay to see something like this? Then again, people pay much more to see wrestling matches. At least with pillow fighting you don't have to listen to Vince McMahon.

ABNORMALITY: 7 STUPIDITY: 8 ENTERTAINMENT: 7

220 Aleister's Komputer Magick
members.aol.com/pgrsel2/aleister/frames.htm

Early twenieth-century occultist Aleister Crowley (no relation, trust me) has returned from the dead to work his magick on your komputer (Aleister was obviously fond of Ks). "Writing from my own experiences, I describeth the methods and theories of modern magickal computer practices, I shall manageth to persuadeth thy that Magick Komputing is a scientifick reality—and that it worketh." In other words…um, I have no idea. The one thing I do understand is that the site senselessly protests against the "Dark Forces" of the evil "Master of Oracle Software." There's also an "esoteric incantation" that will allow you to become a Komputer magick master. The "incantation" is comprised of many computer-related terms and popular websites, along with many exclamation points.

COMMENTS: It's somewhat disconcerting, and at the same time kind of cool, that I share my last name with Aleister (or "Mr. Crowley," as he's called in the Ozzy Osbourne song). Still, I don't think Komputer Magick will save my Windows computer from crashing. But, if Aleister's magick works for you, let me know.

ABNORMALITY: 9 STUPIDITY: 8 ENTERTAINMENT: 8

219

Nobody for President
nobodyforpresident.net

This website endorses the campaign for the presidency of one candidate: Nobody! "Nobody will be running as a member of NO party...except the parties he is going to throw at the White House!" That's right! Nobody is running for president in 2008. So vote for Nobody! According to Nobody, his vice president is going to be Everybody, so that therefore Everybody can rule the country. Nobody's biography states: "I was born to be a career politician because I hate to work. I've never been in the military, and I did inhale." And yet, Nobody still has positions on war ("nobody wants peace with everybody"), gun control (he thinks we should give everybody water guns), taxes ("you should be able to keep the money you earn and do what you want with it"), and all of that other junk that politicians prattle on about.

COMMENTS: I have no idea what or who Nobody is, or who he's supposed to be. But sometimes, Nobody ruling our country might be better than Somebody.

ABNORMALITY: 8 STUPIDITY: 8 ENTERTAINMENT: 7

218

The Great Cosmic Joke
www.thegreatcosmicjoke.com

This is one site I just don't get.

It's The Great Cosmic Joke, and it has a number of odd things on it relating to life and the universe. It says that life is meant to be a joke, although at the same time it says it's not supposed to be a joke. There are also such profound quotes as, "Our heads are round so our thinking can change directions." Right, sure.

COMMENTS: I honestly can't determine the purpose of this site. It's more confusing than a Maya Angelou poem. Is it meant to make people laugh? Is it meant to make people think? I'm just confused. I'll go now and watch a movie where things blow up and there's no plot whatsoever. That will make sense.

ABNORMALITY: 9 STUPIDITY: 7 ENTERTAINMENT: 7

217

Free College Degrees!
freedegrees.webdare.com

This site makes the argument that you shouldn't have to work hard and pay some fancy university to earn a college degree. You should just get it for free from this site!

Here, you can "earn" a free honorary college degree. There's info about the campus, the president, the mission, the different departments, and, of course, a disclaimer. Plus there's no need for boring undergraduate work. You can earn a master's or a doctorate right off the bat. Check out the "Master of Lying Degree, required for legal and political majors" or get a DDS—a Doctor in Drinking Sciences. Now doesn't this site have it all?

COMMENTS: I agree with this site! Why should we waste money getting degrees when they're just going to end up gathering dust in a box somewhere? Honestly, do you proudly display your college diploma for everybody to see? Heck, some of the most successful people I know didn't even get a college degree.

ABNORMALITY: 7 STUPIDITY: 8 ENTERTAINMENT: 7

216

Caveman's Crib
www.cavemanscrib.com

I can safely say that I despise 99 percent of the commercials I've seen on TV over the past twenty years. The remaining 1 percent that I do like are all Geico commercials. So you can imagine my joy when I got the opportunity to enter the hip penthouse condo of the Geico caveman. This site is an interactive video that allows you to tour the caveman's "crib" and see what he has on his computer, his answering machine, and even his iPod (apparently the caveman is fond of rap, techno, and South American tango-style music—two out of three ain't bad). The caveman's upscale urban pad is, of course, very neat and trendy, and he's got all the latest gadgets and gizmos in his crib. As you tour his home, the caveman will occasionally come along and make a friendly comment, along with a hint of the cynicism he's developed from those traumatizing commercials.

COMMENTS: Ah, the paradox of the Geico caveman. He's intelligent, sophisticated, and fond of the finer things in life—but he's still a caveman. No wonder he's experiencing, in his words, an "existential meltdown."

ABNORMALITY: 8 STUPIDITY: 8 ENTERTAINMENT: 9

FUT
fut.com.au

FUT stands for Faceless Ugly Teddy. What a concept: killer teddy bears with no faces.

Here, you can see a bunch of stuff having to do with the FUT, including its story, an e-zine, and cartoons containing the disturbing adventures of this…thing. There are warnings that FUTs may lurk inside bananas or be disguised as snails. Killer snails? And, of course, once again, there is an alien connection. "They came from outer space. Their mission: conquer the human race!" I would jump off a cliff into the arms of Rosie O'Donnell before I'd conceive of the Faceless Ugly Teddy.

COMMENTS: Australians made this site, so maybe that's why it's so screwed up. Actually, I take that back; stupid Americans can be just as screwed up as stupid Australians. Probably more screwed up.

ABNORMALITY: 9 STUPIDITY: 9 ENTERTAINMENT: 7

Pet Pennies
petpennies.50megs.com/index.html

Distemper vaccinations? Dog food? Heartworm pills? Kennels? Toys? Ha! Forget all that and purchase your very own pet penny!

Now, I know you're thinking, "I can get a penny anywhere!" and "Pennies make horrible pets!" You're probably right on both accounts. However, despite these realizations, this site offers you a pet penny, with a certificate of authenticity, for one dollar. What a great value! There's a rather useless FAQ, with "answers" to questions like "Why can't I just get a pet nickel?" and "Why exactly is the sky blue?" There's also customer testimonials (no testimonials yet; surprise, surprise) and pet-penny forums.

COMMENTS: Any pet, even a goldfish (which I personally view as a useless pet), would be better than a pet penny. It's just a ridiculous concept. Pennies don't even qualify as pets! Still, though, the site is funny to take a look at and see how stupid some people think you can be.

ABNORMALITY: 8 STUPIDITY: 9 ENTERTAINMENT: 6

213

Amtrek.net
www.amtrek.net

This is a pretty funny train-travel parody based on Amtrak—funny enough to merit a long disclaimer before you enter the site. Instead of the high-speed Amtrek service of "Acela," Amtrek runs "Crashela." Here, you'll see news, an unusual travel planner, and a store with tons of train stuff. There are also popular Amtrek features like "Restroom in a Bucket" and special service to "the island nation of New Jersey." This site is stupid and makes no sense.

COMMENTS: This is a weird website that I can't do justice to with a description. Kind of like when William Shatner talks; you don't understand how he's so funny and stupid until you actually hear him.

ABNORMALITY: 9 STUPIDITY: 7 ENTERTAINMENT: 8

212

Church of the Flying Spaghetti Monster
www.venganza.org

Of all the bizarre Internet churches in this book, this one has to be the weirdest. The Church of the Flying Spaghetti Monster (or CFSM) was founded in 2005 when a guy named Bobby Henderson wrote a letter to the Kansas City School Board in opposition to the "intelligent design" versus evolution controversy. After Henderson posted the letter online, it generated thousands of emails, so Henderson decided to make a website spreading his outrageous religion. Since this letter was published, the CFSM site has gotten 350 million hits. Random House has even published a book by Henderson called *The Gospel of the Flying Spaghetti Monster*. The Church believes that humans are evolved from pirates, and "that global warming, earthquakes, hurricanes, and other natural disasters are a direct effect of the shrinking numbers of Pirates since the 1800s." Yar, we prevented global warming! Give us our booty back and you'll help the environment, yar!

COMMENTS: The Church of the FSM proves that a deity made of pasta is the perfect solution for injecting humor into an otherwise heated debate... Has the Flying Spaghetti Monster touched you with His Noodly Appendage yet?

ABNORMALITY: 10 STUPIDITY: 8 ENTERTAINMENT: 9

211

The Official
Doohicky Website
www.angelfire.com/home/doohickys

This is a site that features info on the national animal of Pluto. Yes, the planet.

The animal is called the Doohicky, and this site has a bunch of "facts" on it (facts that, of course, have no substance to them), preservation efforts for the breeds that are endangered, and much more. Once again, I am baffled as to how they found out that creatures of any sort live or lived on Pluto, which leads me to know, I repeat, *know* that this is a joke…I think. Everybody knows that the only planet in the solar system that has life on it is Mars, and maybe the third moon of Jupiter.

COMMENTS: I'm wondering where on Earth they got the name Doohickys. Is it just a random jumbling of words and letters, or does it have an actual meaning? Hmm…I'll have to look into this further. Until then, it remains a mystery.

ABNORMALITY: 9 STUPIDITY: 8 ENTERTAINMENT: 7

210

The Original Densa Quiz
www.pressanykey.com/cgi-bin/jquiz.cgi

This is a rather interesting quiz on intelligence.

Here, you answer twelve questions, all very diverse in nature. Some of them seem quite simple, but don't be fooled. Examples include "Do they have a 4th of July in England?" and "If there are three apples and you take away two, how many do you have?" All of the other questions are similar in that they seem deceptively simple. And I got only five right. You must think I'm an idiot, right? Well, let me just say that like I said before, the questions in this quiz are very unusual.

COMMENTS: I totally expected to ace this quiz. I didn't. Instead, I've been left with an accusation that I'm slow-witted. Which raises a new question: do quizzes like these destroy self-confidence? Maybe they do. And maybe one of these days somebody will file some kind of lawsuit against the people who made this. Hey, after that case where that klutzy lady spilled hot McDonald's coffee on her lap and then sued, I wouldn't be surprised.

ABNORMALITY: 7 STUPIDITY: 7 ENTERTAINMENT: 7

Lobster Liberation Front
www.lobsterlib.com

Geez, I've seen so many "liberation fronts" that it's starting to make me sick. This one's pretty wild: it encourages people to steal lobsters and then release them into the ocean. Sounds outrageous, doesn't it? When it comes to robbing the seafood section of your supermarket, tips include having "a big gun. Those pimply-faced clerks who work at the seafood counter sometimes like to play the role of hero. Big guns curtail this urge." Very good advice, isn't it? There are a number of other tips to help you release lobsters into the ocean, as well as success stories.

COMMENTS: Maybe lobsters have some redeeming qualities that justify "liberating" them. Look at Pinchy the Lobster from *The Simpsons*. Homer initially buys Pinchy to eat him, but loves him so much he keeps him as a pet. Pinchy then becomes a bona fide member of the Simpson family—until Homer accidentally gives Pinchy a "nice hot bath," which instead cooks him. After that, Homer tearfully mourns Pinchy—while eating him.

ABNORMALITY: 7 STUPIDITY: 9 ENTERTAINMENT: 5

The Death Clock
www.deathclock.com

This is a site that has a rather interesting prediction device. It's simple in design. You type in your birthday and select your gender (no other personal information is required), and this site will tell you the day that you will die. There are four different modes on the Death Clock: "Pessimistic" (for those of you who know that the Chicago Cubs will never win the World Series again), "Optimistic" (for those of you who think that it would be great to be on *Who Wants to Be a Millionaire?*), "Realistic" (you know Cher has had lots of plastic surgery), and "Normal" (after what I've seen in writing this book, I'm not sure what that is). Talk about complex.

COMMENTS: What I want to know is how this thing works. Is it based on statistics? Do they hire an out-of-work phone psychic specifically for the device? Actually, I'm sure that's not true, because your death calculation is instantaneous, and those psychics get paid by the minute.

ABNORMALITY: 8 STUPIDITY: 7 ENTERTAINMENT: 7

The "Dogs Playing Poker" Website
www.drunkandretired.com/dogs

Have you ever seen any of the "Dogs Playing Poker" paintings? If you have and you like them, if you're somewhat interested in them, or if you're just really bored and picked up this book to find an amusing site to go to, check out this site. It has all of the versions of the "Dogs Playing Poker" paintings and a link to a biography page of C.M. Coolidge, the original painter of the "Dogs Playing Poker" picture.

COMMENTS: I am an aficionado of fine art, so I love this site. The one thing I would like to do is take a survey of people and ask, "Which is stranger, the 'Dogs Playing Poker' paintings, or what passes for modern art?" One final comment: I wished they had painted "Monkeys Playing Poker." That would have been cool.

ABNORMALITY: 6 STUPIDITY: 5 ENTERTAINMENT: 7

---

206 Mustache Summer 1999
www.mustachesummer.com

It seems that sites dedicated to people's obsessions with things are becoming more plentiful. Anyway, this site has everything and anything on it about mustaches. There are mustache articles, mustache haiku (sounding familiar?), and much more. Be sure to check out the Mustache Prejudice case, in which a criminal described as being "clean cut" when he murdered four people was pictured in the article with a mustache. Prejudice or journalism? You decide. There's even information on Cinco de Mustache, a holiday derived from Cinco de Mayo, except much hairier.

COMMENTS: I know mustaches look good on some people, but why dedicate a website to something on your face? It just doesn't make any sense. Then again, neither do the other 504 websites in this book. Maybe someday when I have a mustache (if I ever do), maybe, just maybe, it'll make sense.

ABNORMALITY: 8 STUPIDITY: 8 ENTERTAINMENT: 6

DisneyTattooGuy.com
www.disneytattooguy.com

This is the homepage of a guy who has more than one thousand Disney tattoos on his body. Yes, you heard me right: more than one thousand *Disney* tattoos.

From Donald Duck to Goofy to Pluto, he's got them all, somewhere on that scarred body of his. Every inch of this guy's body is covered with Disney body art, including a *Little Mermaid* tattoo on his stomach. If you want, you can see a top ten list, pictures, and a list of TV talk shows the Disney Tattoo Guy has appeared on.

COMMENTS: Wow. This guy is the ultimate Disney fan. I mean, who would go so far as to endure all those hours of needles being stuck into his body just for glorifying some entertainment company? Well, I guess that's what circus freaks do, but that's different. That's their job, for Pete's sake! And another thing: if Disney keeps making movies, what happens when he runs out of room to put the tattoos on? Hmm… Why does this guy do it? We can only guess his intentions.

ABNORMALITY: 8 STUPIDITY: 8 ENTERTAINMENT: 6

Tess's Michael Jackson Impersonator Site
www.tess-impersonates-mj.com

This site is home to a female—that's right, female—Michael Jackson impersonator. On this site, you can see Tess's Michael Jackson impersonation performances, news, pictures, and more. I wonder why nobody else thought of a female Jacko impersonator? I mean, it seems kind of appropriate. Wait, isn't Diana Ross really a female Michael Jackson impersonator? Or, wait, is Jacko a male Diana Ross impersonator? I'm getting so confused. Help!

COMMENTS: I think that this girl can do a better impersonation of Michael Jackson than most men could, mainly because Jacko's style seems, well, very close to how a woman sings. I'm not going to say anything more, before I insult someone. Although I probably already have. And I know Michael Jackson has never been ridiculed, never ever!

ABNORMALITY: 7 STUPIDITY: 7 ENTERTAINMENT: 7

203 Star Trek Convention Photos
www.convention-photos.de

We've all heard of them: the Trekkies. *Star Trek* fanboys that are so obsessed with the series they're in the same category as Comic Book Guy from *The Simpsons*. "Worst convention photos ever!" Here, you can see (obviously) a bunch of photos from various *Star Trek* conventions. There are more than four hundred, including such wastes of film as aluminum shuttlecrafts (yeah, I'm sure that something that costs ten bucks can go to warp eight), Spock ears (which is about the only thing cool within five miles), and more.

COMMENTS: Don't get me wrong, I like the series. But these Trekkies don't have a life outside of it. If *Star Trek* suddenly ceased to exist and all records of it were destroyed, these losers would think of themselves as bigger failures than Paris Hilton's music career. And if that would be the case, I wouldn't be surprised if they all gave up any hope of success forever.

ABNORMALITY: 5 STUPIDITY: 6 ENTERTAINMENT: 6

---

202 Hammertime with Tom DeLay
hammer.cf.huffingtonpost.com

It's Hammertime! But this time, it's not with MC Hammer—it's with former U.S. House Majority Leader Tom DeLay. "Representative Tom DeLay (R-TX) has announced that he is resigning. Unfortunately, he's a little reluctant to leave, and is hiding in the house chambers." Your job is to go into the chambers with a hammer to try to coax Tom out by smacking him in the head. Tom pops up in many places in the House chamber; the further back he is, the more points you get for hammering him. Be sure not to hit any other prominent House representatives, or you'll lose points (although, politics aside, it is tempting to just smack Nancy Pelosi).

COMMENTS: Ah, the irony. DeLay was called "The Hammer" for so many years, and now there's a game where everybody can smack him with a hammer. This is a pretty fun game that pokes fun at politics. And that's something that needs a lot of poking.

ABNORMALITY: 7 STUPIDITY: 7 ENTERTAINMENT: 8

201

Make Me Watch TV
www.makememewatchtv.com

Not many people have the opportunity to be forced to watch TV. But that's exactly what Aric McKeown has done with this site. "Make Me Watch TV is the site where you get to force me, Aric McKeown, to watch whatever TV show you please. Not only that, but you can watch me watch TV!" Aric works from home as a cartoonist, a voice actor, an animator, an actor, and a video game columnist (this guy is a jack-of-all-trades, isn't he?) during the day, but at night he'll watch whatever show you want him to. Why exactly is Aric doing this? "In being forced to view the good and the bad programs, I hope to become more educated in exactly why so much TV is horrible. By blogging about different varieties of shows, I think we'll all discover something about the state of entertainment." So, Aric is a scientist, too? Fascinating.

COMMENTS: This guy may sound lazy at first. But when you think about it, he's a good sport for watching bad TV against his will. The last thing I want is being forced to spend a perfectly good evening watching *Fat Pets* or *Reba*. But if you want Aric McKeown to watch *Reba*, you can make him watch *Reba*. That's not laziness, my friends. That's courage.

ABNORMALITY: 7 STUPIDITY: 8 ENTERTAINMENT: 8

200

What the Bob
whatthebob.com

I know what you're thinking: what the heck is What the Bob? The site is as simple and primitive as it sounds. Videos, pictures, and games—all incredibly stupid—comprise the bulk of this site, along with the favorite pastime of moronic guys—football (no offense to the intelligent football lovers among you). Games include "Alpha Bravo Charlie," a crappy arcade-style helicopter game, and "Geek Fighter," another crappy game with two stereotypical geeks fighting each other. It's jocks picking on nerds all over again. Sigh...

COMMENTS: One word describes this site perfectly: average. The people who run it, the site's design, the content—all average. Not good, not bad. Not painful, not pleasurable. Just average. Unless you want an average Internet experience, What the Bob should be low on your web-surfing priority list.

ABNORMALITY: 6 STUPIDITY: 7 ENTERTAINMENT: 5

199

The Twinkles Hakim Archives

www.geocities.com/Hollywood/Picture/3822

These are tales from a rabbit who travels with Miss Piggy.

It's basically a bunch of insane articles about a cartoon rabbit named Twinkles Hakim and his misadventures with Miss Piggy, from the Muppets and other assorted creatures. Articles include "How I Tried to Bite off Miss Piggy's Ear" (maybe a take-off on the Tyson/Holyfield match a while back?) and an article about Twinkles's arrest for attempted molestation of a "rare emerald octopus at Sea World."

COMMENTS: If there is any shred of purpose in this site, you will be hard-pressed to find it. I could find more meaning in the *Dukes of Hazzard* movie (didn't Jessica Simpson win an Oscar for that one? Or was it a Razzie?) than on this page.

ABNORMALITY: 9 STUPIDITY: 9 ENTERTAINMENT: 6

198

Fellah Whose Big Toe Could Predict Earthquakes

pacificcoast.net/~rick

It's commonly known that unusual animal behavior is often a warning sign that an earthquake is about to occur. Well, the creator of this site has unusual behavior that predicts earthquakes as well. According to this guy (whose name is Rick), he broke his big toe in the sixties during a soccer game, and later in the nineties, a vise fell on it (wow, would I hate to be that guy's toe). "Sometime in between, a terrible *itch* arose… The itch at times was quite unbearable, which led to some bizarre scratch-ing." Rick claims that his toe "is somehow bio-mechanically attuned to the geo-magnetic phenomenon associated with faultlines. As the stress builds within the earth, the magnetic forces increase and so does the *itch*. When the stress is relieved by an EQ, the *itch* stops. Honest!" We believe you, Rick. Really, we do (snicker).

COMMENTS: I get the impression that this guy really believes in his toe/earth-quake theory. I suppose if my toe starting itching like crazy for some unknown reason, I'd conjure up some wild explanation for it, too.

ABNORMALITY: 9 STUPIDITY: 7 ENTERTAINMENT: 8

197

Pennsylvania History— The Real Story

user.pa.net/~nrwing/Pennsylvania

This is quite a different take on the history of this state. It tells how William Penn sailed to the New World "in a few ships he borrowed from a Spanish guy," and how Pennsylvania resident Ben Franklin invented both "welfare and the delicious Franklin Mint." Here, you can learn a twisted version of history, including the Civil War, where people could watch the battles progress on an electric map (funny, because I don't remember that in Civil War history class), and how the discovery of black water was "invented" into oil and gasoline by a man named Pennz. Get it? Pennz-oil. Isn't that a real knee slapper?

COMMENTS: These guys have a twisted vision of history; they probably think that the Civil War soldiers had lasers and Amish people had credit cards. Anyway, this is a somewhat, I repeat, *somewhat* funny take on history, and I'd recommend seeing it once or twice.

ABNORMALITY: 9 STUPIDITY: 8 ENTERTAINMENT: 6

196

Cloud Kissing

www.cloudkissing.com

Cloud Kissing is a "well established but largely overlooked organisation which has been operating for several million years." On this site, you can learn about how you can purchase your own clouds for surveillance, destruction, pleasure, and even to impress your friends. Now won't they be impressed when you have them take a look at your very own cloud? If they don't show suitable amazement, you can arrange a "courier cloud" with the ever-popular "plague of frogs." I wonder if I can use my cloud to hack into the Microsoft servers and discover their plan for world domination?

COMMENTS: I'd like to have my own cloud. I'd like one that I can shape to look like whatever I desire, like ordinary people shape their personalities to appreciate really slimy people with lots of money. If it happens in real life, why can't it happen with clouds? Unfortunately, most of these clouds are probably really expensive. Or are they? I wonder.

ABNORMALITY: 8 STUPIDITY: 7 ENTERTAINMENT: 8

195

SoupCan Universe

www.geocities.com/dracothevampyre/Soupcanindex.html

Here, you can learn all about how the "Great Soup Can" spawned everything we know today in the universe. "It all came from a very large can of Chicken and Stars soup. About the size of oooohhh...Cleveland." They claim that the contents of the soup can shaped how things appear to us today, and that if it had contained, say, tomato soup instead of chicken, things might be quite different today. From all the planets to McDonald's Quarter Pounders, this site claims a soup can brought everything, and I mean everything, into existence. Not just any soup can, mind you. The "Soup Can."

COMMENTS: I never would have guessed that everything in this universe came out of a soup can. Talk about convenience! Of course, there's a good probability that this site is just the mad ramblings of someone who is stupendously stupid, or maybe someone who just really, really, really likes soup.

ABNORMALITY: 8 STUPIDITY: 8 ENTERTAINMENT: 7

194

Mesk's Used Couch Emporium

www.picturescape.co.uk/mesk/mesk%20frame.htm

On this site, you'll find an ancient Middle Eastern (Egyptian or Sumerian or something) used-couch seller and king. His name is Mesk, and if you want to find a used couch from the times of the pharaohs or from when the Hanging Gardens of Babylon existed, he's the guy to go to! Mesk also has such contemporary wares as the "chat couch," for Internet chat room usage, that "extends into the 5th dimension to accommodate an infinite number of chatters," and the multi-use "Swiss Army Couch." You can also see Mesk's family tree and more interesting tidbits on this ancient ruler/salesman.

COMMENTS: How an ancient Sumerian got into this time period and started using the Internet is beyond me. Maybe someone from the future went back with a time machine. But wait, wouldn't the space/time continuum be disrupted with the interdimensional...dang it, I hate time travel!

ABNORMALITY: 9 STUPIDITY: 8 ENTERTAINMENT: 6

193

Billdonia
billdonia.tripod.com

This site is home to the independent online nation of Billdonia, as well as the Stupidco Inc. art gallery.

This is a well-presented page that is, unfortunately, chock full of meaninglessness and idiocy. It's quite obvious that the supposedly real nation of "Billdonia" is fictitious, unless the entire world has fallen victim to a Billdonian stupidity curse.

COMMENTS: I'll believe that Lyndon LaRouche has a decent chance at winning the presidency before I'll believe that Billdonia exists. The art gallery is entertaining, though, and the story behind this fabricated nation also has a bit of humor in it.

ABNORMALITY: 8 STUPIDITY: 9 ENTERTAINMENT: 7

192

The Funny Hitman
www.funnyhitman.com

This site features a ton of random generators, including a random comment generator so you can have an easier time picking up girls. Another one is a random Mexican restaurant–name generator. When you want another one, simply hit Refresh. That's all there is to it.

COMMENTS: This is kind of like those phone services that promise you custom horoscopes and predictions for your future, but really instead generate random, prewritten gibberish that they paid some loser ten bucks to "create." They're empty promises, just like those weight-loss infomercials. Still, they are fun to see.

ABNORMALITY: 7 STUPIDITY: 7 ENTERTAINMENT: 8

191
Bring Back Kirk.com
www.bringbackkirk.com

According to the makers of this site, Captain Kirk's death in *Star Trek: Generations* was unacceptable, and it must be fixed. "*Star Trek: Generations* was supposed to bridge the gap between the two eras of Trek," they whine. "Instead, it created a chasm from which the franchise still has not recovered to this day." Pretty wild accusation, isn't it? There's all sorts of other information on this site that is supposed to encourage fans to try to bring back Captain Kirk, such as letter-writing campaigns and even Bring Back Kirk displays at *Star Trek* conventions. Now that's taking things a little to the extreme.

COMMENTS: People, people! Kirk is dead! Accept it! Besides, we all know Captain Picard was ten times better than Kirk in the first place (and let the mountains of Trekkie hate mail in my mailbox begin). Therefore, I'll just go along and evaluate the site. It's a funny site, mainly because the fans are fighting for something they'll never get. Shatner is too busy as an insane law firm owner on *Boston Legal* to ever become Kirk again. So, for all you dreamers out there, sorry to burst your bubble.

ABNORMALITY: 7 STUPIDITY: 8 ENTERTAINMENT: 7

190
The Spidler Site
www.angelfire.com/in4/spidler

This is an odd page where you are greeted by a very angry cat.

Afterward, you are introduced to miscellaneous absurdities, including how to take care of your very own giant pet squid, the mystery behind the photograph of the "Irish Horse," and, of course, the "Dancing Strawberries"!

COMMENTS: This site is kind of amusing—at least to me it was. I am baffled at the "mystery" of the "Irish Horse." Why is he there in the field? What are those cows doing there? And what is that little round black thing on the ground in the far right corner of the picture? Like the success of Justin Timberlake, this remains a mystery.

ABNORMALITY: 8 STUPIDITY: 9 ENTERTAINMENT: 8

189

Lunatic's Fridge
www.lunaticsfridge.co.uk

On this site, you'll find nothing but a white page with a handle along the left side (it's supposed to be a refrigerator, I'm assuming) with a bunch of random crap on the page. Among the things on the page are a picture of an apple, a cartoon of a rapping beetle, and a picture of an electric oven range abandoned on the side of the road. And, this lunatic doesn't use fridge magnets to attach them. He uses tape and gum! Oh, the horrors! The horrors!

COMMENTS: This sounds like what Cletus the Slack-Jawed Yokel from *The Simpsons* would put on his fridge (you know, the one outside the mobile home). All I know is all the crap on this fridge is enough to put even a yokel to shame. Do yourself a favor: if you do visit this page, spend about ten seconds there, if that.

ABNORMALITY: 9 STUPIDITY: 9 ENTERTAINMENT: 6

188

The Daily Blah
members.lycos.co.uk/dailyblah

It's more obvious that this site is fictional than it is that professional wrestlers are merely a bunch of semiathletic horrible actors.

Here, you'll find a plethora of products, news stories, and various other pieces of material in this fabricated, Web-based magazine. One product that is available in the classified ads is the "Lava Lamp of Doom" with an "angry clown" base. It's a not-so-kid-friendly night light that steals your soul. Also available is the "electro roof" for blasting those pesky freeloading birds with 240 volts. As an added bonus, the electro roof "also acts as a Santa deterrent." This site is pretty well done, and you might want to come back again to check if they have updated it.

COMMENTS: This is more proof that people have way too much time on their hands. Next thing you know, somebody will make a page about mutant zombie ninjas from the planet Jupiter! Well, now that I think about it, there probably is something out there to that effect…and that just scares me.

ABNORMALITY: 8 STUPIDITY: 9 ENTERTAINMENT: 8

187

Tailor of a Cat
www.petoffice.co.jp/catprin/english

We've seen some weird pet outfits (like Poodle Disguise Kits, number 118), but when it comes to sheer scariness, Tailor of a Cat takes the cake. Half of the site is in Japanese, while the other half is in broken English, with tons of creepy drawings and pictures throughout the site. So, what is Tailor of a Cat? "CAT PRIN – the tailor for a cat you know – it is- fact which will become clearer than former if cat has clothes on." Confused yet? It gets worse. "Don't you doubt? Although I want to dress with dress extravagant with my cat, doesn't a cat dislike having clothes on?" Cats do dislike having clothes on—especially these. The outfits for cats here include frog hats, rainbow rabbit ears, a leopard hat with ears and a scarf, and even a necktie set.

COMMENTS: Why do all the Japanese things seem so weird? It's probably just cultural perception. What's normal to them is weird to us, and vice versa. If I were Japanese, I would probably have found it really weird when all of our serious twenty-four-hour news channels aired nothing but coverage of Paris Hilton going to jail for hours on end.

ABNORMALITY: 10 STUPIDITY: 8 ENTERTAINMENT: 8

186

Rate My Mullet.com
www.ratemymullet.com

This is a site about mullets and the people who have them. You know, that crazy haircut, short in the front, very long in the back.

From the Asian midget who is obsessed with basketball to the regular ol' mullet man, this site has a bunch of very stupid people with stupid-looking mullets, as well as a numeric rating code for them. There are also sections for "senior mullets," "junior mullets," and the mullet store where you can purchase products to help keep mullets in style (wait a minute…they're already out of style). There are also short biographies of the people who have the mullets.

COMMENTS: Man, oh man, when are people gonna learn! Mullets went out of style years ago. Stop obsessing over them! It's not like they're cool. If anything, they're something to be ashamed of. Well, all this site has done is provided us with a lot of "hair don'ts" to laugh at and make fun of.

ABNORMALITY: 7 STUPIDITY: 9 ENTERTAINMENT: 6

185

The Mostly Ruthless Destruction of the 1981 Dodge Omni

www.sixfoot6.com/omni

This is a story about how at the end of one summer five friends decided to destroy a car. Don't ask why. On this site, you can find a detailed description of how this ugly Chrysler car was destroyed. They started off by analyzing the car and learning its capabilities. After that, they completely beat the crap out of it. After several off-road driving tests through rough terrain and mud, this little car was forced to suffer further indignities: the "Side Impact Test," where a shopping cart loaded with a large person was slammed into the car's door; the "Heat Endurance Test" using a blowtorch; and the ultimate degradation of "The Sledgehammer Test."

COMMENTS: Now my question is this: who would want to destroy a car? Why not just sell it for parts? Anyway, this is a somewhat funny humor site that you'll enjoy if you like seeing things being destroyed.

ABNORMALITY: 7 STUPIDITY: 9 ENTERTAINMENT: 7

184

The World According to Porcupine

worldaccordingtoporcupine.com

It's all of the confusing mysteries in this world explained by a porcupine named Porcupine Smith. Here, you'll find a bunch of odd stuff, all supposedly written or spoken by a porcupine, or at least themed around the porcupine. There is poetry, photographs, and a drawing of Alfred E. Newman from *MAD* magazine. There are even philosophies of the porcupines, all available on this page for your enlightenment. That is, enlightening if you actually believe that a rodent with needles sticking out of it can enlighten you.

COMMENTS: This site has as much wit, wisdom, and substance as an episode of *American Idol* without any nasty comments by the evil Simon Cowell. (But, gee, gosh, and golly, isn't that Paula Abdul ever so nice?)

ABNORMALITY: 8 STUPIDITY: 7 ENTERTAINMENT: 5

183

Hatchoo
www.hatchoo.com

Do you…Hatchoo? These Dutch web comedians created Hatchoo! (named for "the Dutch sound of someone sneezing") as a parody of the ultra-popular Yahoo! website. Everything is meant to be a parody, even the FAQ, which has questions like, "Have you been sued for making a parody yet?" "No, but now we're operating in the USA, [so] that can happen any minute!" Sections of Hatchoo! include Spammers Anonymous, an Internet support group for people who can't stop sending spam emails, and a section for the "Mersedes-Renz," the "first affordable stuntcar" that's designed to flip over and crash. ("We pay celebrities to die in our cars" is a "company secret.")

COMMENTS: This is a pretty funny parody site. The one thing I would have added is a Hatchoo! Personals section. You could have profiles for people so hideous and horrible in every way, looking for love.

ABNORMALITY: 8 STUPIDITY: 8 ENTERTAINMENT: 8

182

Blue Screen of Death Gallery
daimyo.org/bsod

This page is a gallery of yet another sight Windows users are familiar with: the infamous Blue Screen of Death, or BSoD. The screen that basically says, "Just give up now and restart your computer." There are pictures of the BSoD in various public places, including a McDonald's register, billboards, Circuit City, and even in the middle of New York City. There are also odd screens of death, including a BSoD in a jar, and even the rare Red Screen of Death. There are also non-BSoD error messages on other devices, including the Sony PSP and a computer/TV hybrid system.

COMMENTS: Why did Microsoft have to make error messages so complicated? Why not just say, "Your computer is screwed up, restart it now"? Instead of "Error 404: Page Not Found," why not just say, "The Internet isn't working, fix it"? Bill Gates must have a fetish for weird error messages.

ABNORMALITY: 6 STUPIDITY: 8 ENTERTAINMENT: 7

181

Hoppy's Bag
members.tripod.com/weevilnet

Feed the walrus, make a *Star Trek* script, and see the "filosofy" (that's meant to be spelled that way) are all things you can do on this odd site.

Basically, it's a bunch of gibberish mish-mashed together in order to amuse you. Now whether it will or not depends on your personality, but I will say for sure that it is stupid, and that you will become less intelligent if you choose to view it. Don't say I didn't warn you.

COMMENTS: I wish I had the browser plug-in so I could feed the walrus. I wonder what that would be like in real life, feeding a walrus. Maybe I can watch a zookeeper feed a walrus sometime. Or, I could always watch the portions of the old *Roseanne* show where she eats.

ABNORMALITY: 9 STUPIDITY: 9 ENTERTAINMENT: 7

180

The Love Calculator
www.lovecalculator.com

Ever wondered what your chances of a relationship are with another specific person? Ever wanted to play matchmaker and see how it turns out? This site lets you do both.

Here, you enter in two names and the love calculator will give a short paragraph, along with a percentage number telling how likely a relationship is between the two. Try any two names, and you'll get something. Whether it'll be accurate or even sane is not guaranteed, but still.

COMMENTS: I personally like to enter in the names of celebrities. For example, I tried Bill Clinton and Janet Reno. Not too successful, obviously; a 28 percent match. On the flip side, I got very similar results with Bill and Hillary. Coincidence? I think not.

ABNORMALITY: 6 STUPIDITY: 7 ENTERTAINMENT: 8

179

Seven Peas
www.sevenpeas.com

I've seen a lot of weird stuff, but this is up there with the weirdest.

It's a picture of seven peas with smiley faces and a peapod in the background. The peas keep moving around to the tune of some relaxing guitar music. That's it. That's totally it. What's stupid is the fact that it makes absolutely no sense at all. I mean, why would peas be floating around? What force would cause them to do so? And why peas? Why not carrots or sprouts?

COMMENTS: It's a shame there are sites like these on the Internet; they're wasting space. On the other hand, I'm having quite a nice time watching peas floating around to the tune of a guitar, so I'll stop complaining. Ahh…so relaxing.

ABNORMALITY: 10 STUPIDITY: 9 ENTERTAINMENT: 6

178

YPL Insensitivity Cards
www.iamlost.com/features/ecards

Most cards you buy for unpleasant events try to pussyfoot around the bad nature of the situation: "Sorry for your loss," "Hope you feel better." *These* cards, on the other hand, are in your face and insensitive. "Our wide selection allows you to mock the unhappy circumstances, embarrassing failures, and painful experiences of a friend or relative, and to share that derision with almost anyone on planet Earth through the wonders of email."

The cards are a free service, so being unbelievably offensive doesn't cost you a penny here. Examples of cards include a bandaged up cartoon boy with half an arm in a cast, which says, "Maybe next time you'll listen," and a group of people drinking beer with the text, "At least one of us still has a license!"

COMMENTS: I like these cards. They cut the crap and get right to the point. You don't see that too much nowadays. Everybody's so worried about being offensive there's no room for free and honest expression anymore. Like cartoons, for example. A lot of them used to have tons of innuendo and suggestive themes in them. Now, cartoons are bland and boring. But I digress. If you want a card that doesn't mince words, look no further than YPL Insensitivity Cards.

ABNORMALITY: 8 STUPIDITY: 8 ENTERTAINMENT: 8

177 The World's Funniest Budgie
www.worldsfunniestbudgie.homestead.com

This site is home to a parakeet comedian named Victor.

Here, you can hear audio clips from Victor's latest performances, as well as some funny jokes (like "'Twas the Night before Christmas: the Redneck Version"). You can view funny video clips (proof that he is for real), Victor's story, and my favorite section: "Free Stuff!" Free stuff is always cool!

COMMENTS: I just don't get how parakeets can understand the concept of humor. They're birds, for crying out loud! Monkeys, maybe, but birds?! It's a mad, mad world out there, I tell ya.

ABNORMALITY: 8 STUPIDITY: 7 ENTERTAINMENT: 7

---

176 Celebrity Veg
www.celebrityveg.4t.com/index2.htm

Ever seen a vegetable that looks like a celebrity? If not, head over to this site for a personal first.

Basically, you can see several vegetables that look like celebrities, and vice versa. Although almost all of them are carrots, they're still fun to see. Check out the carrot that looks like Homer Simpson and the picture that proves the site creator's friend Chris bears an eerie resemblance to the orange vegetable.

COMMENTS: Goodness, what's next? Cucumbers that look like Jay Leno? Of course, cucumbers are far from proportionate; it would take three of them just to make up his chin.

ABNORMALITY: 9 STUPIDITY: 8 ENTERTAINMENT: 7

175

Human Thumb Quiz
quizstop.com/askthumb.htm

This site attempts to answer this question: What would your lover look like as a human thumb?

Okay, so maybe it's not the most pressing question that needs attention. Still, this short quiz is worth your time if you ever wondered what your significant other would look like as a body part, or if you're just into stupid quizzes. Answer some basic questions about body type: plump/slim, and attitude: conservative/wild, and out comes a sketch of your thumb-mate.

COMMENTS: This is a website that deserves to exist less than Kid Rock and Pamela Anderson's relationship. Do any of us need to know how somebody would look like as a thumb? Maybe something like "Which *Friends* friend are you?" or "Which *Simpsons* character are you?" but not anything that has to do with a body part.

ABNORMALITY: 8 STUPIDITY: 9 ENTERTAINMENT: 5

174

Whoops! Movie Goofs
www.jonhs.com/moviegoofs

This is a site full of bloopers from movies. This site catalogs such slips as buildings appearing in a film set years before the building was constructed and microphones appearing in the background of a shot.

You can see examples of bloopers from movies such as *Ace Ventura: Pet Detective*, *Halloween*, and even *Saving Private Ryan*. Such bloopers include the movie *Pay It Forward*, where Haley Joel Osment is supposed to be eleven, yet he is in the seventh grade. He should really be in only fifth or sixth grade. Not the biggest blooper, but it still counts.

COMMENTS: It's funny to see what mistakes were made in movies, particularly the really serious ones. It adds a tone of humor to the movies when they're so darn grim. This site deserves a place among your favorites, especially if you're a film fan or, better yet, a film critic.

ABNORMALITY: 6 STUPIDITY: 8 ENTERTAINMENT: 9

173   Darth Vader's Homepage
members.tripod.com/darthvader_7

This is the dark lord of the Sith's first attempt at HTML, so bear with him here.

Here, you'll find a lot of personal info on Darth Vader. There are two funny parts about this site. One is that he's all-powerful, but that his page is crappy as heck. The other aspect that makes it funny is that he just sounds like a normal guy, when he's actually an evil supervillain. The website is a bit small, but it's under construction, so expect more soon.

COMMENTS: This is proof that the evil Dark Jedi Master isn't too adept with the Web. I suspect that maybe he shot some force lightning and used his lightsaber on his computer when he got frustrated making this page, or when the satellite dish on his Star Destroyer didn't work. Listen to me; I'm making the *Star Wars* universe sound like a DirectTV commercial.

ABNORMALITY: 5 STUPIDITY: 7 ENTERTAINMENT: 6

---

172   The Church of the Gerbil
www.corg.org/main.htm

This is yet another "church" that believes we should "spread the holy word of the sacred gerbil."

Sacred gerbils? Yes, gerbils. Here, you'll find all things gerbil, including the Ten Condiments (no, not the Ten Commandments, the Ten Condiments). The Condiments are profound statements like "Thou shall have no fuzzy creatures before me" and "Thou shall not microwave." Why we can't microwave gerbils is something I'm not sure of, but I'm thinking I might break that rule. Soon. Get thee to a pet store!

COMMENTS: This is probably the stupidest church I've ever seen. Who would worship fuzzy little rodents? Not me, that's for sure. What's more, they're carrying out a "Holy War" on rabbits! Rabbits don't deserve to be enemies of anybody! I guess I'll never understand the twisted minds behind The Church of the Gerbil. Seriously, though, this is a funny web page that I would recommend taking a look at. Who knows? You might just become a convert.

ABNORMALITY: 8 STUPIDITY: 9 ENTERTAINMENT: 8

171

MC Hawking
www.mchawking.com

Yo. What. Is. Up. My. Ho. Mies. It's MC Hawking, and he's coming to pimp out all the competing theories! For those of you who ain't down wit the Hawkman, MC Hawking is the creation of a computer programmer who uses physicist Stephen Hawking's synthesized voice to make rap albums. Is this for real, you ask? "Of course it's real!" However, "Professor Hawking had absolutely nothing to do with the creation of this site or the songs on it." What up wit dat, posers? The MC Hawking discography shows a strange mix of songs on his albums, with titles like "All My Shootin's Be Drive-Bys" and "Crazy as F*ck" alongside "Dark Matter," "Black Holes," and "A Brief Dissertation on Gravitational Entropy, Quantum Cosmology, and the Anthropic Principle." Try saying that five times fast. There are also poorly Photoshopped pictures with Hawking alongside prominent rappers such as Eminem and Run D.M.C. I be pimpin' that shiz-it, yo!

COMMENTS: This site has torn my soul in two. The one thing I absolutely despise, rap music, paired with a prominent figure in theoretical physics, one of my favorite subjects to study—even on my own time. It be straight up wrong, yo—more wrong than being whisked past the event horizon into the singularity of a super massive black hole. I ain't down wit dat! In any case, I may not like rap, but MC Hawking can chill in my crib anytime. Word.

ABNORMALITY: 9 STUPIDITY: 9 ENTERTAINMENT: 9

170

The Keepers of the Lists
www.keepersoflists.org

This is a site that, quite simply, has a ton of lists.

This site includes "Top 37 Signs You've Eaten Too Much" (I don't think you need a list for that), "Top 19 Reasons Why Goths Rock" (don't ask), and my personal favorite, "Top 44 Things You'd Like to See Done to the Members of *NSYNC" (I can think of more than forty-four…). There are a ton of lists just like these on virtually every topic imaginable. There's also a way to browse their previous archives.

COMMENTS: There are more lists here than the number of movies that Kevin Bacon has been in (for info regarding that topic, see number 490). The lists definitely have some humorous ideas on them, and some of them are quite clever.

ABNORMALITY: 6 STUPIDITY: 8 ENTERTAINMENT: 9

169

This site attempts to answer the question, "What is a real car?"

According to the site, a real car is a car that's beat up, is partially broken, has high mileage on it, or is just a piece of crap. Having a '91 model car today with broken AC would be a good example, or an '84 model with the windshield cracked and the heating shot. Anyway, this site has examples of these "real cars," pictures, and info on how you can get one. My dad had a real car. It was a '72 Maverick Grabber with just one bucket seat and no front bumper. It was kind of like one of those clown cars; he would take it to college parties and stuff as many people as humanly possible inside.

COMMENTS: Maybe they should make a "Cars Gone Bad" series. You know, like the "Girls Gone Wild" series? It would be pretty much the same, except not as many drunk girls flashing people and making fools out of themselves. Wait a minute…is that a good thing or a bad thing?

ABNORMALITY: 7 STUPIDITY: 7 ENTERTAINMENT: 7

168

Searching for the Mars-Earth Connection

mars-earth.com/cydonia-egypt

This person has a few nuts and bolts loose in his head.

The creator is trying to find proof for his theory that we are descended from a technologically advanced race from Mars who migrated here thousands of years ago after a cataclysmic event on the red planet. OK, it sounds like this guy has watched one too many '50s B-movies. On the site, you can find evidence including ancient Egyptian artifacts, which "proves" that the Martians were the first civilization to inhibit this Earth.

COMMENTS: I don't think anybody on this planet is from Mars, with the possible exception of Richard Simmons. Actually, I take that back; he's more of a Frankenstein-type creation gone bad. Yeah, from the way he behaves, that sounds about right.

ABNORMALITY: 9 STUPIDITY: 8 ENTERTAINMENT: 7

Reverse Speech
www.reversespeech.com

We've all heard of the subliminal messages of reverse speech on rock and roll albums. (Remember the whole "Paul is dead" thing with the Beatles?) But David John Oates, an Australian "twenty-year veteran" of the so-called reverse speech field, claims that understanding reverse speech can help us reveal hidden thought patterns and enhance therapeutic treatments. The testimonials for Reverse Speech are dicey, with endorsements from little-known psychologists and PhDs. *The Daily Texan* says that "Oates is downright evangelical when it comes to the practical applications of his research." And that's a good thing how?

COMMENTS: Another "special" technique that's guaranteed to fix all the problems in our lives. Of course, the only way to learn how to decode Reverse Speech is through expensive training courses and software. Why am I not surprised?

ABNORMALITY: 9 STUPIDITY: 8 ENTERTAINMENT: 6

166

The Original Mojave Phone Booth Site
deuceofclubs.com/moj/mojave.htm

"Welcome to the *Original* Mojave Phone Booth Site!" Original? Does that mean there's more than one? The story began when some guy was at a club seeing a rock band called Girl Trouble. A member of the band gave him a magazine to read while they were hanging out together. In the magazine, there was a letter that gave the number of an old phone booth in the Mojave Desert used during mining operations during World War II. This guy started calling the phone booth every day for a month, until a woman who worked as a miner answered. The rest of the story is basically an obsession with this phone booth. He even visited it once (on the way to Burning Man, at that), and left a "Girl Trouble" sticker "in honor of the band that started it all." There's even an opportunity to buy your own phone booth!

COMMENTS: The Mojave Phone Booth Site proves that strange obsessions that lead guys on a cross-country road trip make for a very interesting website. Even if you don't like the site, at least now you know where to go if you want to buy a phone booth.

ABNORMALITY: 9 STUPIDITY: 8 ENTERTAINMENT: 7

165   Silly Star Trek Obsession
allyourtrekarebelongto.us/contents.html

Ever thought there was something, well, weird going on between Kirk and Spock, or Kirk and any woman on the show? For those of you who think (or know) so, this site is for you.

This site is full of '60s-style *Star Trek* innuendo, as you see pictures of original *Star Trek* episodes, including a picture of Kirk looking at a shirtless Spock, with a speech bubble saying how good Spock looks. Other examples of this humorous text must truly be seen to be believed.

COMMENTS: Geez! Looking back, this show was pretty racy for its day. Back in those days, having the F word in a movie gave it an X rating.

ABNORMALITY: 9   STUPIDITY: 8   ENTERTAINMENT: 8

---

164   Big Heads in Yahoo News
www.jwz.org/bigheads

According to Jamie Zawinski, "I often scan through the wire service photos on Yahoo News, and over the years I started noticing a really strange trend. Many of the photos follow the same form: a picture of a person in the foreground, and on the background, a GIANT HEAD…was it always the same photographer? No, it turns out, it's not. So my best guess at this point is that one of the photo editors just has a GIANT HEAD fetish of some kind." To prove this unusual theory, there are several pictures from Yahoo! News stories. Indeed, there are many giant heads in the pictures—Elmo, the Mona Lisa, and Howard Dean are just a few of the giant heads shown (although Howard Dean has a big head to begin with). There are literally dozens of Yahoo! News pictures from 2004 alone—all with abnormally inflated heads.

COMMENTS: At first this seemed hard to believe. No news organization can have that many huge head pictures, right? But the evidence here is pretty solid. Strangely, there aren't many big head pictures in Yahoo! News today. Did they fire their photo editors after they realized their odd obsession? Or did they simply stop without noticing it was even happening? We may never know.

ABNORMALITY: 9   STUPIDITY: 7   ENTERTAINMENT: 8

163 Canadian World Domination
cwd.ptbcanadian.com

Canadians taking over the world. Canadians? Now I don't know what to say.

This web page is home to the efforts of our northern neighbors to rule the planet. They have a detailed plan, including communications (launching a satellite to destroy all non-Canadian news stations), then the troop deployment (distribute free beer to those questioning mobilization…how convenient…and how tasty), and the invasion itself. The site also has what the predicted cartography of Canada will be after the invasion (including "Land du Beaver" and the province of Molson) and much more.

COMMENTS: With all due respect, guys, I don't think you Canucks are going to be taking over the world any time soon. We've got enough problems already; we don't need to deal with a Canadian conspiracy for world domination through the use of such Maple Leaf icons like back bacon and hockey pucks. Still, this site is pretty darn funny.

ABNORMALITY: 8   STUPIDITY: 8   ENTERTAINMENT: 8

---

162 Compendium of Abandoned Shopping Lists
www.redhotscott.co.uk/shoppinglists

Ever wondered what happens to those shopping lists people toss at the end of a supermarket trip? Chances are they end up in this guy's "Compendium of Abandoned Shopping Lists," available for all to see here. "This site has been inspired by the kind of people who abandon their shopping list at the end of a trip to the supermarket. I collect their shopping lists. If you're American you probably refer to these as grocery lists, which strikes me as a bit strange because not all the items on the lists are groceries. Anyhow, I won't worry myself about it if you won't." Those Brits have to rag on us for everything…

COMMENTS: This site has made me more conscious of what I do with my lists when I'm done shopping. The last thing I want is my shopping list ending up in the hands of somebody like this guy. Note to self: throw my shopping lists away in my garbage.

ABNORMALITY: 8   STUPIDITY: 8   ENTERTAINMENT: 7

161 Flat Earth Liberation Front
www.cca.org/woc/felfat/index.html

This is another site that is very, very odd. The mission of these zealots? They are "determined to fight the evil that has spoiled this once-great world, and to bring humanity back to the ancient utopian state which it deserves."

The Front claims that Earth was once flat, and that the only way to understand Earth and the things that exist on it is to think "within the context of an entirely flat Earth." OK, I don't get it. Could somebody please explain what these psychos are saying?

COMMENTS: I'll believe that there's a government conspiracy to assassinate Leonardo DiCaprio before I'll believe any of the crap that this website has on it. I mean, scientists have proved many things. Einstein's theory of relativity, the benefits of exercise, and the fact that Al Gore is a robot are among the many valuable truths that science has verified. But the fact that Earth was once flat? Try again, fools.

ABNORMALITY: 9 STUPIDITY: 8 ENTERTAINMENT: 6

---

160 Lost Frog
lostfrog.org

This incredibly strange site begins with childlike writing and drawing seeking a lost frog named "Hopkin Green Frog." It also says, "P.S. I'll find my frog; who took my frog," as if to threaten the potential frognapper. From there, it's a descent into madness, covering comic books about missing frogs as well as various themed lost frog pictures. *Lord of the Rings*, tough bikers, error messages, Indiana Jones, lottery tickets, and CNN video are just a few of the images edited in this mad mosaic, all centered on an obsession with this lost frog. The frog even appears in crop circles and Soviet propaganda posters. There are dozens of these pictures, each one stranger and creepier than the one before.

COMMENTS: What is this whole lost frog thing supposed to be? Is it some kind of interpretive art thing? A subliminal message? Or is it just the work of some forlorn, highly disturbed guy who lost his frog? So many unanswered questions.

ABNORMALITY: 10 STUPIDITY: 8 ENTERTAINMENT: 8

159

Industrious Clock
www.albinoblacksheep.com/flash/clock.php

This is one interesting clock.

It displays the time via a unique way: a continuous rolling video of several boxes clustered together. Each box contains either a handwritten number or a video of the number being written by hand. The weird thing is that each number is written extremely fast, even to the second, so it keeps up with actual time. If you don't understand what I'm saying, visit the site for yourself.

COMMENTS: I'm not entirely sure what the purpose of the clock is, but what I want to know is this: Who is that person writing the numbers? Is it Calista Flockhart? It seems skinny enough. Then again, you can't see the hand quite well, so nobody but the person who wrote it can be sure. Another intensive and well done, but ultimately worthless, use of the Web. A digital watch from Burger King does the same thing with a lot less effort.

ABNORMALITY: 8 STUPIDITY: 6 ENTERTAINMENT: 6

158

Pregnant Bellymasks
www.bellymask.com

Being proud when you're pregnant is one thing; but what about buying a Pregnant Bellymask? "A bellymask is an heirloom sculpture created right on your pregnant torso in a simple one-hour process. Made of plaster gauze, it is an exact replica of your pregnant form. Women are making bellymasks as a celebration and honoring of the profound experience of creating human life." You can order a "Do-it-yourself" kit to help you make the bellymask, or you can have a mask-making session with Francine Krause, who runs this silly service.

COMMENTS: This seems a bit too weird. What will happen when the kid the mask was made for grows up? What will his or her friends think when the mom proudly shows them the bulging bellymask and tells them how wonderful it was to have her little baby inside it? One word: embarrassing. Especially for guys. I can only imagine the horror if my mom did something like that when I was born. Note to potential bellymask customers: think of the kid, and not yourself, if you decide to make this mad mold.

ABNORMALITY: 8 STUPIDITY: 8 ENTERTAINMENT: 5

157

The Incredible World of Navel Fluff
www.feargod.net/fluff.html

This guy has a museum of navel fluff, also known as navel lint.

Here, you can see his extensive collection of lint that he's obtained over the years displayed in large glass jars, as well as several 3D galleries (no confirmation on whether they actually are 3D). Inexplicably included are some views of scenic Washington state, a cow gallery, and much more.

COMMENTS: Now who would collect lint and then have the nerve to call it navel fluff? I don't know why, but I think he actually does attract more people with the term "navel fluff" rather than "navel lint."

ABNORMALITY: 9 STUPIDITY: 9 ENTERTAINMENT: 7

156

Stick Figure Fighting
www.stickpage.com/stickfights.html

This is one action-packed kung-fu video! The only thing that's *not* incredible about it is that the participants of the video are stick figures.

Here, you'll see one stick-figure man take out an army of ninja minions using flips, kicks, swords, and everything else imaginable to achieve total dominance. There are also a number of videos to check out, and you can actually play a game based on this video at a website described previously (see number 356).

COMMENTS: Now *this* is action. Too bad it's with stick figures; it would be simply incredible if it were normal people. Better than Jackie Chan. Better than Bruce Lee. Better than Arnold? No. The action doesn't stop for a second, and you'll get a kick (no pun intended) in some way or another from watching the video, whether it comes from amazement or laughter.

ABNORMALITY: 7 STUPIDITY: 6 ENTERTAINMENT: 8

155

Vector Park
www.vectorpark.com

These are a few games that make no sense at all; sometimes they are boring, slow, and stupid; sometimes they are a little fun; but they are not very useful.

The games are weird. One includes a person with a handheld telescope, where you click on various objects to view them, and click on them again to interact with them. Another game is where objects fall out of the sky, and then you can "hook" them onto a scale suspended in the sky. I know it sounds like it doesn't make sense, and believe me, it doesn't.

COMMENTS: These games are weird, but mildly fun for short moments. Kind of like a bear riding a unicycle—weird, but fun as heck. Anyway, these games may or may not be for you, but they're kind of fun to see just how different they are.

ABNORMALITY: 8 STUPIDITY: 7 ENTERTAINMENT: 7

154

Rent a Midget
www.rent-a-midget.com

If you Google the words "rent a midget," you will get 650,000 search results. This is just one of hundreds of places on the web where you can rent a tiny person for your next party, bar mitzvah, or bowling banquet. So what makes this one different from the others? For one, they claim to be "The #1 Midget Rental Service." Well, if nobody else claims that title, it must be true, right? (Actually, most of the other midget rental sites claim to be "number one.") Midgets available for rent include "Don," "Little Jon," "Dan," and "Drevon." There's a video of one of the midgets as an elf at a Christmas party, so you can see just how "high-quality" these small show-men are. This all sounds great, until you consider the price: "one hour of midget fun" is two hundred bucks. That's a thousand dollars for a five-hour party! They may be small people, but their prices sure aren't.

COMMENTS: This is a humanitarian outrage! I hope these midgets get their fair share of the outrageous profits this service must make. Otherwise, I may have to report them to the government. There must be some agency that prevents the unjust exploitation of these tiny troopers.

ABNORMALITY: 9 STUPIDITY: 8 ENTERTAINMENT: 6

153

Meat Mation
www.meatmation.com

If you're looking for a place to express your love of beef, pork, chicken, and other meat products, prepare to be disappointed. This site has nothing to do with meat at all, but rather "the amazingly disturbed photography of Stephanie Rose." And boy, is it ever disturbed. If you know Stephanie (which I hope you don't, for your sake), "then this page makes complete sense. If you don't know her, then play Freud and you should be able to figure her out quick enough." Freud, channeled through me, would say, "I think it's an unconscious fixation on the oral stage of child development, with an Electra complex centered on her father's love of carnivorous cuisine." Wasn't Freud a genius?

COMMENTS: Why do certain writers and artists have a penchant for such unsettling works? On the other hand, the idea of a man made of meat who eats his own family is kind of funny—in a very perverse sort of way. Maybe we all have a dark side that appreciates this kind of thing. The bottom line is that Meat Mation definitely will appeal to people who appreciate dark humor. Especially the dark meaty kind.

ABNORMALITY: 10 STUPIDITY: 9 ENTERTAINMENT: 8

152

The Bad Scary Place
www.silverladder.com/links/badscary/intro.htm

This is one disturbing website. Be careful, as this site claims: "44,931 people went in and never came back."

This is probably one of the top sites that I cannot do justice to by describing it with words alone. Imagine a number of disturbing, stupid, and downright weird objects, with some fancy HTML tying it all together. Sound like a decent explanation? It shouldn't; this page is downright psycho.

COMMENTS: Marilyn Manson is closer to normal than this site is (OK, maybe that's going a little too far). Want a better idea of the site? Okay, here it goes: one of the images is a picture of a guy with a huge hairdo with a caption that says "Clown Hatred." Frightening, yet strangely fascinating. Repulsive, yet compelling.

ABNORMALITY: 10 STUPIDITY: 9 ENTERTAINMENT: 7

151

SmilePop
www.flowgo.com

Yet another variety site with a ton of fun material.

Here, you can see SmilePop's take on the news and some great Flash videos (including one with an annoying singing bug that is a personal favorite of mine. I highly recommend it). There are forums on various weird topics, including one guy who doesn't really get the concept of Thanksgiving (the name kind of gives you a hint, buddy). And finally, a really cool feature: email free food to your friends!

COMMENTS: Plenty of fun. The Flash movies are good, and it sounds like there are some interesting topics of discussion going on in the forums (use caution if you intend to join; your IQ may suffer). Take your time here to observe all of the stuff that showcases our wonderful world of stupidity with lots of enthusiasm and verve.

ABNORMALITY: 8 STUPIDITY: 8 ENTERTAINMENT: 9

150

People Are Morons
people-are-morons.tripod.com

Let's face it, my friends; people are morons! (The sites listed in this book are ample evidence of that, now aren't they?)

This site contains some classic examples of moronity. Wait a minute…that's not a word! See! There's an example right there! *I'm* a moron! And I'll bet you are, too. You just have to think moronically. Anyway, this site has a section called "Darwin Awards," which describes deaths that were "innovatively moronic": a section called "Criminally Moronic," similar to Dumb Crooks; and some other random examples of human stupidity.

COMMENTS: I think there's a little bit of stupid in all of us. Whenever we watch dating shows, *The Real World*, or professional wrestling (although believe me, I know several very intelligent people who watch professional wrestling), it shows we're all slowly reverting back to Neanderthal stupidity, bit by stupid bit.

ABNORMALITY: 7 STUPIDITY: 9 ENTERTAINMENT: 8

149

How to Eat Rocks
www.vgg.com/tp/tp_030801_eatrocks.html

This is a beginner's guide to one of the finer arts in the culinary world: eating . . . rocks? "Greetings and welcome to this handy guide to eating rocks for beginners. A lot of this guide is just good ol' plain common sense, but you'd be surprised how often people make the same stupid mistakes eating rocks." I know the first mistake of eating rocks: eating rocks. The first piece of advice to prospective rock eaters is to "start small. I know, I know, you're excited, you want to eat a rock…but you simply must pace yourself!" The second "mistake" beginners make is that they don't clean the rocks, another result of "enthusiasm." Who would be stupid enough to be enthusiastic about this to begin with? The guide goes on to list more mistakes, and then at the end wishes you "good luck and bon appetit."

COMMENTS: There must be countless reasons to not eat rocks. They must taste horrible, not to mention the potential health hazards. Hopefully, you're not dumb enough to follow the advice of this guide. If you do, have fun trying to digest those rocks.

ABNORMALITY: 9 STUPIDITY: 10 ENTERTAINMENT: 7

148

Witwords
www.witwords.com

This site is a collection of short stories and various other objects of entertainment, but the real attraction of this site, in my opinion, is "the Fictionary." In it, you'll find invented combination words that mean a cross between the combined things, such as "absane" (a cross between absurd and insane) and "aquadextrous," (the ability to turn on the bathtub with your toes.) Are you "tanorexic" (obsessed with being tan)? Or are you simply a "fadnatic" (a person compelled to follow every fad that comes along?) Whatever your interest, there's a word for you.

COMMENTS: Where the words in the Fictionary come from is a mystery, much like why people like Eminem's music or why nudists exist. All I know is that the people who created the Fictionary are somewhat creative, in a weird sort of way. I mean, it takes a bit of skill to make any word up, much less a funny word.

ABNORMALITY: 8 STUPIDITY: 7 ENTERTAINMENT: 8

147

Rapper Dentist Daddy
www.rapperdentist.com

The concept of a rapping dentist daddy is sad enough. What's even sadder is that it appears to be the page of a real dentist.

This is the page of a cosmetic dentist who apparently specializes in putting the "bling-bling" in the smiles of rappers and wannabes. You can get a special "22 karat alloy" tooth with "high quality diamonds." Gee, I'll rush right over, doc! Locations, nearby attractions, and more are available, as well as information on how you can get hooked up with some of the wonderfully useful platinum teeth we associate with today's rap "artists." There are also links to hip-hop magazines and a rapping record label.

COMMENTS: If you want to be a cosmetic dentist who specializes in diamond teeth or whatever, that's fine. But don't set up your website so you look like a total poser. This dentist is embarrassing himself in front of the entire world. This page is funny to check out if you want a classic example of someone trying all too hard to be cool.

ABNORMALITY: 7 STUPIDITY: 9 ENTERTAINMENT: 5

146

Whimsical IceBox
www.whimsicalicebox.com

Here, once again (and again and again. What is it about the Internet that attracts these clowns?) are the mad ramblings of a couple of really weird guys.

On this page, you can see a lot of random senseless junk, all of which looks ridiculous, but is hilarious nonetheless. This site supposedly was started by "the world's most obscure comedy group." Let's hope they stay obscure, please. Random stuff includes a weather report and articles about when the Whimsical IceBox boys attended the Delaware Author's Day, which I'm guessing is some kind of convention. They probably caused a ruckus and got thrown out.

COMMENTS: This is crazier than the amount of money Bill Gates earns off of his bank-account interest. (Seriously, if you do the math, you'll hate the guy for receiving a ton of interest just for sitting on a pile of cash.) Still, it's funny, and that kind of excuses it from being stupid.

ABNORMALITY: 8 STUPIDITY: 9 ENTERTAINMENT: 8

145

Eat Babies
eatbabies.com

Remember Fat you-know-what in the *Austin Powers* movie series that liked eating babies? If you thought he was disgusting, wait until you see this site. It opens with several pictures that are just plain wrong: a baby covered in lettuce, along with an animation of a baby with an apple in his mouth turning into a hamburger and being eaten by a sharp set of teeth. They claim that they got the idea from "the chicken," who appears to be a leader of some kind for these wackos. The site contains baby recipes, polls, and fan art, one of which includes a "Baby Food Pyramid."

COMMENTS: Fortunately for everybody, this site is a joke. A pretty sick joke, but still a joke.

ABNORMALITY: 9 STUPIDITY: 8 ENTERTAINMENT: 8

144

Why I Will Never Have a Girlfriend
en.nothingisreal.com/wiki/ Why_I_Will_Never_Have_a_Girlfriend

Tristan Miller of the German Research Center for Artificial Intelligence has written a thesis of why he will never have a girlfriend, explaining, "I am convinced that the situation can be readily explained in purely scientific terms, using nothing more than demographics and some elementary statistical calculus." And he wonders why he doesn't have a girlfriend. He insists that his standards are not too high, and proceeds to narrow down the demographics (using advanced mathematical formulae, of course), and finally arrives at a potential pool of 18,276 women who are compatible with him. That seems like a high number, but he reasons that he would have to go on a blind date every week for 3,493 weeks before he would find a potential match. He ends by giving his email address, and tells women who are "deluded enough to think that you and I have a chance together" that they can give him a try.

COMMENTS: Words aren't adequate to describe how sad this guy is. Besides the fact that he's obviously an egotistical jerk looking for the perfect woman (and nobody's perfect), reducing women to statistics doesn't exactly paint a sensitive and caring picture of him.

ABNORMALITY: 8 STUPIDITY: 9 ENTERTAINMENT: 7

143

The Official Steps Vegetables Site
www.cordle.net/stepsvegetables

This is a site about a British singing group who were turned into vegetables.

Here, you can learn all about them, including how they originated, the story of how they got stolen, and the quest to get them back. This nutty British site chronicles reported sightings of the vegetables (or is it the band itself?) and invites you to make your own vegetable creation using a band member.

COMMENTS: I could write a lengthy thesis on the varied beard-trimming patterns of Amish furniture makers easier than I could figure out the reason for this site. I mean, I just don't understand singing vegetables. But I suppose if they want to stay as vegetables, they can. Anyway, the Steps Vegetables website is weird, yet it has this strange appeal, kind of like freak shows.

ABNORMALITY: 9 STUPIDITY: 8 ENTERTAINMENT: 7

142

For Sale by Mental Patient
www.total.net/~fishnet

This site features items for sale—by a patient in a mental institution. "I am Mental. I am a Patient. I like to sell things!" Simple concept.

Here, you can buy a number of items that obviously prove that the maker either is a mental patient or should be. A "Pocket Urinator" (a small pet mouse); "Ludwig Van Beethoven," a musician who can play almost any song imaginable in a funky tune (a cell phone with unique rings); and a "Barkless Tomato" (don't ask) are among the objects for sale.

COMMENTS: I think this guy is more unstable than Anne Heche. The objects for sale are ridiculous, senseless, and useless. This site might just cause you to become institutionalized if you linger too long.

ABNORMALITY: 8 STUPIDITY: 10 ENTERTAINMENT: 7

141

Skinema.com
www.skinema.com

No, this site is not about cheesy skin flicks. It is about skin and movies, though. Combine dermatology and cinema and you get "skinema." Besides "skinema" being the most God-awful attempt at a joke I have ever heard in my life, this site has pictures of famous celebrities and movie characters who don't have much hair on their heads ("Why is hair loss considered evil?"), as well as actors who have had complexion problems in movies. Examples range from the bald-headed Mike Myers as Dr. Evil to Elijah Wood in *Lord of the Rings* who had some very minor acne (very, very minor), right down to the bumps on Bill Cosby's face. There are also details on the "Skinnies," awards for best and worst skin conditions as featured in the movies.

COMMENTS: Celebrity skin ailments are a subject that I would rather not talk about. Some things just are too outrageous and unbelievable to be entertaining, like an episode of *Elimidate* or Carmen Electra's acting career. But, if you want to see warts of a rock star or acne on an actor, this is the place to go.

ABNORMALITY: 9 STUPIDITY: 8 ENTERTAINMENT: 6

140

Reality Syndicate
www.reality-syndicate.com

A variety site with a very, very odd twist. "Reality" is in the eye of the beholder. So is humor, and I beheld none. There are some long, lame articles that really belabor their points. A woman was charged with perjury for testifying in a flaming skirt. Why perjury, you say? Because a man in the same situation would be a "liar, liar pants on fire." Very stupid joke, very stupid site. Here, you can also see a weird word, an unusual article, stupid art, boring films, and, unfortunately, much more. One of the few entertaining features of the site is a funny video telling how to drive a big black pickup truck, with a French songstress crooning along.

COMMENTS: A lot of weird stuff on this website. Almost as weird as the fact that former MTV VJ "Downtown" Julie Brown continues to find employment. No, wait, nothing could be *that* strange. "Wubba wubba wubba"? Get her off the tube, please!

ABNORMALITY: 8 STUPIDITY: 9 ENTERTAINMENT: 8

139

IShouldBeWorking.com
www.ishouldbeworking.com/panicins.htm

Shouldn't you be working?

Okay, maybe not. But still, this is a great site for those who need a little workday diversion, but still want to look busy if the boss checks up on them. Simply browse through the site's extensive library and enjoy. When the boss approaches, hit the "Panic Button" feature and hit the panic button in the upper left-hand corner. The panic button will immediately switch your screen to a site that looks like legitimate work.

COMMENTS: This is really creative! It's one of those little perks that make something that would be otherwise ordinary great, much like the "buy a vowel" option on *Wheel of Fortune*, or the hydraulics on those low-rider cars that bounce up and down. Gee, I love those cars. And I love vowels.

ABNORMALITY: 6 STUPIDITY: 8 ENTERTAINMENT: 8

138

JustAddBrains.com
www.justaddbrains.com

These are some forum and discussion pages with a ton of hilarious content: "A rich aroma of satire, humor, and good old ranting." From general rants (what genius thought up the idea of drawing targets like bull's-eyes and crosses on World War I biplanes) to a do-it-yourself storybook where one person starts a story out with some lines, then the next poster adds another few, and so on, there is much to savor. The best part about this is that if you want to post your own stupidity, no sign-up or money is required!

COMMENTS: One of the rantings was that we supposedly sent tobacco to the countries that lost World War II to addict them to American cigarettes. I don't believe it's true, but it makes sense. I still don't get why people smoke. Sure, spend more than twenty or thirty bucks a carton to inhale carcinogens and kill yourself. Makes sense to me.

ABNORMALITY: 6 STUPIDITY: 7 ENTERTAINMENT: 8

137

The Dork Pages
www.pdrpip.com/nowse/dork.html

If you're looking for ultimate examples of horrible taste, this is the site to visit.

There are several sections on this site, featuring photos of dorky, weird things, mostly from the '80s. In the "records" section, see E.T. The Extra-Terrestrial and Michael Jackson in the same photo (that's Michael Jackson *before* the plastic surgeries), along with a photo of people dancing on carpet squares. Also find *Willie Jackson-E.S.P.*, a freaky album whose cover features a lady in exercise gear bending over a crystal ball. Another feature is "postcards," with photos from different locales such as the "Tourist City Motel" (all rooms equipped with TVs and carpeted floors!).

COMMENTS: Why Jacko and E.T. are in the same photo is a mystery to me. I would imagine that E.T. would run away screaming, "Must phone home! Must phone home! Psycho singer on the loose." The lovable alien looks content enough at his side, however. It really makes me wonder if Jacko isn't from another planet. That might explain things.

ABNORMALITY: 9 STUPIDITY: 9 ENTERTAINMENT: 8

136

Sheila Moss, Humor Columnist
www.humorcolumnist.com/

This is a page that's home to a "skilled" humor columnist.

There are a number of things on this website to keep you busy, from Sheila's mildly amusing personal takes on various subjects to semi-humorous cartoons to a whole section dedicated to fireflies. Now, this site is pretty, but why fireflies? Once again, this site proves that anyone can pass for "humorous" when the content is put on the Web.

COMMENTS: One of Sheila's columns was on a thing called Spamguard that's been put in place by various email providers. Her take is that Spamguard can do almost anything for us, much like the *Saturday Night Live* parody of Al Gore's famed "lockbox" from the 2000 election. Was there anything it couldn't do? I have a hard time remembering.

ABNORMALITY: 5 STUPIDITY: 7 ENTERTAINMENT: 8

135

Antitomato.com
www.antitomato.com/index.cfm

Why do people hate certain things so much? Why can't people just coexist with a juicy red vegetable?

This time, the humble tomato is the victim of prejudice in this site advocating everything anti-tomato. There are anti-tomato facts such as the fact that tomatoes don't make ketchup (ketchup is 60 percent sugar), anti-tomato stories like a person who tripped and fell on a tomato (it's your fault, buddy…), and much, much more.

COMMENTS: This is one website where I sympathize with their cause. I hate tomatoes! They are a foul-tasting vegetable, which I wouldn't eat if they were the last food on Earth. Tomatoes are stupid. Maybe I should join this club. I never realized how much I hate tomatoes.

ABNORMALITY: 7 STUPIDITY: 8 ENTERTAINMENT: 8

134

The Brothers Grinn
www.brothersgrinn.com

This is yet another variety site with a ton of material that's best described as odd, in a fairy-tale-parody sort of way. Hence, the name, I guess.

Here, you can see a bunch of cool stuff, including a full-length parody of *The Lord of the Rings*, which I must say is pretty funny. You can find more at this "home of Chicken Soup for the Soulless," including a horoscope with a twist, a reader's forum known as Monkeybrains, and much, much more.

COMMENTS: You might be wondering what the twist is on the horoscope. Well, let's just say that my "Chinese vegetable horoscope" told me I'm an "artistic carrot" who could be a priest or a politician. Interesting description, no? I wonder what Angelina Jolie would be. She'd probably be the "tattooed ragweed of death who survived being married to Billy Bob Thornton."

ABNORMALITY: 8 STUPIDITY: 8 ENTERTAINMENT: 8

133

Finger Jousting
www.fingerjoust.com

"Finger jousting is a sport where two consenting players square off in an attempt to prod their opponent with their lancing (right) index finger before the opposing player can." Consenting is an issue here? Does that mean people have tried to force their finger jousting on others? The origin of finger jousting is a mystery, but "some historians believe" that finger jousting was started in ancient Israel, where it was called "Finger Spearing." There is supposedly evidence for this in one of the apocryphal (unofficial) books of the Bible called the Book of Phalanges. Sounds like keeping that one out was a good choice. You can see the rulebook of Finger Jousting, browse through Finger Jousting news, and even apply for membership in the Federation. You'd better start practicing now if you want to beat the pros.

COMMENTS: With real jousting, I can understand the interest. Seeing two people trying to whack each other with long poles reminds me of knights in armor, or those old pirate movies. And everybody knows that pirates are awesome (as shown by the Church of the Flying Spaghetti Monster, number 212). But finger jousting must make people look like idiots.

ABNORMALITY: 8 STUPIDITY: 9 ENTERTAINMENT: 7

132

Cats in Sinks
catsinsinks.com

"What is Cats in Sinks? It's obvious. It's about cats. And kittens. Who like sinks. And basins." A site that gets right to the point. I like it already. It's as simple as it sounds. You're shown a picture of a cat in a sink or basin. Click "Show me another cat in a sink!" and you'll get another picture. There are countless types of cats—thin ones, fat ones, white ones, black ones (I sound like Dr. Seuss now) in bathroom sinks, bathtubs, and basins. Some of the cats look very comfortable in their sinks. Others look confused or suspicious. Still others look contemplative. So simple, yet with so much depth…

COMMENTS: Those owners better not have forced them into those sinks. It's blatant animal abuse! The media should be notified immediately of this outrage! OK, so maybe it's not that bad. But I still don't understand Cats in Sinks.

ABNORMALITY: 8 STUPIDITY: 7 ENTERTAINMENT: 7

131

Stupid.com
www.stupid.com/index.html

This is the page whose domain name is stupid…literally.

There's tons of funny, bizarre, and, of course, stupid stuff on this page. Stupid toys, stupid food; you name it, they've got it in stupid form. They include various examples of stupid candy, inventions, jokes, and tools. The actual collection is quite extensive, and there's an online store, too.

COMMENTS: This website is full of stupid stuff and is naturally a great website to visit. Stupid stuff seems to be getting more and more popular these days. Look anywhere, and you'll see something stupid. SpongeBob SquarePants is a perfect example. Even the world of children's television contains tons of stupidity. You'll get a kick out of a lot of the stuff here and may even be persuaded to buy something.

ABNORMALITY: 7 STUPIDITY: 9 ENTERTAINMENT: 7

130

WeinerDogRaces.com
www.weinerdograces.com

These are some of the oddest races you'll probably ever see.

Lovable Dachshund dogs compete in a number of different races, each with a bizarre result. When you're done viewing one race, just click a button and you'll have another ready to amaze you with its stupidity. Here's a hint: the dogs are joined in their race by cartoon aliens, bees, fish, and other assorted objects added by these ignoramuses. Or is that ignorami?

COMMENTS: Like the reason Kevin Federline keeps popping up on TV, this site is a mystery to me. If there is a reason, I don't want to know what it is. But the dogs are cute.

ABNORMALITY: 8 STUPIDITY: 9 ENTERTAINMENT: 8

129

GetBubbaTeeth.com
www.getbubbateeth.com

This is a store dealing with artificial redneck teeth.

This site has all of your teeth needs. From redneck baby-teeth pacifiers to plain ol' redneck teeth (they look about the same), you can find all kinds of artificial teeth here on this site. What's even better is that this is an actual store! You can actually order teeth! Four out of five dentists do not recommend Bubba Teeth.

COMMENTS: They have hockey-player teeth on this site. They look like what old hockey players' teeth look like, especially back in the old days, when they wore no mouth guards and the goalies had no masks. Hockey's a great sport. People are tough and willing to beat each other up, and they get to carry sticks. Think of how much better baseball would be if the players got to carry the bats on the bases and whack the shortstop to foil a double play!

ABNORMALITY: 7 STUPIDITY: 7 ENTERTAINMENT: 6

128

The Unnatural Enquirer
www.trygve.com/enquirer.html

This is home to an e-zine similar to the *National Enquirer*.

The site is updated regularly with content that is sure to make you laugh, smile, and appear confused and puzzled. "Films You Don't Want To See" and "All About Computers" are some of the categories. A favorite was "The Visible Barbie," where a Barbie doll was cut into cross sections with a bandsaw. Stupid and crude? Yes, but undoubtedly enjoyable and informative.

COMMENTS: One of the films you don't want to see is the "Trekkie Terror Picture Show," a cross between *Rocky Horror* and *Star Trek*. Yes, that movie would be quite disturbing. In fact, I want to stop thinking about it before I have nightmares. Wait…it's too late. Dang it.

ABNORMALITY: 9 STUPIDITY: 9 ENTERTAINMENT: 9

Leia's Metal Bikini
www.leiasmetalbikini.com

Return of the Jedi introduced us to what became the ultimate nerd fantasy: Princess Leia in a metal bikini. But outside *Star Wars*, this scant swimsuit didn't see much attention—until now. "This website is dedicated to the costume worn by Princess Leia following her capture by the crimelord, Jabba the Hutt, in *Star Wars, Episode VI : Return of the Jedi*... Clad in a skimpy dancer's outfit and kept on a short leash, Leia endures her captivity with a natural, inner strength..." I'm sure "natural inner strength" is the real reason for this site. There's a gallery of pictures featuring Leia in *Return of the Jedi*, as well as artwork and an opportunity to make or buy a metal bikini of your own, presumably to use for some weird fantasy.

COMMENTS: I feel sorry for Carrie Fisher. I can only imagine the shame she feels when she sees a site like this. At least they didn't decide to put Luke Skywalker or Han Solo in a metal loincloth. That would have probably killed *Star Wars* right there, although it would have made Karsten pretty happy (see number 276 for her site).

ABNORMALITY: 9   STUPIDITY: 8   ENTERTAINMENT: 8

The Final Retribution
www.finalretribution.com

If yo really hate somebody's guts, you could come up with some original insults for them, or you could just use this website. The Final Retribution is the ultimate "flaming" letter (a term used in online forums for severely insulting somebody), letting your worst enemy know just how horrible he/she is. "You swine. You vulgar little maggot. What is that tripe you call your opinions? What is that scrofulous little tumor you call a brain? I would rather kiss a goat than be seen with you."

COMMENTS: This is close to the vilest string of insults I've ever seen. And it doesn't even use profanity. The bottom line here is that if there's a big worm in your life that needs a good flaming, just copy and paste this letter and you'll be set.d take that long. Then again, with the way the Web is, I wouldn't be surprised.

ABNORMALITY: 6   STUPIDITY: 7   ENTERTAINMENT: 8

125

Museum of Unnatural History

www.unmuseum.org/unmain.htm

This site is home to a museum of the odd, the strange, and the paranormal.

UFOs, odd archeology, ghosts, and the like are the norm in this museum. You can take a virtual tour through any of the museum's weird exhibits. The UFO exhibit, the "Lost Worlds" exhibit, and the "Seven Wonders of the Ancient World" exhibit are among the few on this site. There are also some semi-amusing cartoons about "LGM—Little Green Men."

COMMENTS: There's lots of stuff here—not really anything here that's totally stupid, but as some elderly college professors would say, it's "prodigious, yet undisciplined and largely useless." Still, this is some of the most unnatural stuff you'll ever see. Be sure to click on the "mini-links" within the exhibits; they link you to some cool places.

ABNORMALITY: 9 STUPIDITY: 6 ENTERTAINMENT: 8

124

MicroAngela

www.pbrc.hawaii.edu/bemf/microangela

Ever wondered what unseen creatures live throughout your house, your car, and even on your skin? Well, this site has the answer.

This site has information on all sorts of microorganisms, including the black ant, the fruit fly, mold, bacteria, and all of the organisms that play a vital role in the soap opera that plays out in the functioning of our bodies. Except in this soap opera, the ant's sister isn't sleeping with the fruit fly's brother who's secretly in love with the bacteria's mom.

COMMENTS: Once again, it's not so much that this site is stupid; it's just that it's so weird and interesting! There's a touch of humor to each little "article" on each organism. Check this site out; it's educational *and* weird.

ABNORMALITY: 8 STUPIDITY: 5 ENTERTAINMENT: 6

A Gadzillion Things to Think About
www.gadzillionthings.net

This is *the* ultimate variety site.

It's a site with, virtually, a gadzillion things to think about. I mean, think of the mental dilemma posed by the question, "When you choke a Smurf, what color does it turn?" or the infinite Zen of "What would life be like without rhetorical questions?" Whether you want to ponder over work, entertainment, advertising, holidays, or anything else imaginable, this huge and comprehensive site has it. If you intend to view everything, park yourself in front of that computer screen and stock up on snacks; you're gonna be there awhile.

COMMENTS: One question: how does the laugh track know when the sitcom is funny? The laugh track is controlled by a psychic entity. It can read into the minds of viewers and tell when someone thinks something is funny. So somewhere, even on a horribly bad sitcom, when the laugh track comes on, some idiot is laughing.

ABNORMALITY: 5 STUPIDITY: 6 ENTERTAINMENT: 9

Stuff and Me
www.stuffandme.com

This site is from the same guy who bought us Make Me Watch TV.com (number 201). Here he is offering to sell himself for anybody who wishes to use him for advertising. "Stuff and Me is an experiment in web advertising. This site is in place to serve entertaining ads to people who like entertainment. And joy. And sunshine. And hugs." If you want to advertise on Stuff and Me, follow these steps: "Step 1: You buy an ad on this page. Step 2: I take a funny picture of myself and you. Step 3: The funny picture is placed on this page. Things that have been advertised on Stuff and Me include M&Ms, "Scary-Go-Round," which appears to be some off-color humor cartoon, and *Running with Scissors* magazine, whose website doesn't seem to exist anymore.

COMMENTS: This Aric McKeown guy is all over the place. Besides Make Me Watch TV.com and this, he has a site for his cartoons, his acting career, his video game review site… I hope he makes good money off of this stuff.

ABNORMALITY: 7 STUPIDITY: 7 ENTERTAINMENT: 7

121   **Dear Aunt Nettie**
www.dearauntnettie.com

Here is the home of the oldest lady on the Internet.

You can see the question of the day, ask a question yourself, browse Aunt Nettie's question archives, view fables and wisdom, and more. One thing to keep in mind when you're asking Aunt Nettie a question; she's a bit senile after all these years, so don't be surprised if the answer she gives you is a little odd.

COMMENTS: Pretty funny stuff. Funny like a *Jerry Springer* episode. Sure, you know the families on *Springer* are probably screwed up beyond the point of recognition, but it's so stupid it's funny. Anyway, Dear Aunt Nettie is the place to go if you want a second opinion on what *not* to do.

ABNORMALITY: 7   STUPIDITY: 8   ENTERTAINMENT: 7

---

120   **Save the Bald Beaver**
www.savethebaldbeaver.org

We've all seen movements to save rare species of wildlife: whales, manatees, elephants, snow leopards—all pretty understandable. But when you see a movement to "Save the Bald Beaver," you just have to laugh. The story is that the North American Bald Beaver, which is "the official symbol of Berlow, Canada" (ah, it's those crazy Canadians again), was hunted to near extinction back in the late 1600s and early 1700s during the peak of the fur trade. Strangely enough, the site itself implies that the Bald Beaver no longer needs saving, as it is currently "common" and "the danger of extinction seems remote." The Bald Beaver population has even "reestablished itself to nuisance proportions" in some areas. There's also legislation protecting the creature. So…why does it need saving again? In addition to the background information, there's a kids section (very disturbing!), as well as sections for photos, a shop, and a help section, which has links to wildlife organizations like Greenpeace and the National Wildlife Federation.

COMMENTS: Don't get me wrong; saving endangered wildlife is a noble goal. But why do we have to save the Bald Beaver when the site itself admits that it doesn't need saving?

ABNORMALITY: 7   STUPIDITY: 8   ENTERTAINMENT: 6

119

The Worst Website.com
www.theworstwebsite.com

Warning: this site contains adult content.

Well, not really. That's the warning message that you're given to begin with, which is only the first in a long line of monotonous pop-up window messages. It's quite a helpless feeling to be at the mercy of this evil person as you bear all those error messages…(sniff).

COMMENTS: This site is probably a good candidate for the worst website ever. Yet once again it's—you guessed it—strangely amusing. One thing's for sure: this guy has a serious lack of creativity and an excess of idiocy.

ABNORMALITY: 8 STUPIDITY: 9 ENTERTAINMENT: 7

118

Stickman Murder Mysteries
normandcompany.com/stickman

This is one really weird game.

You can choose from a number of mysterious cases where you can then investigate to find out what caused the crime. The game has some purpose, and there's a lot of humor added along the way to keep things fresh. Mysteries include "Cadaver at Stickville Dump" and "Arson in Stickville." This is definitely not a game for Playstation or Xbox fans. No action, bad graphics.

COMMENTS: I played this game and it was pretty boring, but I was in kind of a rush. I guess the bottom line is that if you have some time to kill, and if you feel in a mood to solve a mystery, head over to the Stickman Murder Mysteries site.

ABNORMALITY: 6 STUPIDITY: 7 ENTERTAINMENT: 7

117 Tax Jack

www.hypegames.com/casino/9881/tax-jack.html

Blackjack meets the IRS.

Yes, I know you can almost see your money burning in a proverbial bonfire, but the game is actually pretty fun. Although, I might just be saying that because I got really lucky and won almost every hand. The dealer is an IRS agent, and you can do things related to taxes to increase (or decrease) your pot.

COMMENTS: Take that, big tough *Infernal* Revenue Service agent! Ha! Anyway, like I was saying, this game can be fun if you get lucky, plus it gives you a chance to laugh in the face of a computerized IRS agent. Hey, it may not be the real thing, but it's close enough. Now if only they had "Torture the Auditor."

ABNORMALITY: 5 STUPIDITY: 6 ENTERTAINMENT: 8

116 Husker Elvises

www.huskerelvis.net

Ladies and Gentlemen, the King has returned! Unfortunately, he's not here to sing "Jailhouse Rock" or "You Ain't Nothing but a Hound Dog"; he's come back to cheer on the Nebraska Cornhuskers. Oh yeah, and there's four of him this time, too. "The Husker Elvises group is made up of the four Brew brothers (Larry, Steve, Ron, and Gerry). Dressing up in Husker Red and white Elvis jumpsuits, wigs and capes; they show up at Husker games to cheer on 'Big Red' and promote team spirit." This site consists of pictures with these overweight Elvises, as well as links to the few newspaper articles that have been written about them. The Elvises are also available for entertainment at parties. The only cost you have to pay is for their travel expenses, and excess money is donated to a scholarship fund for the University of Nebraska-Lincoln. They're Huskers *and* charitable. What's not to love?

COMMENTS: Normally, I'd rant about how pathetic these guys are. But, seeing as I have a certain relative who is, on occasion, a Husker Elvis, I'll take pity on the Husker Elvises and say that they're only marginally pathetic. Aren't I a nice guy?

ABNORMALITY: 7 STUPIDITY: 8 ENTERTAINMENT: 8

115

The Ahhhhhh Page
www.steveratcliffe.me.uk/ahhhhh/index.html

Ah, the Ahhhhhh Page. Sounds relaxing, but what is it? "This page plots the number of results obtained from Google for words of the form a{n}h{m}. For example aaahh would be represented by 3,2 and is found on the grid below at 3 down and 2 across. Hover over the square to see the number of Google results, you can also click to see the results in Google for yourself." The graph contains hundreds of variations of the expression, from the simple "ah" to versions that are 50 characters long (the maximum length of the Google search field). Red squares contain the most results—over eight thousand—while orange squares have less results than red, yellow squares less than orange, and so on. Another interesting fact is that "there is a lot more ahhh'ing than argh'ing." There's also a link to "The Aargh Page," which inspired the Ahhhhhh Page. All these aarghs and ahs are giving me a headache. Argh...

COMMENTS: It's interesting to see how many variations of words like ah and argh there are. No wonder English is the hardest language to learn.

ABNORMALITY: 8 STUPIDITY: 7 ENTERTAINMENT: 8

114

The Hoff Gallery
www.hoffgallery.com

This site makes me cringe. It's nothing but pictures and animations featuring David Hasselhoff! The horror, the horror! Claiming to "help build a better world, one Hoff at a time," there are literally dozens of pictures featuring Hasselhoff, all divided into different categories and subcategories. The "Classic Hoffs" collection contains "Seasonal Hoffs," "Hoffelaneous," and most disturbing of all, "Sexy Hoffs." I shudder at the mere words. Even worse is the "Twisted Hoffs" category. Sections include "Hoffverts," which contain advertisements edited to feature Hasselhoff (the "Beef Stroganhoff" ad is enough to shatter even the strongest of wills), and "Hoffalikes," with pictures where Hasselhoff is edited to look like other celebrities. ("Luchoffer," where Hasselhoff is edited to look like Satan, is the only appropriate one.)

COMMENTS: When an actor is reduced to a cameo in a cartoon movie about a talking sponge, you know he's hit rock bottom. Visit this site if you dare, but unless you like Mr. Horrid Hasselhoff, you may be scarred for life.

ABNORMALITY: 9 STUPIDITY: 10 ENTERTAINMENT: 7

113

Kiss My Floppy
www.kissmyfloppy.com/pages

This is a site that's home to some great computer jokes.

The best of the best computer jokes are here on this site. From cracks and cartoons on Microsoft to jokes related to everyday matters such as gender (check out the one that tells why computers may be females; it's a classic), this site has plenty of stuff to keep you occupied. Check out the pictures of crazy computer cases created by computer nerds with too much time on their hands. Very entertaining.

COMMENTS: With plenty of jokes, cartoons, and stories, this site has a ton of content that will place it in with your favorites. This is true without even mentioning the fact that the site has plenty of Microsoft insults. That is an aspect that alone makes it worth visiting in my book.

ABNORMALITY: 6 STUPIDITY: 7 ENTERTAINMENT: 8

112

Trifle-Hut
triflehut.iwarp.com/index.htm

This site is dedicated to the trifle, a type of dessert dish. According to the site, a trifle is a multi-layered dessert with sponge cake, fruit, jelly, and custard. Sounds delicious enough. The only question I have is this: WHY DEDICATE A SITE TO IT? Some people never learn.

COMMENTS: This world is going nuts, I tell you. I mean a site that states its purpose as "to develop an understanding of the role of cream-topped sweets in the twenty-first century, whilst attempting to entertain and amuse"? Don't give in to insanity, my friends! Stop the madness before it's too late!

ABNORMALITY: 8 STUPIDITY: 8 ENTERTAINMENT: 6

111

Journal of the King's Royal Food Taster
web.superb.net/thetaster

This site is actually quite…interesting. Especially if you enjoy reading about vomiting.
It's the Journal of the King's Royal Food Taster. His job: to taste food for the king to make sure it isn't poisoned. Sounds like a lovely job, doesn't it? My only question is, what would happen if he did get poisoned…yes, yes, that would not be nice. Anyway, the site is written in journal form, and it tells a sort of story from the perspective of the taste tester. Someone amazingly put in a good deal of time and effort on this drivel.

COMMENTS: Actually, I do have one other question: if he's supposed to be a poison tester, shouldn't he be "The King's Royal Poison Tester" then? That's what confuses me. Oh well. Anyway, this site is kind of funny, although I wouldn't want to spend a great amount of time looking at it.

ABNORMALITY: 7 STUPIDITY: 7 ENTERTAINMENT: 5

110

The Blue Brick
www.thebluebrick.net

Their motto is "All the News that's made up."
It's the Blue Brick, and they've got fake news up the wazoo, or something like that. From a story about Wal-Mart greeters using "Whazzup?" and "Welcome to the Shizzy" to welcome customers (never heard that when I've gone to Wal-Mart), to "Ford Shelves New SUV, No Good 'E' Names Left" to even more irreverent stories like "Pretty Girl Realizes She Is Neither Interesting, Funny," there are a number of full-text stories to keep you busy. They also have guest editorials from famous celebrities, including Ashton Kutcher's "Old Chicks Rock!" (yeah, we noticed) and my personal favorite, Mel Gibson's "I'm Pretty Sure that I'm Not Crazy!" (whatever you need to tell yourself, Mel…).

COMMENTS: Anyway much like the famous Onion periodical, this site has a great mix of witty satire and completely senseless and irreverent articles. Check back on this site regularly; it'll always have great content. A Christmastime article, "Santa Claus Goes on Atkins Diet, Asks Families to Leave Low-Carb Snacks This Year," was especially funny.

ABNORMALITY: 8 STUPIDITY: 8 ENTERTAINMENT: 9

109

This site has some great military humor.

From Murphy's Laws of Combat Operations ("friendly fire—isn't" or "if at first you don't succeed, call in an air strike") to daily military jokes, this site has something for everyone. The people who will most appreciate this site are people who were once, or who are currently, in the military, since they can relate to the situations described here.

COMMENTS: Regardless of whether you've been in the military or not, you'll enjoy most of the jokes here on this site, unless you're like Rosie O'Donnell and you hate the military and you hate guns (even though her bodyguard carried a gun). Go figure.

ABNORMALITY: 5 STUPIDITY: 5 ENTERTAINMENT: 8

108

Golfjokes.co.uk
www.golfjokes.co.uk

It's a golf site! An English golf joke site! Smashing, wot?

This U.K. site has tons of hilarious golf jokes. From caddy jokes to the less…conventional jokes, this site has tons of jokes for your viewing pleasure. You can share them with your driving, putting, or golfing mates later on. You can also submit your own jokes.

COMMENTS: Even if you don't golf, you owe it to yourself to visit this site. It's got plenty of golfing humor to make you want to at least play a game at your local mini-golf course. After all, who doesn't like mini-golf? Of course, you can't go if it's wintertime, with the snow, and the cold, and the…yeah.

ABNORMALITY: 6 STUPIDITY: 7 ENTERTAINMENT: 8

SportsPickle.com
www.sportspickle.com

This is a sports satire site. Here, you'll find tons of stuff that makes the world of sports seem wilder than it really is. From Saddam Hussein's rumored baseball-card collection to hilarious pregame football predictions, this site has everything a sports fan needs to keep his or her funny bone in tune with favorite sports. This site even lampoons the ridiculous trend toward Taj Mahal luxury stadiums. "Sports Designer Bucks Retro Trend, Builds Mid-'70s Copy" is a funny parody on the supposed construction of a new venue in Philadelphia.

COMMENTS: Let me explain my favorite part of the website. After suffering through several horrendous Thanksgivings watching sports on the tube, the best poll question was "What's the worst part about Thanksgiving?" The answer is simple: the Detroit Lions!

ABNORMALITY: 5 STUPIDITY: 8 ENTERTAINMENT: 8

Herself's Super Hideout
www.geocities.com/Heartland/Valley/2337/index.html

It's a variety site that, while made by an amateur, is really quite good.

Pictures, jokes, and other fun stuff can be found on this site, all available for your prying eyes. From the Canadian's idea of deer hunting (sitting next to a deer-crossing sign…seems logical) to a rubber face that makes George W. and Dick Cheney look like Beavis and Butthead (heh heh, heh heh, we're morons dude, heh heh, heh heh), the site has a ton of creative material.

COMMENTS: This site manages to be funny, but you know what else is funny? The Pillsbury Doughboy. He's just so cute, it's almost as if he begs to be poked. I don't know why I mentioned that; the thought just crossed my mind. Anyway, this site is pretty good, despite its somewhat generic status, so be sure to stop by.

ABNORMALITY: 7 STUPIDITY: 7 ENTERTAINMENT: 8

105

Mobile Cooking
www.wymsey.co.uk/wymchron/cooking.htm

Looking for a quick meal on the go that doesn't consist of re-heated pizza and fast food? If you're in an adventurous mood, you may want to try this kooky culinary site. "Many students, and other young people, have little in the way of cooking skills but can usually get their hands on a couple of mobile phones. So, this week, we show you how to use two mobile phones to cook an egg which will make a change from phoning out for a pizza. Please note that this will not work with *cordless* phones." Well duh. If you want to fry with your phone, you'll need two phones (they don't have to be on the same network), an egg cup (remember not to use stainless steel; you don't want to put yourself in danger doing this, do you?), and an AM or FM radio. After you've gotten those, follow the instructions here and enjoy! Hopefully, you'll live to tell the tale.

COMMENTS: Doesn't this seem a little dangerous? Cooking an egg using microwave radiation from a cell phone doesn't seem like a smart thing to do. Even if it works, those eggs could be bad for you. Anyway, try this at your own risk, but if it works, more power to you.

ABNORMALITY: 9 STUPIDITY: 8 ENTERTAINMENT: 8

104

Sheep 101
www.sheep101.info

This site is your first stop for a highly important subject that everybody should be educated on: sheep! Sheep 101 is "a web site to teach students, teachers, 4-H and FFA members, beginning shepherds, and the public about sheep and shepherding." Start with the About Sheep section, which answers burning questions such as "What's the difference between sheep and goats?", "Why don't sheep have tails?", and most importantly, "Are sheep stupid?"

COMMENTS: Well, I certainly know more about sheep than I did before. There is a somewhat disturbing picture in the products page, though, with "fresh American lamb—meat lovers know" and a picture of a half eaten rack of lamb. Shame on you, Sheep 101! I thought you exalted sheep, not encouraged their consumption!

ABNORMALITY: 7 STUPIDITY: 6 ENTERTAINMENT: 8

103

Miss Behaved
www.missbehaved.com

Here's advice from someone who's not exactly careful with what she says.

She's Miss Behaved, or as you could call her, Miss Politically Incorrect. From insulting how family letters have given way to websites of the caliber that I am reviewing in this book (that's not a compliment) to "Fine Dining Tips for the Baby" (I don't even want to know), Miss Behaved has something for everyone. The site is updated regularly.

COMMENTS: What a little harpy! Does she know nothing of family values or warmheartedness? Apparently not. Then again, who does these days? What is this world coming to?

ABNORMALITY: 7 STUPIDITY: 8 ENTERTAINMENT: 6

102

Engineer Jokes
www.inflection-point.com/jokindex.htm

Who would have thought of engineer jokes?

This site has a different engineer joke every day. While some of the engineer jokes are dated, they are funny. One was a thirteen-question quiz relating to a fictional show called *Who Wants to Marry a Software Engineer?* much like FOX's *Who Wants to Marry a Multi-Millionaire?* There's also a way to browse archives of past jokes.

COMMENTS: I hate how network shows rip off each other like that. For example, FOX ripped off *The Bachelor* with *Joe Millionaire*. This was obviously meant to be *Who Wants to Marry a Multi-Millionaire?* meets *The Bachelor*. And they call these things "reality TV"? What rip-offs. Why don't we get a real "reality" show like *How Can I Meet a Sober Blonde?* or *Where the Heck Is My Raise, You Cheap Skinflint?*

ABNORMALITY: 6 STUPIDITY: 5 ENTERTAINMENT: 8

101

The Cat Machine
www.catmachine.com/live

Don't ask me how cats can form a machine, but they've managed to do it…or so they say. Once again, the English have created a stupid, meaningless, confusing website.

On this variety site, you'll find a cat newspaper featuring "Gossip, bizarre outrage, scandals, breasts," and much more. From an article describing some things that Ben Affleck is thankful for to all the latest on the holidays at the White House, this site has a ton of stuff for you to sniff out, read, and see.

COMMENTS: There's a funny picture showing a news-show anchorman with the head of a cat. I don't know why that's funny. Maybe it's because the cat's head isn't very proportional to the newsman's body. Maybe it's because a news anchor with a cat's brains would rank above average in terms of intelligence when compared to his blow-dried brethren. Or maybe it's because the cat has better hair than Ted Koppel.

ABNORMALITY: 7 STUPIDITY: 7 ENTERTAINMENT: 8

100

Comedy Zone
www.comedy-zone.net/links/index.html

Here's an unbelievable variety site with a cute little clown.

The Comedy Zone has all you need for a laugh, including jokes-a-plenty, quotes-a-plenty, T-shirts-a-plenty, and anything-else-a-plenty you can think of. There are also more than two thousand links, with a number of the sites included in this book. You can order T-shirts with such profound sayings as "time is never wasted when you're wasted all the time." You can look up lawyer jokes, chicken jokes, and drunk jokes. It's all here.

COMMENTS: It's great to laugh. Everybody needs a good laugh once in a while. What should you do when somebody trips on a banana peel? Laugh! What should you do when you trip on a banana peel? Laugh! What should you do when Mr. T trips on a banana peel? You can laugh, although you might have to deal with serious consequences afterwards. Fool!

ABNORMALITY: 6 STUPIDITY: 5 ENTERTAINMENT: 10

Cult of Cod
www.cultofcod.com

Welcome to the Cult of Cod, the new religious movement that has been "Washing your brain better than other leading cults since 2001." I like it already! The cult was "originally founded in the year 1337 by a religious fanatic with no tongue and no hair." The teachings of this great prophet were mistaken for nonsense, and he eventually died "after being stoned by an angry mob for the crime of 'saying something we don't understand.'" All seemed lost until 2001, when a "soon-to-be-university student" received a vision from Cod Himself, and the Cult of Cod was born.

COMMENTS: Most of the Internet churches I've seen have left me unimpressed. But this site almost succeeded in converting me. That brainwashing formula almost got me. In fact, it was pretty successful for a while. But I'm too dedicated to good old-fashioned voodoo to become a follower of Cod.

ABNORMALITY: 9 STUPIDITY: 9 ENTERTAINMENT: 8

98

Acme Vaporware, Inc.
www.acmevaporware.com/acme.htm

Corporate technology encounters of the weird kind are the best way to describe this site. This site has a whole bunch of weird inventions and creations that are supposed to give you luck with other technology. Like a machine that gives your LANs and WANs "chi." or, (Think of it as Feng Shui for Microsoft products; gotta make them work somehow, right?) You can also go to the vaporware store and "behold things that will help make the world a Perry Como HOLIDAY PARADISE," like sweatshirts and teddy bears. Perry Como? Definitively bizarre.

COMMENTS: The Vaporware things I like the most are the interactive ones. This is partially because the options allow you to choose, to a certain degree, how weird the results are going to be. Take the "AVW Tech—Tarot Deck," for example. It allows you to be a latter-day Nostradamus with the aid of your computer! Well, kind of. You can also make virtually any corporate leader speak "geek" with the help of the "Acme Vaporizer High-Tech CEO Quote Generator." Visit this site if you're looking for some weird technology humor.

ABNORMALITY: 8 STUPIDITY: 8 ENTERTAINMENT: 7

Renegade Llama
renegadellama.tripod.com/llamahome.htm

Yes, I know. I don't have a clue either.

It's the life and loves of Larry the Llama, and these are his daily adventures. The site has a short profile on Larry and his "love interest," Debra the Donkey. From there you are catapulted into a wild world of random animal stupidity. The outlandish claims on this site include a report that musician Kenny G is Larry's long-lost son (don't ask), that Larry is smuggling SPAM into Ireland (that mystery meat is all over the Web), and that Larry watches (of course) *Larry King Live*. Larry King? He should make a second career as a wedding planner or a divorce advisor; after all, he's had a lot of experience with both.

COMMENTS: One picture features a train with a caption that says Larry has been living on a train for the past few weeks. Funny, I haven't heard anything on the news about a llama on a train. Of course, it could be in some place like Kuala Lumpur where that's common. You never know.

ABNORMALITY: 9 STUPIDITY: 9 ENTERTAINMENT: 7

---

96 Pylon of the Month
users.tinyonline.co.uk/bigh/bigh/pylonof.htm

This electrifying site is "dedicated to the humble electricity pylon, whose beauty remains tragically unrecognised." Tragic, indeed. Pylons also have the honor of providing "children and adults alike with the opportunity to engage in the fascinating and rewarding hobby of *electricity pylon number collecting*." Strangely, the site doesn't describe what pylon number collecting is. Whatever it is, it sounds boring. The namesake pylon of the month is included here, along with a guest book, a chat room (which, not surprisingly, is inactive), and links to other pylon sites, most of which are dead.

COMMENTS: It's a wonder that this site is still up. How many people actually go out and catalog pylons as a hobby? But the most disturbing part of this site has to be the guestbook. Let's just say that people who signed it have an interest in pylons that extends beyond a casual hobby (they call themselves "pysexuals"). Disturbing indeed.

ABNORMALITY: 8 STUPIDITY: 8 ENTERTAINMENT: 5

95

Bad Cookie
www.badcookie.com

You might say that these aren't fortune cookies, but misfortune cookies.

Usually, when you open a fortune cookie, you receive a message that has some profound, often positive, meaning. However, these fortune-cookie messages definitely don't foretell a good future and are often nasty and negative. Examples include, "You have little understanding of arts and music," "All your hard work will not pay off," and, my favorite, "Bad luck and extreme misfortune will infest your pathetic soul for all eternity." If you wish to curse others with bad fortunes, you can email a fortune cookie to a "friend" or relative.

COMMENTS: Most of these cookie messages aren't even fortunes; they're just insults. "You will have difficulty finding outlets for your minor creative abilities." Note the use of the word "minor." I didn't know you could get mad at a Chinese dessert cookie, but these people have somehow made it possible. I sense the work of some very hateful people. Check out this site, but beware; extreme misfortune may befall you.

ABNORMALITY: 7 STUPIDITY: 8 ENTERTAINMENT: 8

94

The Dubbinternet
www.dubbin.com

Dubbin is a wonderful thing. The question remains though: just what is it?

I have no clue, and the people at the official site of this product, or thing, or animal, or whatever it is don't seem to be helping. Based on this site, I'm sure that "dubbin is not shoe polish," "dubbin is illegal in Wales, for very good reasons," and that Oscar-winning actor Richard Dreyfuss "uses dubbin to attract seahorses." Categories on this bizarre site include uses for dubbin, celebrities who are fans of dubbin, a dubbin FAQ (which creates more questions than answers), and more.

COMMENTS: Maybe Dubbin is a magical time-traveling substance that can send you through the space-time continuum while ripping it to proverbial shreds at the same time. Or, maybe it's just a shoe cleaner. From the sound of things, it could be anything. These people are nuts.

ABNORMALITY: 9 STUPIDITY: 8 ENTERTAINMENT: 7

Bob the Angry Flower
www.angryflower.com

Flowers usually are associated with pleasant, calming, and/or romantic experiences. Bob the Angry Flower is not one of them. This web comic strip is about a talking flower who, true to his name, can get very, very angry. Actually, "angry" is not a good word to describe Bob. "Bipolar" would be more accurate. One minute, Bob will be talking casually with a friend or random pedestrian; the next, he will burst into a profanity-laced fit of rage. (Bob is quite obscene at times, so keep the young and the easily offended away from this one.) The settings of the comics are varied, ranging from casual, everyday situations to sci-fi storylines and warlike settings. Humorwise, they range from mildly amusing to very funny. A new comic comes each week, along with a little about what's happening in his life, and an occasional movie review or political rant. Ah, political rants. The best part about having your own website.

COMMENTS: Bob the Angry Flower is one of the smarter web comics I've seen. There's a good mix of crude adult humor along with some witty pop-culture references and social commentary. If you're not too offended by adult humor, try checking this one out. Don't worry, Bob will be nice to you—maybe.

ABNORMALITY: 9 STUPIDITY: 8 ENTERTAINMENT: 9

FALnet
www.fal.net

Their motto claims that this website is for "smart people with extremely bad taste." Regardless of whether you're smart or not, though, this site is stupid. Features include the "misfortune cookie," with such Oriental witticisms as "With the rate you give people headaches, you should buy stock in Excedrin," or "You have a big future in food service." There is also a rhyming tale by Edgar Alan Seuss (a grisly take on the beloved children's author Dr. Seuss) and a listing of some sick take-offs like "One Death, Two Death, Red Death, Blue Death." Bad taste indeed.

COMMENTS: With more bad taste than people who watch *The Weakest Link* reruns, this site has stupid, brainless stuff galore. Just click anywhere, and your IQ will magically drop one or two points. When compared to this site, an episode of *Kathy Griffin: My Life on the D-List* is like *Masterpiece Theater*.

ABNORMALITY: 8 STUPIDITY: 9 ENTERTAINMENT: 7

91

ET Medical
etmedical.com

Do you have a terminal illness? Any kind of incurable disease? Most doctors probably would have trouble treating you, but not Adrian Dvir. You see, Adrian has a specialist team of doctors that is literally out of this world. "Alien medical teams from other realms or dimensions cure humans at Healers-Mediums alternative medicine clinics. Patients feel strange sensations during the treatments (itching, heat or cold, increase or decrease in gravity sensations, and many more) and some even see and communicate with the Alien medical teams." According to the biography, in 1994, Adrian Dvir "became aware of spirits, ghosts, light entities, aliens, and other multi-dimensional beings" and began working with them to treat human medical conditions.

COMMENTS: This site is simply laughable. Channeling alien messages? Multi-dimensional beings? Alien doctors, operating out of an alternative medicine clinic in Israel? If you've got an incurable disease and you're incredibly desperate, you could try finding this Adrian guy. But don't say I didn't warn you.

ABNORMALITY: 10 STUPIDITY: 9 ENTERTAINMENT: 7

90

Noise Monkey
www.noisemonkey.com

It's a monkey. And it's writing news. Well, not really. It's writing "manufactured music news," with an emphasis on "manufactured."

"Were the Beatles a Government Conspiracy?" cites proof that the British government manufactured the Fab Four. The Sex Pistols punk-rock anthem "God Save the Queen (She Ain't a Human Being)" is revealed to be a touching love song to England's ruler. This U.K. site pokes fun at British bands that aren't really big in the U.S., so that portion may be hard to comprehend for Americans. But this is some pretty funny fake news in most cases.

COMMENTS: My personal favorite article is in Issue 24: "Stereophonics Frontman to Run for President." (Stereophonics is a Welsh rock band with a particularly dashing lead singer—and they have pretty good music, too.)

ABNORMALITY: 8 STUPIDITY: 8 ENTERTAINMENT: 8

Vaughan Lloyd III's
Evil Sledge Website
vaughan.lloyd3.users.btopenworld.com

"My name is Vaughan Lloyd III. I am fifty-seven years old. I live in a modest country house in Hertfordshire…I believe that the former pop group Sister Sledge are living in the gravel in my garden. I am NOT mad." Sure you aren't. The diary tells the story of how Lloyd hunts the "evil Sledge" and tells about the people who help and hinder his "Sledge-Hunt." Lloyd sounds highly paranoid throughout the story, believing that "the ants are traitors" and condemning a man named Edgar who "believes my archaeological hero Indiana Jones to merely be a character in a film played by some actor called Harrison Ford." The story eventually goes on to involve time travel, leprechaun and pixie tribes, and incantations from mystical books.

COMMENTS: I hope this is just a very inventive work of fiction. If this guy believes what's happening to him is real, he should be put in a mental institution ASAP. Even if Sister Sledge were living in his garden, it wouldn't be that bad. If somebody like Michael Jackson were living in his garden, though, I could understand his insanity.

ABNORMALITY: 10 STUPIDITY: 9 ENTERTAINMENT: 8

ASCII Babes
www.asciibabes.com

This site is dedicated to pictures of attractive women (don't worry, parents, there's no nudity). The difference is that these pictures are made up not of pixels, but keyboard characters. "Sometimes it's as simple as a 'email sig' or an emoticon :-) But in the case of asciibabes.com it's a portrait of a person. With an average of 80,000+ keyboard characters. There's a lot happening there, so you might have to move AWAY from the screen to be able to see the detail." Portraits of female celebrities here include Alyssa Milano, Jessica Alba, and Tyra Banks.

COMMENTS: These portraits are actually pretty realistic, considering they're made of numbers and letters. The Steve Irwin picture in particular is disturbingly true-to-life.

ABNORMALITY: 8 STUPIDITY: 6 ENTERTAINMENT: 8

87

Old Coot.com
www.oldcoot.com

This video series is basically *The Muppet Show*, only with a deranged, clumsy old hick instead of Kermit and Fozzie. It's also a hundred times less funny. The videos are about an old man named "Granpa Cratchet," who is constantly caught in comically awkward situations revolving around his old age. There's information here on a "Live Tour" of Old Coot, a place to purchase Old Coot DVDs (who would pay to see this nonsense?), and a children's website (sure, teach kids to laugh at a clumsy old man).

COMMENTS: What is it with people laughing at the misfortunes of old people? If anything, young people deserve more to be laughed at for their constant stupidity and ignorance. If I had a quarter for every time I heard a teenage guy laugh at a dumb bodily function joke, I'd be a billionaire. Besides, these videos are bad to begin with by comedy standards. I've seen much better shows and movies making fun of old people.

ABNORMALITY: 6 STUPIDITY: 9 ENTERTAINMENT: 5

86

Location Earth Dog Tags
www.earthbounddog.com

This site asks the ultimate question: if aliens abducted you, how would you get back to Earth? For a safe return after alien abduction, the simple solution, according to this site, is the "Location Earth Dog Tag"! The die-stamped aluminum tags contain instructions on how to get back to our blue planet via a handy star chart that any alien race could easily decipher. The tags also locate Earth within our solar system, show the various landmasses of our planet, and have other helpful features to help guide you back. Want proof that the creators of this product are confident that it works? They offer this ironclad guarantee: "Should you ever be abducted by aliens while wearing Location Earth Dog Tags and not returned safely to Earth, you will be entitled to a full refund of the purchase price." Talk about standing behind a product!

COMMENTS: What I don't get is how you could get back to Earth unless the aliens were willing to transport you. If they took you from Earth, wouldn't they know how to get back here?

ABNORMALITY: 8 STUPIDITY: 9 ENTERTAINMENT: 6

85

Things My Girlfriend and I Have Argued About

www.mil-millington.com

The writer of this site gives us a list of examples of things he and Margaret (girlfriend) have argued about. The list is literally fifty-plus pages long. There are, of course, the traditional boyfriend/girlfriend arguments: that he doesn't spend enough time with her, doesn't communicate enough, and so on. But some of the arguments are just ridiculous. These include "How one should cut a Kiwi Fruit in half (along its length or across the middle)," "Our telephone number," or "Which type of iron to buy," although he insists that "price wasn't an issue, it was the *principle*."

COMMENTS: This makes absolutely no sense to me. If he and his girlfriend argue so much, why doesn't he just break up with her and get a new one? I'm sure the fact that they've had two children and spent sixteen years together has something to do with it. But even then, wouldn't it be better to break up and reach some agreement instead of living with constant arguing?

ABNORMALITY: 6 STUPIDITY: 8 ENTERTAINMENT: 7

84

Two Men and a Wooden Duck Called Geoffrey

www.twomenandawoodenduck.tripod.com

This is a story about two men and their wooden duck named Geoffrey.

Yes, I know it sounds like it has no plot. Well, you are most definitely right. It is nothing but a bunch of poorly written gibberish about these two guys, a wooden duck, and the adventures that they have. One of the guys was born in Australia, so his stupidity is forgivable. I'm not sure what happened to the other guy.

COMMENTS: This story makes less sense than a Monty Python movie. I mean a story with "a wooden man called SPAM" (SPAM again?) and a "giant mechanical raccoon"? It is just so stupid! Check out this story if you're looking for something that doesn't have a shred of logic or value in it. In fact, it is perfectly stupid.

ABNORMALITY: 10 STUPIDITY: 10 ENTERTAINMENT: 7

Spidey and Bunbun
spideybunbun.tripod.com

Here's a superhero who literally fights in his underwear!

I'm not sure what the rest of the website is about, but I was able to decipher that much. "Diaper Bunny (Bunbun) vs. That Wrestler Guy" is a disturbing spread of pictures showing a guy in underwear and bunny ears grappling with another guy in a wrestling uniform. With these sites getting weirder and weirder, nothing surprises me. Anyway, this site is about Spidey, Dressboy, and Bunbun, and their "adventures" fighting the forces of evil!

COMMENTS: Wouldn't a superhero be very bashful about fighting crime and stopping evil while in his underwear? I know I couldn't do it. I guess Bunbun is just one of those folks who takes that superhero underwear thing a little too far. Or maybe he's just an exhibitionist.

ABNORMALITY: 8 STUPIDITY: 9 ENTERTAINMENT: 7

Smash Our Stuff.com
www.smashourstuff.com

What red-blooded American guy doesn't like smashing stuff? Unfortunately, the boundaries of society prohibit us from smashing extremely expensive items—until now. Smash our Stuff.com offers four distinct sections: Smash my iPod.com, Smash my PS3.com, Smash my Wii.com, and Smash my Xbox.com. For each website, the creators started a donation pool to buy the specific item. Once they had enough money, they went out, bought each of the items, and then videotaped themselves smashing it to pieces. Each site has a news section, forums, and of course, a hate mail section. What site is complete without a voluntarily added hate mail section?

COMMENTS: These videos are stupid, senseless, and make these guys look like cavemen, and not the sophisticated type of caveman seen in the Caveman's Crib (number 216). Yet, the videos have a slight flicker of genuine humor and creativity. Such is the paradox of smashing things.

ABNORMALITY: 7 STUPIDITY: 9 ENTERTAINMENT: 8

81

Galactic Defenders of the Universe

www.4gdu.com/index1.html

Be afraid! Be very afraid! The aliens are among us! (Yes, again!)

This is an organization dedicated to fighting back the alien hordes that are conspiring to take over the galaxy and turn us into robot zombies. "Don't be fooled by their seeming sincerity, they have only one objective. They want to enslave us." Join the cause and donate money, learn about strategies for alien defense, and learn something that George W. Bush, the Backstreet Boys, and Hillary Clinton have in common.

COMMENTS: I don't know if I am afraid of aliens, unless they're trying to take over Pizza Hut or Domino's! If that's the case, I will get mad and things will not be pretty. I will take up arms for pizza if I have to! Keep your hands off my cheese and sausage, you alien scum.

ABNORMALITY: 8 STUPIDITY: 8 ENTERTAINMENT: 8

80

Is There a Duck on the Web?

www.notduck.com

"Look, up in the sky. It's a bird! It's a plane! It's a...well you were right, it is a bird. A duck to be exact. NOT Duck to be even more exact." So, it's a duck, and at the same time, not a duck? Wow, that's deep. This Not Duck, or NOT as he is called, appears to be a plush Beanie Baby-like animal. He is described as "*the* world traveler," making the Travelocity gnome's journeys look like a "walk in the garden." In his travels, Not Duck has been to all seven continents (including Antarctica), forty-six countries, and all fifty states. He has also been aboard the Weinermobile and the Nutmobile, seen over half the Capitol buildings, and has mingled with many celebrities, including several *Simpsons* stars, Gene Wilder, and even the Blue Man Group!

COMMENTS: You wouldn't believe all the places and people this duck has seen until you see the pictures. He certainly does get around. I can only imagine the horrible jet lag he has. But, I'm sure meeting Corey Feldman was more than worth the effort.

ABNORMALITY: 7 STUPIDITY: 7 ENTERTAINMENT: 8

Basic Jokes
www.basicjokes.com

"Clean jokes for a dirty world" is their motto.

Nevertheless, they manage to put up one funny site. Jokes of all categories are here available for your viewing, each one with an individual rating based on a five-star system. One joke I viewed was when Newt Gingrich, Dan Quayle, and Bill Clinton were teleported into Oz, and…well, you'll just have to see.

COMMENTS: With more jokes than there are brain cells in the Backstreet Boys group, this site should keep you occupied for a little while. And while according to my description it doesn't seem like much, you'll be content with what's here.

ABNORMALITY: 6 STUPIDITY: 7 ENTERTAINMENT: 9

ChandraKClarke.com
www.chandrakclarke.com/thecolumn.htm

More opinionated babble from a self-proclaimed "humor writer" running a website.

She's Chandra Clark, and her column is here to spare no one and nothing in her quest for humor. And a lot of nothing is what you'll find, like boring story archives, a column that's updated regularly, and a list of books written by Clark, including a science-fiction novel and a book on the subject of humor writing.

COMMENTS: A lot of comedians tend to pick on certain types of people for their humor. Ever notice this trend? I guess it's just human nature that some people are just funnier than others, like old ladies who keep lots of cats, or people who can't locate the United States on a blank world map, or Barbara Walters trying to act like a comedian, such as when she had her two-hour "bloopers" special (it's not that she's funny at all, but the attempt itself is amusing).

ABNORMALITY: 5 STUPIDITY: 7 ENTERTAINMENT: 7

77

Nave Humor
www.navehumor.com/php/home.php

No, this is not somebody talking about the Navy who can't spell. It's another joke site.

More jokes by the hundreds, including stuff on marriage, animals, the military, and money. Simply click a category that you're in the mood for laughing about and presto! You'll have an assortment of jokes available for viewing.

COMMENTS: I don't know why, but I was never very good at telling jokes. Leave that to the comedians. I'm better at recognizing different types of humor, like pointing out the fact that the '80s were the worst disaster in fashion history. Really and truly. Just look at some old photos of yourself.

ABNORMALITY: 5 STUPIDITY: 6 ENTERTAINMENT: 9

76

Homemail
www.parodie.nl/homemail

The worst free email service! Ever!

It's Homemail, and it is by far the worst email program there is. Password problems? This site has a feature to help you forget your password. Who should sign up? "People who are very stupid" or people who already have an email service. In fact, the website itself admits nobody should sign up for this service.

COMMENTS: Just what the world needs, a parody email service that doesn't work. Stupid, stupid, stupid. Just another wanton waste of bandwidth.

ABNORMALITY: 7 STUPIDITY: 9 ENTERTAINMENT: 4

75

Pathetic Personals
www.patheticpersonals.com

Internet dating, like the regular dating world, has some bad apples. In the case of Pathetic Personals, there are a LOT of bad apples. "Here you'll find the cream of the crap; that special something that's magically captured the essence of life in their Internet dating profile." The page has a dating search engine that allows you to "find shirtless singles near you," along with a picture of a man that bears a disturbingly uncanny resemblance to Right Said Fred. You can say that you are a Klingon, Democrat, Canadian, or Jackass in search of a Cashier, Tool, Life, or Way Out. Well, I'd be seeking a way out if I were Canadian too. The personals themselves are indeed pathetic. One includes a fat guy seeking an "intimate encounter" who says, "I may look scary but give me a chance." How about no?

COMMENTS: This site gives Internet dating a bad name. While I do know people who have had successful relationships that started online, it's kind of discouraging for potential online daters when they see profiles like these. But, if you enjoy laughing at how pathetic other people are, Pathetic Personals is second to none.

ABNORMALITY: 8 STUPIDITY: 8 ENTERTAINMENT: 8

74

The Partygoers
www.thepartygoers.com

Are you ready to party?

Or is it "par-tay"? I'm not sure. Anyway, if you are willing to find out what some rocking parties are like, this is the site to go to. "The Partygoers are dedicated to spreading goodwill through the spontaneous visitation of social gatherings and celebrations." Here's how it works: these San Francisco "partygoers" visit parties and document them. It's like a personal party scrapbook on the web. How unique. How novel. How stupid.

COMMENTS: You know that song by the artist formerly known as the artist formerly known as Prince who is now known as Prince? You know, the one where he says, "Tonight we're gonna party like it's 1999"? What happened in 1999 that was so great? What relevance does the song have now? We can only wonder.

ABNORMALITY: 6 STUPIDITY: 8 ENTERTAINMENT: 8

73

Pundefined.com
www.pundefined.com

What do a cold, a bill, and coffee have in common?

This website answers that question. Here's how it works: you click on a word, and you will be given a "pun" on the word. Some are amusing, many are stupid. Click on "baker" and you'll find the "punny" response "a person who works because he kneads the dough." Click on "beverage." The pun is "How old a beaver is." (Can you figure it out?) And, of course "gladiator" leads to a pun about a happy cannibal. If you're stumped, click the blue "pronounciation" button for the answer.

COMMENTS: This is quite a creative website that's more fun than fishing. I mean, seriously. Who wants to fish? I mean, sure it's cool when you catch something, but what about the other 95 percent of the time? That's not fishing, that's patience. I guess some people just like sitting and doing nothing in the middle of a lake.

ABNORMALITY: 6 STUPIDITY: 5 ENTERTAINMENT: 9

72

Feline Follies
www.felinefollies.com

These are news articles with a twist: they're written by cats!

That's right! Feline Follies delivers you a pussycat's perspective of the planet—a cat's-eye view, so to speak. You'll find everything that a cat would say on this website. Although how they actually taught a cat to write is beyond me. The site features an advice column, "Ask Butterscotch," and a fashion report, "Style by Cosmos."

COMMENTS: Although cats don't really make good reporters, I will admit that some of the stories are mildly amusing. Such as the strange outfits the cats on the site are wearing: seeing a cat with a British army-style helmet and camouflage gear is somehow sad and funny at the same time.

ABNORMALITY: 7 STUPIDITY: 7 ENTERTAINMENT: 6

71

Opportunities
www.bullworks.net/invest/invest.htm

You could be rich beyond your wildest dreams! At least, this website does a good job of trying to make you believe so. Here, you are given a number of "investment" opportunities, among them "Marge's Barges" (a twisted transport service) and "Snow Globes" (like those happy glass-enclosed winter scenes, except real ugly). Click on any of these products, and you will be taken to a rather humorous investment profile.

COMMENTS: The "fine print" in these pages is nothing but a bunch of garbled letters with some occasional words thrown in. Well, basically that's what fine print usually is, legal gibberish from high-priced lawyers. Like when the announcer on the radio talks really, really fast to fit in all the catches in the deal. It sounds too good to be true, and always is. Only the fine print here actually has some value, since it includes things that will actually happen to you, like "you will lose all your money" and "you'll lose your home, too."

ABNORMALITY: 8 STUPIDITY: 8 ENTERTAINMENT: 6

70

Hollywood Humor
www.caryn.com/biz/caryn-biz-humor.html

"Lights, camera, action!" Isn't that all that really needs to be said?

You'll get a bizarre answer to that question from this site. Here, you'll find the best of Hollywood humor, including "Things I Learned from the Movies," which is about stuff that always seems to happen in movies for no apparent reason. Isn't it always true that "at least one of a pair of identical twins is born evil," or that "the Eiffel Tower can be seen from any window in Paris"? Other categories include Hollywood's Famous Last Words, a collection of stupid comments by Hollywood insiders, like the classic, "Who wants to hear actors talk?" uttered when studio head and silent-movie fan H.M. Warner of Warner Brothers predicted that movies with sound would fail.

COMMENTS: Hollywood can be a wonderful place if you can look past certain disaster movies, like *The Poseidon Adventure* or *Dirty Love* (any movie that is written by, produced by, and starring Jenny McCarthy has to be awful). This site features the best and the worst of Hollywood humor, past and present.

Insanity: Home to All Things Funny

www.angelfire.com/in4/insanity/index2.html

It's awful! It's insulting! It's incredibly funny!

It's Insanity, and like it says, it's home to all things funny. Well maybe not everything, but nobody can have everything. Except maybe Bill Gates. And why isn't he sharing it with me, that cheap, lousy son of a gun? He could buy his own country if he wanted to, why can't he buy me a small city? Anyway, this page has tons of things to fit your comedy needs, including jokes, one-liners, and more.

COMMENTS: Humor is addictive, much like Krispy Kreme's jelly-filled doughnuts. Mmmm, doughnuts! Oh, just thinking of those doughnuts, hot off the fryer, melting in your mouth and oozing with creamy goodness. No wonder people run across crowded highways to get them. Anyway, now that I'm over that very unnecessary (and unfortunately, very unpaid) promotion, let's get to the rating!

ABNORMALITY: 5 STUPIDITY: 8 ENTERTAINMENT: 8

Freaky Folk

www.polarboy.pwp.blueyonder.co.uk/freakyfolk

It's the attack of the freaks!

Go there and you can see some really scary people with unusual talents, from the bizarre "leopard man" to the woman who can pop her eyes halfway out of their sockets to the man with the seventeen-foot pigtail, "washed every December to ensure good luck." This site has something for fans of circus freaks and the bizarre everywhere.

COMMENTS: We've finally found something that's stranger than SpongeBob SquarePants. And that's saying a lot. This site has that special something for those looking for the really, really weird, wild, and freaky. There are plenty of common weirdos out there, but only a few select "freaky folk."

ABNORMALITY: 9 STUPIDITY: 7 ENTERTAINMENT: 7

67

Chimpage
chimpage.tripod.com/chimpage

A bizarre radio show that has monkeys on it! What more could you ask for?

This is the official site of Chimpage, a weekly updated radio show by two guys named Andy and Tom. The show was created while Andy was sitting in a bar thinking about "cabbages, varnish, and fruit pastilles." Tom walked in and the rest is history. Here, you'll find everything from merely stupid topics to strangely weird ones to downright insane ones. Don't forget to join the search for a certain chimp that recently went missing.

COMMENTS: What is it about monkeys that is so funny? Perhaps it's because we're the closest to them genetically. Or it might be because they're cute and they can jump really high and hang from trees. That makes anything funny. Wait, is a chimp a monkey?

ABNORMALITY: 7 STUPIDITY: 8 ENTERTAINMENT: 7

66

Patent the A
www.patentthea.com

Next time you use the letter A (oops, I just did), you'd better check with these guys first. If you don't, you could get sued for copyright infringement. "On the first of April 2003 The Ecchi Patent Company applied for a patent on the letter A. This Patent has now been formalized and all users of the letter A (in either capital, lowercase, or any variation thereof) must immediately obtain a license or discontinue use of the aforementioned letter forthwith." The A patent has been ratified in the USA, Canada, Mexico, and all of the European Union countries, so if you write a love letter to Anna Alva Anderson in any of those countries, you'd better be prepared to pay big time. There is also a payments page where you can send your money to these wackos if you intend to use the A heavily.

COMMENTS: Although this is obviously a joke, it would be pretty bad if the A were actually patented. I can only imagine how hard encyclopedia makers would be hit. On the other hand, if letters were patentable, that would be a great way for cunning entrepreneurs to earn some extra cash.

ABNORMALITY: 8 STUPIDITY: 9 ENTERTAINMENT: 7

65

Churches ad hoc:
A Divine Comedy
www.efn.org/~hkrieger/church.htm

Here, you'll find a bunch of photos of the outside of churches, each with its own unique caption that makes it funny. For a church with a "motorcycle parking only" sign in the foreground, the caption reads: "Our Lady of the Hell's Angels." A house of worship at the corner of Church and State streets is simply captioned "disestablishment." And while the other ones are a little more subtle, they're still funny.

COMMENTS: Pretty funny for a site that manages to be humorous, yet respectful and very appropriate. Then again, if they weren't, God could strike them dead, now couldn't he? For those interested in more secular pursuits, there are links to some interesting and compelling photo essays like "A Day in the Life of a Mobile Veterinarian."

ABNORMALITY: 5 STUPIDITY: 6 ENTERTAINMENT: 7

64

Windows RG
www.deanliou.com/WinRG/WinRG.htm

This site is an overexaggeration of how Windows seems to work sometimes. Or not work.

Here, you can see Windows RG, a really, really dysfunctional version of Windows. Error messages are everywhere. Any form of entertainment is nowhere in sight. As errors constantly pop up and remind you of Window's familiar, flawed nature, you'll see that "art" does indeed imitate life. Plus, the "help" feature is about the same as you will find in Windows. Any attempt at accessing a "help" question leads to the "blue screen of death" and a general protection fault. Sad, but true.

COMMENTS: This certainly does seem to be the way Windows works for me almost all the time. Thank goodness I got a Mac laptop, which, in all honesty, is superior to a Windows computer in almost every way. Those witty commercials with the trendy Mac guy and the nerdy Windows guy do have a kernel of truth to them. Now that I'm done with another unnecessary (and once again, unpaid) promotion, I will say that if you've experienced problems with your Windows computers, you should definitely check out this site.

ABNORMALITY: 6 STUPIDITY: 8 ENTERTAINMENT: 6

NiceCupofTeaand ASitDown.com

www.nicecupofteaandasitdown.com

Would you like some tea? Or maybe some biscuits? If so, this site is for you.

Here, you'll find a bunch of information on tea and biscuits, and how they affect the world. Don't ask me what relevance this has to ordinary, everyday life. It has none. I mean, who in their right mind would ask if the dinosaurs were "wiped out by some sort of tea-related catastrophe"? Sorry, not my favorite topic of conversation. And, well, I really don't plan on observing "Biscuit Tin Awareness Week." This site also attempts to answer just exactly what those "little pink wafers" are. Interesting.

COMMENTS: The only redeeming feature of the site was the "Apocalypse Rabbit vs. Kitchen Appliances" game. Short, sweet, and stupid, it had nothing to do with tea or biscuits. I think that's why I liked it.

ABNORMALITY: 8 STUPIDITY: 9 ENTERTAINMENT: 7

Hollywood Extra

www.thehollywoodextra.com/index.html

He's one of those guys you see walking in the background on TV shows, and he loves it. Or at least he wants you to believe it.

This is "Phil Schwartzetti's" documentation of his "life" as a Hollywood film extra. Don't know Phil? Then I'm absolutely sure you would recognize him by his "stage name" of Donovan Swing. Now, I have yet to see any of "Phil's" actual movie credentials on this site, and it doesn't look like I'm going to find them any day soon. "Mr. Swing" also has posted pictures "proving" the existence of UFOs. Imagine that. More aliens. I'll believe in aliens before I believe the drivel on this pathetic site.

COMMENTS: Why do people make sites about themselves when they're not interesting? Why do people create vanity pages that aren't funny or interesting? On the other hand, if you want to tell your life story in a bit of your spare time and want to post drunken party pictures on the Web, you too can totally embarrass yourself. Just make sure you don't make this guy's mistake. Have a good-looking photo of yourself to put on the page. Or at least a funny one.

ABNORMALITY: 5 STUPIDITY: 7 ENTERTAINMENT: 6

61

Quark Dance
pdg.lbl.gov/quarkdance

What do particle physics and polka have in common? The answer is this site. The site shows a number of strange shapes—which are apparently quarks—dancing to "Go Man Go" by Big Lou's Polka Casserole. The polka music can't be turned off while the site is open, and it gets quite sickening after a few minutes. Actually, more like a few seconds. There are also links to serious sites related to particle physics.

COMMENTS: I hope that real quarks don't look and act like this. It's unsettling to think that when I'm drinking a soda or listening to music that what I'm hearing, seeing, and tasting are made up of little colored shapes dancing to some inaudible polka music. And why polka music? Maybe polka is the fifth force of matter in the universe. Polka could be the key to solving the secrets of the universe! It's exciting and unsettling at the same time. More unsettling, though.

ABNORMALITY: 9   STUPIDITY: 8   ENTERTAINMENT: 6

60

The Supreme Court of Common Horsesense
www.edwardbaskett.com

Now this is one weird site.

It's…well…I don't know what it is. It's basically this guy who shares a bunch of his weird "knowledge," philosophy, and "horsesense" with you. I mean anyone who says that Hillary Clinton bears an uncanny resemblance to Sharon Stone really makes me want to get away from him. Get away fast, real fast. Mr. Baskett lists some of his "potential audiences" as "Christian Scientists…lawyers…investigative reporters (and) gay activists."

COMMENTS: Well, this site has plenty to offer those who like to be confused and bewildered. In fact, I will bet you a thousand bucks that you will be dazed and confused beyond all recognition. But don't quote me on that.

ABNORMALITY: 9   STUPIDITY: 7   ENTERTAINMENT: 7

The Warp
thewarp.studentplanet.com

Let's do the news warp again!

Okay, so it's not the greatest joke in the world. Still, that's the name of this odd satirical newspaper, *The Warp*. Articles include how the Kool-Aid pitcher man trampled seven children when he burst through a wall at a birthday party, and how defective tires are running Microsoft Windows (don't ask).

COMMENTS: After reading that article, I do recall watching those early '90s ads where the giant Kool-Aid pitcher burst through the wall. And regardless of whether he tramples children or not, mothers can't be happy with him. I mean, sure Kool-Aid is marginally healthier than soda, but do you know of any soda cans that burst through walls causing possibly irreparable damage to small children? I rest my case.

ABNORMALITY: 8 STUPIDITY: 8 ENTERTAINMENT: 9

58
The World's Smallest Website
www.guimp.com

There's no way to make it bigger; this *is* the world's smallest website.

In this little quarter-inch square, you'll find the smallest HTML job ever. You must use the small, one-word menus to navigate the site. Features include miniature pictures, the world's smallest Pong game, and much, much more!

COMMENTS: Those of you who have a hard time with their sight should not go to this site (no pun intended). You won't be able to see it at all. Try to find some new glasses, or get one of those four-second laser surgeries that costs $2,000. You might be disappointed, though, if you did that just for this ridiculous site.

ABNORMALITY: 8 STUPIDITY: 7 ENTERTAINMENT: 5

57

How to Be a 'Web' 'Designer'
www.ex-parrot.com/~chris/design.html

Here's a very outdated guide to making a website. The sad thing is that it was written recently. At least, as far as I can tell.

You'll find everything you need to get your site online, including which book to buy (he doesn't exactly recommend the greatest book), which computer to have, and more on this new "cutting edge technology" known as the Internet.

COMMENTS: This reminds me of the days when the Internet was a luxury, and ISPs charged by the minute. Now look at us! We have so much time on the Internet that people just like you can spend endless hours making (or, in your case, looking at) unbelievably stupid web pages.

ABNORMALITY: 7 STUPIDITY: 8 ENTERTAINMENT: 5

56

Lobster Man from Mars
www.lobstermanfrommars.com

The ultimate in B-movies is here on this site!

It's the Lobster Man from Mars, and he's coming to take over the movie industry! This is apparently an actual movie, released in January 1989, with stars such as Tony Curtis and "little person" Billy Barty. Patrick Macnee, from the old *Avengers* TV series, takes a turn as "an outer space crustacean expert." On this site you can see reviews of the movie, see stills of the cast and crew, and see how the film went from being an absolute total flop to just a plain old flop with a moronic website. You can even buy the monstrosity of a movie.

COMMENTS: With an extremely corny story, the likes of which I haven't seen since *Attack of the Killer Tomatoes*, this movie's site is no better than watching the real thing. This is mainly because the site concentrates on the movie so much. In this case, this movie deserves no recognition. The movie's producer is quoted as saying, "Basically, no one has seen it." Let's keep it that way, OK?

ABNORMALITY: 8 STUPIDITY: 9 ENTERTAINMENT: 5

55

Sounds of Pasta
www.geocities.com/Heartland/Farm/9258

The hills are alive with the sounds of…pasta?

Apparently so in this bizarre site where you can hear sound clips about pasta. Now, why the noises that pasta makes sound good enough to put on a website is something I'm not familiar with. Still, this site does have some nifty pasta info.

COMMENTS: The language of lasagna! The sounds of spaghetti! The rhythm of ravioli! All tunes you can find on this site, and some other ones you might not expect. With less relevance to the real world than, well, MTV's *The Real World*, this site is hardly worth visiting unless you like to actually listen to pasta. I mean who could possibly resist the lure of listening to "8 ounces of elbow macaroni being poured from a cardboard box into a plastic container"?

ABNORMALITY: 8 STUPIDITY: 7 ENTERTAINMENT: 4

54

The Unofficial Captain N Home Page
ldloveszh.tripod.com

This site is meant to do a number of things. What it seems to do best is show you an example of a truly pathetic life. Even though, as a computer-games geek, I'll probably end up this way, I stick by my opinion. Here, you'll find out all about this geek and his quest to bring back the TV series *Captain N: The Game Master*. According to this site, *Captain N* was an NBC cartoon series that aired in the late 1980s and early '90s. A game-playing kid is sucked into the TV and becomes a character in "Videoland." I have no idea who would want to bring back a series that only nerds could enjoy. There is also a Captain N photo gallery, links to other Captain N pages (my, my, I can't wait to see that…), and more.

COMMENTS: *Captain N: The Game Master* sounds like something Comic Book Guy from *The Simpsons* would enjoy. "Worst series ever!" But I am worried. I mean, how can I live knowing that I may never see Captain N in "When Mother Brain Rules" or "The Trouble with Tetris"? Will my life be meaningless if I miss out on Wombatwoman battling Eggplant Man?

ABNORMALITY: 7 STUPIDITY: 7 ENTERTAINMENT: 4

53

G.I. Joe Fan Fiction

www.joeheadquarters.com/fanfiction/index.shtml

God help us all: fan fiction about a plastic action figure.

Here, you'll find the worst and the, well, worst of G.I. Joe fictional stories, straight from the minds of the people who like to play with the action figures themselves. Stories include a G.I. Joe "romantic" Christmas story; "Holographic Convergence," which is a two-part story (only part one exists, part two will be written "after Maryann graduates"); and several more scintillating tales with characters like Zarana, Mainframe, and Wet Suit trying to stop humans from being turned into snakes.

COMMENTS: What's next? A Barbie soap opera? If you got together enough characters, sure. "Ken, why did you dump me for Joey? Why?!" And Ken would say, "I did it because, well…Barbie, your cousin is my brother and Skipper is really my sister!" And then Barbie would freak out and ask for more outfits and accessories.

ABNORMALITY: 8   STUPIDITY: 8   ENTERTAINMENT: 6

52

UFOIndia.org

www.ufoindia.org

Aliens are invading! They're not starting at Roswell, they're not blowing up the White House, and they're not storming Area 51. They're landing in…India? Forget about extraterrestrial intelligence, I'll settle for *any* intelligence, anywhere.

The land of the Taj Mahal, sacred cows, and decorated elephants is being targeted for alien invasion, according to these fellows. Here, you'll find a comprehensive sighting database for UFO incidents in India, crop circles, and more. You'll even find reports on attacking alien "muhnowchwa," which means "something that pinches the face" (really, that's what it means!). If face pinching makes someone an alien, then those creepy aunts who embarrass characters on TV must all be from another galaxy.

COMMENTS: Why would aliens start landing in India? Maybe they want to land someplace where the people still believe in myths and legends and stuff (although India is quite civilized). Or maybe they're just not thinking. Or maybe they don't exist at all. I'm inclined to think that the aliens haven't landed…yet.

ABNORMALITY: 9   STUPIDITY: 8   ENTERTAINMENT: 8

Dr. Toast's Amazing World of Toast

www.drtoast.com

More goodness on a lightly crisped slice of bread.

It's Dr. Toast's Amazing World of Toast, and the doctor answers all of your questions about toast, and some questions about other things. Features on this site include Toast haiku (haiku certainly is popular on the Internet, isn't it?), toast recipes, and an opportunity to ask the famous Dr. Toast himself a question. This site even has a link to the Toast Bible, with the Ten Commandments of Toast: "Thou shalt not place unnatural condiments on toast." And, of course, "Thou shalt not covet thy neighbor's toast."

COMMENTS: I don't see what's so heavenly about a slightly crisped piece of bread. Why not Pop-Tarts? Or waffles? Toast is just so…plain. Still, the opportunity to ask somebody a question about food is worth the stupidity.

ABNORMALITY: 9 STUPIDITY: 9 ENTERTAINMENT: 7

306WD.com

www.306wd.com

This is a complete waste of time for both you and this site's maker.

Here, you can find several features to waste your time, including "Meet the Cars," where you can view "Taco Tim's" exciting Honda Accord, and "MK's Neon." Specifications of the car include "weight of garbage inside," "candlepower" (as opposed to horsepower), and "snowbank kills to date." Now that last statistic scares me.

COMMENTS: My favorite game on the site is "Can you spot the Lunch Lady?" It is fascinating, despite its simplicity. It gives you a bunch of common properties of lunch ladies, including how they smell like sloppy joes (haven't you ever noticed?). It's fun to pick out who would and wouldn't be a lunch lady. It's pretty easy too, particularly when they have that ugly appearance like Roseanne Barr Arnold Whatever or "Lunchlady Doris" from *The Simpsons*.

ABNORMALITY: 7 STUPIDITY: 9 ENTERTAINMENT: 7

A Little Laughter

www.geocities.com/SouthBeach/
Lights/3099/ffunnies.html

More comic goodness that, like Campbell's Soup, warms you all over. (Trademark issues prevent me from using the actual phrase. Surprise, surprise.)

This comedic site includes several jokes about the Clintons, including one about a waitress where he accidentally "misreads" the menu. Another example is an animal joke where one of two bears swallows a Czechoslovakian and a lawyer has to tell the sheriff which one the Czech is in. Let's see if you can figure this one out. "The Czech's in the male." Duhh. Stupid.

COMMENTS: There are some funny comments about work in here. One favorite is "When I take a long time, I am slow. When my boss takes a long time, he is thorough." Just remember, "work" is a four-letter word. Just another kind of "deep thought" by me.

ABNORMALITY: 5 STUPIDITY: 7 ENTERTAINMENT: 9

---

48 Dan Quayle Quotes

www.quotationspage.com/quotes/Dan_Quayle

The Quotations Page has many quotes from history's greats: Albert Einstein, Winston Churchill, Shakespeare, and countless others. Many of the quote pages here are uplifting, inspiring, and loaded with intellectual thought. Dan Quayle's page, however, is not any of those. Quite simply, Dan Quayle's quotes are just hilarious. Many of them are logical contradictions, such as, "I have made good judgments in the past. I have made good judgments in the future," or, "We have a firm commitment to NATO. We are part of NATO...we have a firm commitment to Europe; we are part of Europe." Right, just like Japan is a part of Africa. Others are unbelievably obvious statements: "For NASA, space is still a high priority."

COMMENTS: It's very ironic that quotes like these come from a former vice president. Politics aside, Dan Quayle is proof that holding public offices doesn't require you to be logical.

ABNORMALITY: 9 STUPIDITY: 9 ENTERTAINMENT: 9

Grundage!
www.grundage.com

All hail the almighty Grund!

What the Grund is, I don't really know, but still, it's something that's interesting to see. These stories make up a collection of comedy writings gathered to form "Grundage!" Examples include "All I Want for Christmas," which is basically a Christmas list with wishes for "Part 2 of every movie ever made," a "food-scented air freshener," and "4-D Glasses," among other things.

COMMENTS: Some of these writings are really bizarre. One entry includes "Car Pick-Up Lines," which are pick-up lines, not about cars, but for cars to actually use. Lines such as, "Here's my license plate number...call me sometime!" Amazing how stupid some people are, eh? This is a lesson you've learned all too well from reading this book.

ABNORMALITY: 8 STUPIDITY: 8 ENTERTAINMENT: 8

46

Bob Saget Is God
www.bobsagetisgod.com

Sound the trumpets and sing hallelujah, because the savior of mankind has returned in the form of...Bob Saget? "Searching for hope, purpose, relief? Or maybe just answers to some of life's most complicated questions? Well then look no further my friends. BOB SAGET WILL SAVE YOUR SOUL!" At the main page, you are greeted by Bob's smiling face shining in a cloud-filled sky, practically filling your soul with the Holy Bob. "Proof" that Bob Saget is divine includes his "power to manipulate people," and cites his ability to manipulate *America's Funniest Home Videos* entries, claiming that he controlled their outcome as well. Plus, they ask, "When was the last time YOUR GOD gave you $10,000?" If you feel compelled to join Bob's followers, you may join the "Church of Saget."

COMMENTS: Bob Saget does appear to be a holy man when you see him on *Full House* or *AFHV*. But in his stand-up comedy routines, Bob is actually pretty vulgar. But even if he is divine, I still refuse to watch *Full House* for more than thirty seconds. Sorry, your holiness, but I stand by my principles.

ABNORMALITY: 9 STUPIDITY: 9 ENTERTAINMENT: 7

45

Squirrel Hazing:
The Untold Story
www.squirrelhazing.squirrelsinblack.org

It turns out humans aren't the only ones who humiliate each other in the search for acceptance and belonging.

Here, you can see tragic examples of "squirrel hazing," including cheek stuffing, where a squirrel tries to fit as many nuts as possible into his cheek pouch, sometimes resulting in "permanent cheek disfiguration." And of course, the classic example of the most dangerous squirrel hazing ritual: running out into the middle of a busy highway. The horror…

COMMENTS: This is a pretty funny take on anti-hazing organizations for humans. I particularly liked the "squirrels in black," or the S.I.B.s. Theories on their existence include a theory that the S.I.B.s are here to prevent squirrels that have been abducted by aliens from telling their story. They even go so far to say that the S.I.B.s are connected to O.J. Simpson.

ABNORMALITY: 9 STUPIDITY: 9 ENTERTAINMENT: 7

44

The Tofu Olympics
www.tiedyes.com/thetofuolympics1996.html

Ladies and gentlemen, let the games begin!

It's the Tofu Summer Olympics, and this is the site to see all of the events from this exciting competition. From the women's "Tofu Balance Beam," which shows a Tofu box with two stick legs balancing on a beam to men's "Tofu synchronized swimming," where two Tofu boxes go underwater and perform stunts in an amazingly spontaneous way, this site is your headquarters for Tofu Olympic action!

COMMENTS: I only have one compliant about this site: each Tofu event only has two or three stunts! What a rip-off! I want to see more extremely bad-looking Tofu boxes performing stunts in little cartoons! Is that too much to ask? Apparently the creators of this site were just too lazy, and as a result they have deprived us of more of this amazing sport. Like Tom Cruise's senseless rants, you can never have too much of a good thing.

ABNORMALITY: 9 STUPIDITY: 10 ENTERTAINMENT: 5

43

Gobbler Toys
www.goblertoys.com

This site is definitely weird toy central. The entrance to the site has an old-time factory that, when you click on it, sprouts a red whistle from the roof that blows out steam. After that, there is an animation with an old man's head juxtaposed on a small cartoon figure dressed in a scientist's lab coat, operating a conveyor belt with the various Gobbler's Toys. Whoever designed this site should seek a psychiatrist. From Louie the Cheese Shark, a shark with a head made of cheese that "blows cheese-scented soap bubbles," to the "Mysterious Spit Brothers—Siamese Saliva Siblings" to a giant horse head to Ethel the Opera Lobster (who screams operatically when she's dipped in boiling water) to Kiki the Fashion Tiki, a Tiki idol with Barbie-like clothes, this site has a bunch of toys you can get to keep demented little tykes occupied.

COMMENTS: There is one thing I do not get about this site. Just exactly who needs a giant horse head, a shark-cheese combination, or a spinning top that holds a person? None of these "toys" has any use! Maybe that's the point. While the site *is* a joke, I'm still mad, because if this company really existed, they'd be at the bottom of my customer-satisfaction list.

ABNORMALITY: 9 STUPIDITY: 8 ENTERTAINMENT: 6

42

Planet Ketchup
www.ketchup.wonderland.org

Ketchup, or "catsup" as some people may spell it, is the subject of this condiment-crazy site. Here, you'll find the home for everything that's ketchup-related, from the amount of money Heinz spent to market its ketchup in 1993 ($1.1 million) to the "did you know" section with such interesting information as the fact that "ketchup is great for restoring the glow to copper pots and pans" and that Baskin Robbins once made ketchup flavored-ice cream. Obviously it didn't sell that well. I wonder why?

COMMENTS: Ketchup is the world's top condiment, and it deserves its place on the Internet. After all, ketchup is found in 97 percent of America's kitchens, according to the facts you'll find at Planet Ketchup. Unfortunately, other condiments may soon demand their own web pages. Now, a site devoted to something like mango chutney would be really weird.

ABNORMALITY: 7 STUPIDITY: 6 ENTERTAINMENT: 7

41

Poodle Disguise Kits
www.attackchi.org.au/kits.htm

"Are you sick of people looking at your breed of dog in fear because politicians and the media are saying things like, 'We want to breed these dogs out of existence,' 'They are killing machines on a leash'…Well, worry no longer, [because] attackchi will be making disguises for all the so-called 'dangerous breeds.'" The most popular "disguise" right now is the "Poodle Disguise for Dobermans." Each kit contains fake fur pieces, black face paint ("safe for dogs"), and a "safe suit fitting method statement and instructions." The pictures on the site show a rather miserable-looking Doberman in a disguise that appears only marginally authentic. Be warned, though, because "dressing your dog like this will increase the chance of it biting you." Gee, you think?

COMMENTS: This site, once again, gives me mixed feelings. I do sympathize with the owners of these dogs. My big sister has a pit bull that's one of the sweetest dogs you'll ever meet (he's actually kind of a scaredy-cat). But these "disguises" seem a little too extreme and ridiculous.

ABNORMALITY: 9 STUPIDITY: 8 ENTERTAINMENT: 8

40

The Uncoveror
www.uncoveror.com

Here you'll find all the stories that "they don't want you to know," although I have no idea who "they" are. From the sensational scoop "Pirate's Treasure Hidden in Cincinnati Park" to "Elmo Busted for Smuggling Meth" to the university professor who says we should celebrate Christmas in February, you can find it all here. This site also takes a humorous look at actual events, such as "Britney Spears has Cooties: They Made Her Hair Fall Out," which refers to Britney's sudden decision to shave her head. (And we thought she was just looking for attention—Britney would never do *that*, would she?)

COMMENTS: It says on this site that ice geysers on Mars are actually vents for underground Martian cities, and that if we don't stop snooping around Mars, the aliens will use their ancient, ultra-powerful weapons of mass destruction to annihilate us!

ABNORMALITY: 8 STUPIDITY: 9 ENTERTAINMENT: 9

39

Generic Cheese and Macaroni Page

www.geocities.com/macandcheesebox

Generic macaroni and cheese! How exciting! How thrilling! How tasty!

Well, not really. Macaroni and cheese is nothing that I really go wild over. At least certainly not any low-rent, "no name" crap. This "cheesy" site has pictures and information on tons of generic, I repeat, *generic* brands of mac and cheese, including Best Choice, Piggly Wiggly (Shop the Pig!), and Kohl's. On their "archive" list, they also have a comprehensive database of both generic and brand-name (Kraft, Velveeta, etc.) products.

COMMENTS: The fact that anybody would want to dedicate a site to macaroni and cheese is weird enough. But generic macaroni and cheese? What were these people thinking? Did they actually like the generic brands that much? Or is there some sort of government conspiracy involving aliens, Cindy Crawford, Hillary Clinton, and Richard Simmons reruns? The answer remains a mystery.

ABNORMALITY: 8 STUPIDITY: 9 ENTERTAINMENT: 4

38

Spud the Traveling Potatohead

www.spudstravels.com

A potatohead who travels around the world? What a great idea!

His name is Spud, and he's a world-traveling potatohead. He's been seen in Peru sitting on a bench in front of a royal palace next to a two-liter of citrus soda. He's been to Easter Island and hiked up to the top of the Rano Kau crater. He's gone snorkeling in the Caribbean. In fact, Spud has been almost everywhere!

COMMENTS: This site was OK, but I personally liked the misadventures of Larry the Llama a lot better (see number 97). Speaking of which, whatever happened to Larry's relationship with Debra the Donkey? I'm curious to see how that turned out. Anyway, as for Spud, the idea of a starch-based food product turned globetrotter is somewhat interesting. He sure does get around.

ABNORMALITY: 9 STUPIDITY: 9 ENTERTAINMENT: 8

37   Be Nice to Penguins Society
www.stormlodder.com/bnps

This site claims that we should not fear penguins, but rather embrace them and give them all that "warm and fuzzy" feeling. The society's stated mission is "to inform the masses about poor misplaced penguins that need kindness." Here, you'll find all you need to know about being nice to these Antarctic birds, including the "Give a Penguin an Ice Cube" program, where you generously donate cubes to penguins with "ice deficiency." The goal of being nice may not succeed, but another goal "to take up bandwidth for a somewhat noble cause" has been achieved. Well, at least the part about taking up bandwidth.

COMMENTS: I agree with this site. Penguins are funny, cute animals, and they deserve our utmost respect. The question is: what kind of respect? Is the penguin's goal world domination, or are they simply searching for happiness? Only time will tell.

ABNORMALITY: 8   STUPIDITY: 9   ENTERTAINMENT: 7

---

36   Turn into a Cabbage
www.geocities.com/Heartland/Plains/2144

This site claims to be able to turn you, yes *you*, into a cabbage. If you have ever "stared mournfully into the coleslaw and thought to yourself 'Gee, I wish I was a cabbage,'" this is the page for you. Here, you'll find all sorts of stuff on how to convert yourself into a cabbage. There's a helpful FAQ that addresses pressing issues such as "Now that I'm a cabbage, can I still eat cabbage?" Are there cabbage cannibals? I don't really know. Or, you can just skip all those questions and go straight to the Cabbage Converter, where you are transformed into an official head of cabbage.

COMMENTS: What a rip-off! All you get is some cheap certificate that says "You are now a cabbage." I really, really want to be turned into a green vegetable! I want to undergo a transformation! Where's all the creepy sci-fi stuff? Where's the blinding flash of light? Very disappointing. I tell you, everything's fine print these days.

ABNORMALITY: 9   STUPIDITY: 10   ENTERTAINMENT: 7

35

Inexplicable Object of the Week

altervistas.com/sites/weird/14

It's the Inexplicable Object of the Week, and I almost can't begin to describe it. Some items are both historical and inexplicable, like the "Kamikaze Attack" action play set, where the carrying case converts to an aircraft carrier that you crash Japanese airplanes into. Or maybe the "Bionic Woman" board game. (More like *bored* game. Do you remember that putrid rip-off of *The Six Million Dollar Man*?) Some are just merely inexplicable, like the ashtray with a picture of a church dome along with the text "Welcome to Boston," which was an advertising item for a "quality shipping service to the funeral profession." Maybe an advertisement for cremation services would have been better?

COMMENTS: This site makes absolutely no sense at all. Maybe something just the slightest bit meaningful about these objects, some kind of silly joke or witty remark, would make this site worth something. But this features nothing but stupidity! Then again, that's what I do in this book. So, here it is.

ABNORMALITY: 10 STUPIDITY: 8 ENTERTAINMENT: 5

34

Idaho License Plates

www.idahohistory.net/license.html

This site is actually an official part of the Idaho State Historical Society. Sad, huh? You can view archives of nine decades of Idaho license plates. From the 1910–19 era to present-day America, this site covers a large portion of the history of cars. In Idaho, at least. There are also photos of special license plates, like the wildlife plates (with elks and bluebirds on them), the snow skier plate, and the coveted Idaho "Famous Potato" plate. The main site also has the official colors of the license plates from 1913 to today.

COMMENTS: I feel very sorry for whoever has the job of maintaining this site. Sure, it's a part of Idaho's history, but that doesn't mean that an archive of license plates isn't stupid. The one strange thing is that there are absolutely no license plates from the '80s. Maybe the ISHS is too embarrassed to show them.

ABNORMALITY: 7 STUPIDITY: 8 ENTERTAINMENT: 5

33

Urinal.net
www.urinal.net

Urinals throughout the world? How exciting! I'm sure you'll be "relieved" to see this site.

Here, you can find pictures and vivid descriptions of urinals throughout the world. There are urinals in bars, airports, private residences, and more. From the Chattanooga Choo Choo in Chattanooga, Tennessee, to the famous Space Needle in Seattle, this site has an amazingly comprehensive archive of places to pee. They even have a picture of a most unusual urinal from Sharm el Sheik, Egypt. It's nothing but a large, long pipe sticking out of the ground! Disturbing, to say the least.

COMMENTS: I would think that, contrary to common sense, it would be easy to take urinal pictures without interference from people. It may be your experience that most public restrooms are never empty for very long, but look at it this way: would you stand in front of a urinal while some guy with a camera was taking your picture?

ABNORMALITY: 9 STUPIDITY: 9 ENTERTAINMENT: 7

32

Pavement Gear
www.pavementgear.com

This site has a mission: to scour the Earth for weird objects and situations and catalog them for your "enjoyment."

On this site, you can see tons of stuff that's been abandoned on the side of the road. From a discarded garden gnome tossed next to some used drug paraphernalia to discarded underpants and boxer shorts to an ordinary pair of pants on a highway, this site has tons of stuff that's inexplicably been left behind. The site even has an international flavor, featuring a picture of a prosthetic leg (yes, a prosthetic leg) tossed in a trash heap in Singapore. You can also see weird happenings related to the road, like "turbo granny" tuning up her vintage '93 Eagle Talon.

COMMENTS: My favorite section is "the agents," whose job is to document and gather this bizarre stuff and "wrap" it into a neat little package suitable to put on this site. It's funny to see these hard-working experts on the job, getting what is basically nonorganic roadkill for your viewing pleasure.

ABNORMALITY: 9 STUPIDITY: 8 ENTERTAINMENT: 8

31 Sugar Packet Collector's Page
www.the.millerfamily.name/sugar

Do you collect sugar packets? If your taste runs toward the sweet persuasion, you might want to check out this site. From the traditional Sweet 'N Low (wait a minute, that's not really sugar) to the U.S. Presidents collectors edition (Lord help us all), this site has all the great sugar memorabilia a saccharine fiend could wish for. This site even has all the information you need to get your own personal sugar-packet collection up and running. So, sucrose slaves unite! Toss off your chains and give in to your obsession. Start collecting sugar packets. Now.

COMMENTS: Who would want to collect a food-sweetening item packed into little paper parcels? The fact that some of the packets are named after presidents is even more bizarre. I don't think George Washington was a sugar-packet collector, do you? Maybe he was a sugar junkie, though. How else would he have gotten the wooden teeth?

ABNORMALITY: 9 STUPIDITY: 9 ENTERTAINMENT: 6

---

30 Brains 4 Zombies.com
brains4zombies.com

You know how zombies eat brains to stay alive? Ever wondered just where those brains come from? Apparently, this is where they are found. At this tasty site you can find all sorts of brains for your zombie friends, although I doubt zombie friends last long. Modeled after Amazon.com, the brain purchase page has a customer rating and comments area as well as a review section. From celebrity brains such as former governor Jesse Ventura's to miscellaneous kinds of brains such as the "outdoor camper" brains or "your ex-girlfriend's brain," this site has all the brains you need to create a tasty treat for your undead desires.

COMMENTS: Mmm…brains! I can just imagine a zombie, like the supposedly human newscaster Ted Koppel, munching on a frontal lobe or two. Too bad these brains are just for munching and not for transplanting. I can think of several people who could use a new brain or at least a portion of a brain. Well, one thing's for sure; we know now where zombies shop for brains.

ABNORMALITY: 9 STUPIDITY: 8 ENTERTAINMENT: 7

Realm of Niftyness
www.niftyness.com

Is niftyness a word? I don't think so. But whatever it is, there's lots and lots of niftyness on this site. So "just lean back, grab a bowl of Cheetos, and watch the time slip away."

Here, you'll see a ton of, well, nifty stuff. From weird articles dealing with how a device should be developed for yelling for pizza (no, not ordering; yelling) to a fresh-baked batch of fortune cookies saying such things as "Next time I'm at the edible eating utensils convention, I'm going to bring peanut butter cups." Don't ask how that's even a fortune, but it's there. There is also an incredibly stupid article entitled "Elvis Is Dead" that proves the death of the King by weaving a tale involving Twinkies, worms, and the Yakuza (the Asian mafia).

COMMENTS: There truly is some nifty stuff on here. I especially liked the fortune cookie that said, "A penny saved is a penny earned, but not even a handful of them is enough to buy a can of soda." Makes ya think, doesn't it? Sure, it's something stupid to think about, but I'd rather think about it than the meanings of 80 percent of the other sites in this book.

ABNORMALITY: 8   STUPIDITY: 8   ENTERTAINMENT: 8

Black Hole of the Web
www.ravenna.com/blackhole.html

Go on, enter…if you dare.

This is the black hole of the Internet. You click on it, and you are plunged into total darkness. Total darkness, except for the presence of a few messages that warned you that you shouldn't have come in. The web link above sends you directly to the entrance of the black hole; so don't say that we didn't warn you!

COMMENTS: Not only did I actually survive the black hole of the Internet, but my Mac didn't even let me go near it! I didn't even have to use the back button, which was necessary for my other Windows computer. Wow, in addition to running efficiently and not freezing up every five seconds, Mac computers can defy the laws of physics! Bet you Stephen Hawking (the famous theoretical physicist who proved the existence of real black holes) didn't know that.

ABNORMALITY: 9   STUPIDITY: 7   ENTERTAINMENT: 6

27

Insect Rights Activists
www.throughwire.net/IRA

It's time to take up arms and join the IRA: the Insect Rights Activists. Insects have rights too, you know!

At least, according to this page they do. This is central headquarters for all of the people who support the bugs, flies, and other insects of the world. They want you to join the "fight to stamp out the senseless slaughter of billions of helpless insects across the world." Features include a "Hit List" of insect enemies such as sea gulls, tequila manufacturers (eat the worm!), and Martha Stewart. Now my question is this: what the heck do Martha Stewart, tequila, and sea gulls have in common?

COMMENTS: One of the funniest features here is the "atrocities" page, featuring such "horrid" things as fly paper and bug zappers. You'd think that if bugs were smart, they'd just stay away from those things. Maybe they know logically that it's a bad idea, but for some reason they're drawn to them anyway. Kind of like me with MTV's *Next* (the speed-dating show where one attractive young person cycles between prospective mates by saying "next!"). It's stupid, pathetic, and probably reduces my IQ by ten points for each minute I watch it, but I just can't resist it for some reason. Maybe we're not that different from insects after all.

ABNORMALITY: 8 STUPIDITY: 8 ENTERTAINMENT: 7

26

TotallyStupid.com
www.totallystupid.com

This page is exactly what it says it is. Stupid. Totally stupid.

There's the "Stupid Cheese of the Month" (you can vote for Feta, Muenster, and Monterey Jack). The "3 Letter Word" page doesn't say that it's stupid, but manages to be nonetheless. However, the most obvious example of the intellectual nature of this site is the stunning revelation that "Stupid People Are Stupid."

COMMENTS: Everything on this site is stupid! They even admit it! It says stupid this and stupid that, so they feed into the fact that their website is stupid! The question is, why do they keep working on it? Some things, like why *The Osbournes* have a trivia game based on their moronic TV show (I'm not kidding; they do!), will remain a mystery. Oh, did I mention that this site is stupid?

ABNORMALITY: 8 STUPIDITY: 10 ENTERTAINMENT: 8

25 The Knuckle Head Club
www.geocities.com/SiliconValley/Lakes/2307

These are the tales of people who are, well, knuckle heads. This is the place to go for a vast variety of crappy tales relating to people who are complete morons. Read about the time a mechanic asked a woman what gear she was in when her car broke down. She replied, "A pair of Pumas and Gucci sweatpants." Or one lady asked why Stonehenge was built so close to the highway. The amazing thing is that many of the stories where the authors accuse others of being knuckle heads are, in fact, peppered with grammatical and spelling errors. So just who's the knuckle head in that case?

COMMENTS: Sometimes it amazes me how stupid people are. Want proof? Take a close look (wait, don't look) at such schlock as the multiple mundane movies of "comedian" Rob Schneider ("classics" like *Deuce Bigalo: European Gigolo,* which sadly enough, is the second movie in the series), or the people who made *Snakes on a Plane*, for thinking that somehow a Sci-Fi-Channel-quality movie would succeed because of viral marketing and Samuel L. Jackson. Knuckle Heads indeed.

ABNORMALITY: 6 STUPIDITY: 9 ENTERTAINMENT: 8

24 The Giant Cows of Wisconsin
www.thom.org/gallery/set/wicows.html

Sometimes, while my family and I have been driving through Wisconsin on road trips, we'll see a giant fiberglass cow on the side of the road near a store. I never gave it much thought until now, when I learned that there is actually a website dedicated to these things. This site gives you the locations of many of these colossal cows, as well as the startling truth that three of the existing "giant cows" are made from the same mold and are therefore clones! Beware the giant cow clones! Are you getting any of this? Because I certainly am not. There's also information on how one cow used to talk (until the speaker for her voice box was shot out) and how there aren't just giant cows in Wisconsin (see the Giant Cows of Georgia link).

COMMENTS: It took a while for me to soak in "everything" that this website has to offer. But, it really just tells you a whole bunch of useless information about giant plastic farm animals on the side of Dairy State highways. This is definitely information we don't need.

ABNORMALITY: 7 STUPIDITY: 9 ENTERTAINMENT: 5

Idiots and Other Aberrations
www.americaworks.net/idiots/index.html

This site is for people who are total "idiots and other aberrations."

On this page, you'll find stuff for idiots and the people who mock them. There's the game "Find the Odd Sheep" (I'll give you a hint: of the five, one's black and barks like a dog). Or maybe idiot stories, like the lady who talked to vending machines. This site has all of these stories and many more features to make you realize how smart you really are. Of course, if you take pride in your ignorance, you can take the "Idiot Test for Professionals." I mean, just think of the prestige in being a *professional* idiot rather than your common everyday amateur moron!

COMMENTS: How about that lady who talked to vending machines! It sounds like she belongs in the loony bin rather than a page about idiots. Everybody knows that only dumb sitcom characters talk to vending machines.

ABNORMALITY: 6 STUPIDITY: 9 ENTERTAINMENT: 8

22

ViewZone.com
www.viewzone.com

UFOs, government conspiracies, and ancient advanced civilizations. What could it all mean? The View Zone explains it all.

Here, you'll find all you need to know about strange happenings in the world. There are theories on ancient civilizations like the questions: "Did the Olmecs come from Asia?" or "Were Ancient Celts in Oklahoma?" You'll find pictures of weird things like mysterious Alaskan lines on the landscape and the "anomalous stones of Peru." Yes, all of the weird stuff you can imagine is here.

COMMENTS: This is probably the most likely place where you'd get information that our society is being infiltrated by kung-fu aliens on the rampage. What that means, I don't know. But you never know. One day, aliens who know kung fu could go on a rampage. You've been warned.

ABNORMALITY: 9 STUPIDITY: 8 ENTERTAINMENT: 8

21

Broccoli Town, USA
www.broccoli.com

It's the official site of broccoli, that wholesome and healthy, notorious and nasty green vegetable that tastes like crap. This is the site to go to if you're looking for info on this nutritious vegetable. You can even take an "exciting tour as we sample the many tastes of fresh broccoli" while cruising through Broccoli Town, USA. Stop the "Food Service" truck to see preparation techniques and recipes. Climb the tree house to the "Kid's Club" (you can tell that isn't gonna last long), where you'll find broccoli coloring books and a game called "The Tower of Hanoi." (Hanoi, like in Vietnam? Where the heck did this come from? "Look out. Incoming! Charlie's got broccoli! Take cover!")

COMMENTS: Isn't a broccoli kid's club an oxymoron? For those of you morons who don't know, an oxymoron is when you put two things together that contradict or cancel each other out, like "dry water," "military intelligence," or "legal ethics." Anyway, broccoli and kids simply do not go together.

ABNORMALITY: 5 STUPIDITY: 7 ENTERTAINMENT: 2

20

Crepes, Food Crepes, Dessert Crepes Galore
www.orbie.com/uni

Need a machine that can make 180 pancakes and/or crepes per hour? Well, this site is for you. You too can "join the trend towards greaseless cooking!"

This is the place to get all your pancake- and crepes-machine needs. Features on these amazing machines include "solid-state speed control" and the ever-popular "cash control" where "tamper-proof digital counters keep track of all products produced." After all, everyone is aware of those hungry hordes of pesky pancake thieves roaming the countryside.

COMMENTS: This website is useless to everybody except restaurant operators, whom I'm sure account for less than 0.01 percent of the population. So, therefore, 99.99 percent of the population will find this website to be useless and stupid. While it's meant to be a serious product sales ad, it still manages to be stupid in a "crepey" sort of way.

ABNORMALITY: 4 STUPIDITY: 7 ENTERTAINMENT: 5

19 The Cephalopod Chronicles
www.angio.net/~reagan/octopus.html

This page is about the world travels of…an octopus? A blue polyester octopus.

No, the world of SpongeBob SquarePants isn't coming to life. Still, this site features the travels and travails of an octopus's adventures through many distant locales. This creature has no name; he is merely "The Octopus." From the octopus's quest to join members of the Appalachian Mountain Club's 4000er challenge, a program where members try to climb various peaks in the White Mountains region, to his trip to the Tuckerman Ravine in Mt. Washington, New Hampshire, you'll find all that you need to follow the octopus on his quest to travel the world.

COMMENTS: This isn't the first site where an inanimate object has tried to span the globe. Spud the Traveling Potato Head (see number 38) was another example. Anyway, it seems so funny to see such lifeless objects like plastic potatoes and stuffed octopi traveling the world. Now all that's missing from the Web is a site for pictures of a world traveling stiff, solemn, soulless robot, like, say, Al Gore.

ABNORMALITY: 8 STUPIDITY: 9 ENTERTAINMENT: 8

---

18 The Fuk Shing Umbrella Co., Ltd.
www.fukshing.com

Enter the world of Japanese umbrellas! Fuk Shing is a leader in Japan's production of these wonderful devices to shield you from the rain. Here, you'll find details on Fuk Shing's product range, including the beach, clamp, and golf umbrellas; the "Japanese umbrella" (is Japanese rain different from American rain?); the "hat umbrella" with safety frames; and, of course, the umbrella gift set, consisting of several different kinds of adult umbrellas packed into tote bags.

COMMENTS: I have no idea why this seems so funny; it isn't meant to be, but it just is. Maybe it's the Japanese mystique. It's kind of like those early B-movie science-fiction flicks that tried to combine a serious task of eliminating the monster along with "dramatic" interactions between the characters. And of course, they ended up on *Mystery Science Theater 3000*.

ABNORMALITY: 5 STUPIDITY: 6 ENTERTAINMENT: 6

17

A Rubber Duck to Every Bathroom

www.students.tut.fi/~cami/Quack/duckpage.htm

This page is for those who believe every bathroom should have a rubber duckie.

No, Ernie from *Sesame Street* did not create it. Still, this site is a strong voice for putting a rubber duck in every bathroom in the world. Their goals are furnishing bathrooms with rubber ducks and to spread rubber-duck awareness regarding the proper way to "use" a rubber duck. A shocking, horrific truth is revealed in a stunning revelation: "Unfortunately, rubber ducks are not made out of rubber." Is there nothing left to believe in anymore?

COMMENTS: Every bathroom? A noble goal, but can it be done? Are there enough rubber ducks to go around? Will Ernie steal all of the rubber duckies and become a rubber-duck thief, much like what the Hamburglar is to McDonald's hamburgers? Only time will tell.

ABNORMALITY: 7 STUPIDITY: 7 ENTERTAINMENT: 7

16

Rusted

www.rustedOnyx.com

This site has "Everything you could ever want to know about rust, in all its forms. Its history, its causes, how to get rid of it, how to create it, how to write poems about it and how not to die from it." The last category is the only one that sounds useful. Here, you can find Rust Images, Rust News, and links to other rust sites. The images section has "Rust Designs," with pictures of rusted car doors meant to be some kind of art form, and a "photovault" of rusting cars, described as "Rust at its finest." There are also links to books at Amazon.com about rust, such as "Images of the Rust Belt," a sixty-four-page book that runs for an amazing $23.75! Almost twenty-four bucks for a book about rust? That's like paying fifty bucks for a pile of paint chips!

COMMENTS: Why are so many sites on the Internet dedicated to the most ridiculously boring things? I'd rather have stamp collecting as a hobby than be interested in rust. And I do not want to collect stamps.

ABNORMALITY: 6 STUPIDITY: 8 ENTERTAINMENT: 5

15   Britney's Guide to Semiconductor Physics
britneyspears.ac/lasers.htm

Who knew that Britney was fluent in semiconductor physics?

Apparently, the people at this site knew. You can learn all about the mysterious workings of semiconductor physics, all while gazing at pictures of Britney Spears. Start out with the basics. Learn about different elements, intrinsic semiconductors, valence bands, and more. Graduate to "vertical cavity surface emitting lasers" and "photonic crystals" while staring at your Britney Spears computer wallpaper!

COMMENTS: Finally, something that makes physics fun: Britney Spears photos! This site isn't quite current, though; Britney has undergone several changes since the photos were taken, including when she went for the Mr. Clean look by shaving her head (see the Uncoveror, number 40, for the real reason behind that one).

ABNORMALITY: 8   STUPIDITY: 9   ENTERTAINMENT: 7

---

14   Immortality Devices by Alex Chiu
liveforevernow.com

The creator of this website claims to have found a device that will make you immortal. "Alex Chiu knows what causes you to age and hereby discovered a great solution to stop you from aging." Through magnetic finger and toe braces that act as positive and negative terminals on your body, the "Eternal Life Rings" allow blood and electricity to flow in order to enhance metabolism, thereby halting the aging process. Yes, I know it makes no sense. I've reluctantly come to accept that from the Internet as I have researched this book.

COMMENTS: I think by now I have made it clear that the Internet is full of wackos and bizarre folks who have no idea what they're talking about. Who would have thought that the Internet would end up as an expressional channel for psychos who think they can make people live forever? Oh well. I like to use the Internet for what it's really meant for: 3D head-to-head virtual-reality poker!

ABNORMALITY: 9   STUPIDITY: 8   ENTERTAINMENT: 6

13

Pop-Tart Blow-Torches
www.pmichaud.com/toast

According to this site, "strawberry Pop-Tarts may be a cheap and inexpensive source of incendiary devices." Here, you'll find a demented and disturbing experiment performed with a strawberry Pop-Tart of the non-frosted variety and an inexpensive toaster. The Pop-Tart was cooked on the darkest setting, with cellophane covering the toaster slots so the Pop-Tart cannot eject. As the Pop-Tart began to burn, smoke rose from the toaster. Soon "the flames steadily grew larger and larger until reaching a maximum height of about eighteen inches above the top of the toaster."

COMMENTS: Why waste a perfectly good strawberry Pop-Tart? They're meant to be eaten, not burned! I guess it just goes to show you that people will resort to incredibly stupid or desperate measures when they're bored. That must explain the popularity of televised bowling tournaments. Actually, people are never really bored enough to justify TV bowling.

ABNORMALITY: 8 STUPIDITY: 7 ENTERTAINMENT: 7

12

Aluminum Foil Deflector Beanie
www.zapatopi.net/afdb

Here, you'll find all the information you need to help you construct a piece of headwear that will make you resistant to psychics, telepaths, and other freaks (although it won't save you from being named to Mr. Blackwell's worst-dressed list). Remember: "The Aluminum Foil Deflector Beanie is the most effective, inexpensive, and stylish way to combat psychotronic mind control." You can also use this practical product on pets. The beanie may especially come in handy during alien abduction. And although it's really nothing more than a little cap of aluminum foil, it's still an idea that deserves recognition…well, probably not.

COMMENTS: While mind control may be the stuff of B-movies, this site seems to have a mission to protect you from manipulation by those who would use your mind for evil, like the Olsen twins. Who knows what this evil duo is plotting next? For all we know, they could be plotting a sequel to *It Takes Two*!

ABNORMALITY: 9 STUPIDITY: 9 ENTERTAINMENT: 8

11

PawSense
bitboost.com/pawsense

Ever had problems with cats climbing on your keyboard and messing things up? If so, head over to this odd site.

This is the place to go for PawSense, a software program that allows you to "cat-proof" your computer. Whenever "cat-like typing" is detected, a window appears that tells you your kitty has been naughty and stops all further typing. It also trains cats not to jump on keyboards by emitting a noise cats don't like. This trains those little critters to stay off of your computer even if you're not there.

COMMENTS: Actually, this may be a bad product. Maybe a cat could accidentally type something really meaningful, like Shakespeare or a Jimmy Kimmel monologue. Maybe the maker of this software is trying to deny the world of fine, cat-created literature. Whatever the reason, someone put a lot of effort into a product with an extremely limited use. Stupid. Very stupid.

ABNORMALITY: 7 STUPIDITY: 8 ENTERTAINMENT: 7

10

I Hate Clowns
www.ihateclowns.com

"Can't sleep, clowns will eat me. Can't sleep, clowns will eat me…"

This site is for people who, well, hate clowns. Whether it stems from fear of clowns (coulrophobia, see number 384), anger, or any other emotion, this website is a sort of support network for people who don't like clowns. There's the "anti-clown store," where you can buy products like the "Clowns Are Humor Challenged" T-shirt, the classic "Can't Sleep Clowns Will Eat Me" shirt, or the "I Hate Clowns" visor. You know why cannibals don't like clowns? They taste funny!

COMMENTS: I wonder what people have against clowns? They're just funny people who like to entertain. I don't see what's wrong with them. Sure, I'd endorse an anti–Ricky Martin organization, but otherwise I'm pretty mild mannered. By the way, whatever happened to that Latin singing guy? I guess he's livin' la vida loser.

ABNORMALITY: 9 STUPIDITY: 8 ENTERTAINMENT: 8

The Official
Sally Jessy Raphael Page

www.sallyjr.com

Sure, the show doesn't make new episodes anymore, but that doesn't mean it's not stupid. On this page, you'll find a bunch of information on the former show hosted by the lady with extremely ugly glasses, known better as Sally Jessy Raphael. The "Ask Sally" column is still active, with such burning questions as, "The worst thing happened between my mom and my boyfriend…they slept together. How do I handle it?" or "Is a 27-year-old too old for a girl of 15?" Good Lord.

COMMENTS: For goodness' sake, woman, get rid of those glasses! They're a disaster. They're so, so ugly! It's not the '80s anymore! I tell you, some people just can't leave the past where it belongs. Mullet men, are you hearing me? Anyway, this site isn't intentionally stupid, but its content is a step below *Jerry Springer*, so I'm putting it in.

ABNORMALITY: 5 STUPIDITY: 7 ENTERTAINMENT: 5

WackyUses.com

www.wackyuses.com

Ever wondered how you can put that Dannon Plain Yogurt to use, other than cooking? Well slather it on sunburn, and you'll soon be soothing your skin. Did you run out of hair conditioner? Use the tangy zip of Miracle Whip. Need to shine your shoes? Use a Huggies Baby Wipe.

On this page, you'll find tons of offbeat uses for everyday household products, like thawing frozen fish with Carnation Non-Fat Dry Milk, or cleaning a toilet bowl with Coca-Cola. There are tons of uses just like this throughout the site, some of which are actually quite useful.

COMMENTS: I never knew you could use Endust to keep your ski goggles from fogging up…wait a minute; what the heck is Endust? I have never heard of it in my life! I've never seen it in stores, I've never seen an ad, and I've never seen anything pertaining to it! I guess there are some things that you just don't know about for good reasons, like why *America's Next Top Model* continues to attract viewers.

ABNORMALITY: 8 STUPIDITY: 7 ENTERTAINMENT: 8

118 Reasons Why Tamara Should Go Out with Rob

www.skirtman.org/tam_rob.html

Can you think of 118 reasons why somebody should go out with you (even if you're not single)? I wouldn't be able to do it, but some guy named Rob did. This is a list made by Rob—who got fifty friends to sign it as a "petition"—of 118 reasons why some girl named Tamara should want to go out with him. Almost all of the reasons are completely stupid and irrelevant (surprise, surprise). The list includes gross reasons ("Hasn't wet his bed for over two weeks now"), senseless reasons ("He subscribes to the theory that the Earth is round"), disturbing reasons ("Has never exploited the tradition of mistletoe to kiss his aunt"), and reasons involving his pointless knowledge base ("He knows the capital of Eritrea").

COMMENTS: If I was Tamara and I got this list, I would move to another city to get away from this Rob guy. At the end of the list, it says, "give me 118 reasons why she shouldn't" go out with Rob. That's easy. All the reasons on this list.

ABNORMALITY: 9 STUPIDITY: 9 ENTERTAINMENT: 7

The World Pumpkin Confederation

www.backyardgardener.com/wcgp/wpc

An organization dedicated to growing giant pumpkins—you know, those eight hundred–pound behemoths you see in magazines. Now I've seen everything.

On this page, you can view the amazingly interesting (a hint of sarcasm, perhaps?) history of the World Pumpkin Confederation, or the WPC. There's a comprehensive list of rules and regulations for the WPC's pumpkin contest. One rule states that the pumpkin must be grown in the country of the contestant's residence. No imported Irish pumpkins need apply! There's also a mailing list and books and videos available to view.

COMMENTS: Pumpkins are a very odd fruit. This page could be very informative if you're into giant pumpkin growing; otherwise it's just plain stupid.

ABNORMALITY: 7 STUPIDITY: 6 ENTERTAINMENT: 4

The Official International Fan Club of Baby Ulf
members.tripod.com/~weluvbabyulf

This baby is "famous just for being famous." Actually, that doesn't make any sense. He's not even famous (at least, not to my knowledge). Still, this page insists on the glorification of the world's first Internet-made baby "celebrity." You can see who he is, join the fan club, and even get updates on how Baby Ulf is doing.

COMMENTS: I don't get why anybody would want to dedicate a page to a baby. The baby doesn't even know that the website exists! Oh well. At least it's an amateur website, so you can rest easy knowing that the creator didn't put in a whole lot of effort to make the site. Still, you wonder why. Vanity sites. You just have to hate them. Oh, and by the way, what kind of a name is Ulf?

ABNORMALITY: 6 STUPIDITY: 7 ENTERTAINMENT: 4

Celebrity Collectables' Celebrity Archive
www.celebritycollectables.com

You might be thinking, "What's so weird about this page?" Lots of people collect items related to celebrities. I'll tell you why it's weird: all of the documents available to purchase here are divorce files, autopsies, or wills of celebrities. Here, you can find Jennifer Lopez's divorce papers (surprise, surprise), Harry Houdini's will (I guess he couldn't work his magic on cheating death), and more famous and infamous documents from the private lives of famous celebrities. You can find Sonny Bono's probate file (a bargain: sixty-three pages for only $15!) but not his will. Sonny died "intestate." That doesn't mean anything naughty; it just means he died without a will.

COMMENTS: This page actually has some interesting stuff. You can find the will of Wilt Chamberlain, who led the NBA in scoring, and also got a lot of points, too. You can gain a great pharmaceutical education through the purchase of John Belushi's autopsy. (R.I.P., Bluto.) And you can glimpse into the truly bizarre and inexplicable with your purchase of the Lisa Marie Presley–Michael Jackson divorce file. Now that union was at the pinnacle of the pointless pyramid.

ABNORMALITY: 8 STUPIDITY: 7 ENTERTAINMENT: 7

White Bread Power
home.uchicago.edu/~narusso/power.htm

Now if this isn't stupid, I don't know what is.

This site is for those who believe white bread is not only the superior bread, but also the superior food. "Those who eat only white bread will some day take over the world and exterminate all those inferior peoples who partake of rye, wheat, and other whole-grain breads." On this site, you'll find valuable and scintillating information on white bread, nutritional data from white-bread scientists, and more.

COMMENTS: All hail white bread! White bread will be the salvation of our world. "When fossil fuels have run out, and an energy crisis ensues once again, everyone will realize the inherent energy and potential in white bread." But seriously, this site is quite disturbing. I mean, I like white bread, but those obsessed with it have to be crazy. Of course, we've seen plenty of other food sites fiercely dedicated to their cause, so this is nothing new.

ABNORMALITY: 9 STUPIDITY: 8 ENTERTAINMENT: 6

Chinese Restaurant Name Generator
www.novia.net/~matt/chinese/restaurant.html

Like any Chinese menu, it's quite simple: pick one from column A and one from column B. Put them together, and voila! You've got a name for an authentic Chinese restaurant. Column A names include Asia, Bamboo, Canton, and Wonton. Names from Column B include Room, Take Out, and Pagoda. Many of the names you might choose are standard fare, but some are not so normal. Take "Beijing Fun." I'm sure all the protesters in Tiananmen Square could attest to the fact that not much about Beijing is fun. And "Ollie's Garden"? Who ever heard of a Chinese guy named Ollie?

COMMENTS: You know, there's a certain "something" about generating Chinese-restaurant names that's fun. You should try it, too. It's very fulfilling, in a weird, stupid sort of way. It still kind of ticks me off that this site doesn't have the luxury of a random, computer-aided generator; you have to do it manually.

ABNORMALITY: 7 STUPIDITY: 6 ENTERTAINMENT: 7

1 The Official Carrot Top Web Page

The horror! THE HORROR!

This is *the* No. 1 most stupid website in this book. From the opening page showing that horrid mop of red hair atop that ugly, twisted face to the bit about the "Mike Tyson Chew Toy," this site screams STUPID! On this sad, sad example of a web page, you'll find Carrot Top's bio: he likes to listen to Hanson in his basement (that's definitely disturbing). His "dancing name" is Cinnamon Spice (also very disturbing). And one of his favorite movies is *Dennis the Menace 2: Dennis Strikes Back* (*very* disturbing). You can also view a photo gallery (why would you want to see more of this cretin?), post a note on the forums (like "Hey Carrot Top: Quit. Now. Before you doom us all to lives as imbeciles!"), and more.

COMMENTS: I have no doubt that this site should be "number one in my book." No doubt at all. It is unquestionably the most stupid site on the entire World Wide Web. Why, you ask? HE'S CARROT TOP! He's a travesty! I've had permanent psychological damage just from viewing this site.

ABNORMALITY: 10 STUPIDITY: 10 ENTERTAINMENT: 6

Acknowledgments

First off, I'd like to thank my editor, Peter Lynch, for helping me put together this book and for suggesting the idea of a second edition. Thanks of course still go to my family: my Mom and Dad, my sisters Colleen and Sarah, Uncle John, the family dog Marnie (eight years old and she still acts like a puppy), and too many others to name. You guys are not only a great family, but great friends too. I'd also like to extend my thanks to my new friends at the Great Lake Zen Center, including Peter, Laura, Mike, Andy, Gretchen, and especially Susi, who had the patience to drive me all the way downtown—every week—until I got my license. I'd also like to thank my friend Ted for, well, being Ted (anybody who knows him will know exactly what I'm talking about). And finally, thanks to Sourcebooks, the fantastic company that publishes this book. They are truly a great bunch of people to work for.

Index

U

V

W

X

Y

Z

About the Author

Dan Crowley is a twenty-one-year-old college student whose hobbies include video games, reading, and, of course, Internet surfing and writing. Dan lives in Wisconsin with his mom and dad, two sisters, and a cute little puppy named Marnie. Since childhood, Dan has frequently written fictional stories for fun. Dan is also the author of The *505 Weirdest Online Stores*, which he completed prior to the second edition of this book.